D1109442

#23

Finding Iris Chang

ALSO BY PAULA KAMEN

All in My Head

An Epic Quest to Cure an
Unrelenting, Totally Unreasonable, and
Only Slightly Enlightening Headache

Her Way

Young Women Remake the Sexual Revolution

Feminist Fatale

Voices from the Twentysomething Generation
Explore the Future of the Women's Movement

Finding
Iris Chang

Friendship, Ambition, and the
Loss of an Extraordinary Mind

PAULA KAMEN

DA CAPO PRESS
A MEMBER OF THE PERSEUS BOOKS GROUP

Photo on page vi is courtesy of the author.

Designed by Timm Bryson
Set in 10 point Galliard by The Perseus Books Group

Cataloging-in-Publication data for this book is available from the Library of Congress.

ISBN-13 978-0-306-81466-2
ISBN-10 0-306-81466-8

Published by Da Capo Press
A Member of the Perseus Books Group
http://www.dacapopress.com

Da Capo Press books are available at special discounts for bulk purchases in the U.S. by corporations, institutions, and other organizations. For more information, please contact the Special Markets Department at the Perseus Books Group, 2300 Chestnut Street, Suite 200, Philadelphia, PA 19103, or call (800) 255-1514 , or e-mail special.markets@perseusbooks.com.

10 9 8 7 6 5 4 3 2 1

Contents

Iris Chang
1968–2004

The Questions

From September 23, 1994, e-mail:

Dear Paula,

I can relate to your comment about being a perfectionist when doing research. This tendency seems to be universal. Consider the following paragraph from Pulitzer Prize–winning historian Samuel Eliot Morison in his book Sailor Historian: *"First and foremost, GET WRITING! Young scholars generally wish to secure the last fact before writing anything, like General McClellan refusing to advance (as people said) until the last mule was shod. It is a terrible strain, isn't it, to sit down at a desk, with your notes all neatly docketed, and begin to write? . . . Nothing is more pathetic than the 'gonna' historian, who from graduate school on is always 'gonna' write a magnum opus but never completes his research on the subject, and dies without anything to show for a lifetime's work. . . . "*

I think you've done enough research for your sex [and gender] book. You may have enough information in your tapes and notes to sustain two or three more books. What you ought to do now is compile an outline of questions.

Ask yourself, what is the single most important question that this book will answer? That will be the thesis of your work. Then ask yourself, what are five to ten questions that must be asked in order to answer my main question? Each of those questions will be the topic of a new chapter. Then break down each chapter by asking five or ten or twenty more questions.

Use complete sentences to pose the questions, such as "What did Jane Doe believe was the most serious threat to sexually active women today?" If you [use] sentence fragments, such as "Jane Doe" or "interracial marriage" or "rape" when writing the outline, then you might get confused later on. When the entire outline is typed up and printed out, then you can go back at your leisure and answer all the questions. . . .

Anyway, feel free to ask questions or bounce ideas off me as your writing progresses. Send me a copy of your outline its [sic] finished!

Love, Iris

My first questions about Iris:

- What possessed her to kill herself?
- Were there earlier signs?
- Could depression come on that suddenly?
- Or was it something more than depression?
- Was it postpartum depression?
- Did the dark topics that she covered in her work drive her to insanity?
- Or, was she murdered?
- Were her fears based in reality?
- Was her suicide preventable?

- Could *I* have stopped it?
- Who was she, really?
- How am I any different from her?

While it was a mystery to me why Iris Chang had wanted to die, I knew why she should have wanted to live.

This thirty-six-year-old woman was the most envied, and enviable, person I knew. She achieved success, by all possible external measures, to an extreme and to an almost farcical extent: She had fame and fortune, a result of her 1997 international blockbuster book, *The Rape of Nanking: The Forgotten Holocaust of World War II*, which sold at least a half million copies and was translated into fifteen languages. She was doing meaningful social justice work and giving formerly anonymous victims of some of the worst war atrocities of the twentieth century a strong voice. She was a powerful and charismatic speaker, able to mobilize audiences with seeming effortlessness. She was beautiful. She was thin. She regularly socialized with filmmakers, the kinds of authors whose books you are assigned to read in college literature classes, and even elite policy makers. Her family was unusually close and supportive; her parents and brother would do almost anything for her. She adored her husband, and he adored her. And she openly expressed delight with her two-year-old son, who already was showing signs of his own genius.

Also, her suicide didn't add up for other reasons. Her family had explained that she had become seriously depressed only in the last several months of her life. I had never known her to be clinically depressed. If anything, she had been one of the most steadfastly positive and exuberant people I had ever known; no one I knew wanted to do more with their life and was more driven. And whenever we had talked about weakness through the years, it was nearly always about me.

The last time I saw Iris Chang was in the spring of 2003, in Chicago, when I went to see her lecture promoting her third book, *The Chinese in*

America. She seemed to be in good spirits, and we had a good time afterward going out for pizza in a small group and hearing about her latest adventures. She was already working on her next project, on the Bataan Death March. I knew the stories she was gathering were intense, like those she had covered from that same World War II period for *The Rape of Nanking.*

The months passed, and I got involved in my own, much lower-key deadlines. In the first week of November 2004, a mutual friend e-mailed me that Iris was trying to reach me, and that she had been sick for the past few months. I had assumed it was some kind of protracted cold, the kind I had over the winter. Coincidentally, I had just been thinking that I hadn't talked to Iris in a very long time, since the summer, when she seemed okay, although the conversations then were uncharacteristically abrupt.

On November 3, she called my cell phone while I was getting a haircut, but I didn't pick up. The wary look in the eye of the hairstylist, who was running late, cautioned me not to get it. Besides, I was relieved to let it ring into voice mail, knowing that if I picked up the phone, the conversation might take hours, and I no doubt would be late for a birthday party that evening.

In her short voice-mail message, which I ended up saving for more than a year, she said:

> *Hey Paula, it's Iris calling. Iris Chang. Hope you're doing well. It's been a long time since we talked, and I want to touch base with you. When you get this call give me a call back at 408 _____. You take care now, bye-bye.*

Her tone was upbeat, as usual. I left her an e-mail message late that night, telling her to call me the next day. Then, three days later, she tried to reach me on my cell phone while I was away visiting friends—a couple and their baby—in Kentucky. When I picked up the phone and simultaneously realized it was Iris via the caller ID, I thought of my friends waiting for me to start dinner in the next room and Iris' typically epic conversations. I immediately cautioned, "Iris, I'm visiting someone out of town and can't talk long. Can I call you when I get back home?"

She cut off my words with: "Paula, I have something to tell you. I have been very, very sick for the past six months."

When I heard the tone of Iris' voice, I wandered outside into my friends' yard for privacy, not bothering to get a coat despite the chill in the air. The bounce in her voice, the one that I had even heard in the voice-mail message from days before, was totally gone. Instead, it was sad and totally drained, as if she were making a huge effort just to talk to me—as if she were a different person. I remembered the comment from a friend that she recently had been sick.

"And I just wanted to let you know that in case something should happen to me, you should always know that you've been a good friend."

Over the next hour, in one of the strangest conversations of my life, I stumbled to ask her about what had happened. She talked about her overwhelming fears and anxieties, including being unable to face the magnitude—and the controversial nature—of the stories that she had uncovered while researching her book on the Bataan Death March. "People in high places are not going to like it. Frankly, Paula, I fear for my life," she said, still maintaining her flat tone.

That was the first time I thought that Iris might be human, after all. Perhaps she wasn't an exception to the rules of nature. Perhaps even she was not able to work nonstop without paying any price. Perhaps I wasn't such a freak, after all.

Despite having told me that she was sick, she described her current vague problem, which I understood as some kind of depression, as the result of "external" forces. It wasn't a result of the "internal." I asked her what others in her life thought about the cause of this apparent depression. She paused and said, "They think it's internal."

"It's got to be external. It just can't be the result of . . . of a book tour," she said, fading out a bit to ponder that question. She was referring to her exhaustion from the more-than–twenty-city tour she'd made in the spring of 2004 for the paperback release of her book *The Chinese in America*. She went on to talk about other fears. "Paula, I've made serious mistakes with my son. I gave him autism with vaccines." The tone of her voice was firm, like she was proclaiming an unassailable guilty verdict on herself from the voice of the highest possible authority.

"What?" I said, totally perplexed at this comment. I understood that autism was the result of the "internal," basic neurology, not external actions. And I had no reason to believe he was autistic.

"I've made some very serious mistakes with my son," she kept repeating.

I fired questions at her, repeating the same ones over and over again—about her son, her research, her state of mind—although I kept hearing all the same answers. I was reeling from the apparent suddenness of this crisis. I thought I had figured her out years ago.

"This is all temporary! It's a storm that will pass. You have to wait it out." I then confessed to her about a period of months in 2001 when I had been immobilized by a depression, which later lifted. I called it a "breakdown," although it probably wasn't technically one. I told her that with some time off, I eventually found a way to manage a root cause of that depression, a chronic and yet untreatable migraine. It wasn't easy, but I was doing the best I could, even in some pretty challenging circumstances. I said that she would read more about those strategies in greater detail in the spring, when my book on chronic pain would be published. She didn't respond.

She talked more about her guilt over her son. At one point, she was silent and then seemed to drift miles away, as if she had been possessed by demons. A faint voice, which did not sound like hers but that of a tiny child, whispered longingly: "Paula, do you ever just want the lights to go out?"

"Yes, of course," I said, stumbling over my words. "These thoughts are normal. But they pass. I would be, I would be devastated if something were to happen to you. I wouldn't, I couldn't. . . . "

There was more silence.

"This is temporary," I said. "This is not how I see you," I assured her. "That's not how you see me? Then, how do you see me?" she said, with sudden intense interest, her voice returning to earth.

"Energetic," I said. "You're someone truly engaged with life. A hero! You've been a total inspiration to me! You've helped so many people."

"Yes, engaged with life," she said, brightening a bit. "Remember that. If anything ever happens to me, people are going to talk, and you have to remind people of that."

I repeatedly asked to speak to her husband, Brett, to get more information, but she said he was busy. Then, we talked more and I felt a bit relieved to hear that her husband and her parents were near. She seemed to come back to me and sound more lucid, and I talked about my pain-coping skills for a while. To start off, I gave the example of Buddhist-like advice an alternative healer had given me. "I know this sounds cheesy, but . . . try to see your fears and anxieties like a fire. You need to acknowledge them, tend them and not ignore them, or else they'll rage out of control. But you have to keep a distance, stand away from them, not stand IN the fire, and then get consumed by it," I said. "There's a lot more to it, but that's just something to start out with."

That sound bite of therapy seemed to resonate with Iris. I promised to e-mail her the titles of some books that had helped me. I also mentioned how so many investigative journalists seem to actually thrive with stress and controversial topics. "What about Seymour Hersh?" I asked, now adding some forced humor to the conversation. "He seems OK, and he criticized a lot of powerful people. He's alive and kicking. I'm sure they didn't like him uncovering all those atrocities in Vietnam, and now he's writing on Iraq."

In return, she perked up a bit and suggested herself that she would look into how famous investigative journalists deal with their stresses.

Yes, and then when I got back to Chicago, I said, we'd talk. She didn't respond. We talked more, and I said I had to go. She plummeted into a deep sadness, sounding worse than she had when she first called. I hesitated to end the call and we continued the conversation.

Before we finally hung up, she said one last time: If anything happened to her, I had to let people know what she was like before this happened. And I said I would.

This book—seeking truth about Iris' glorious life and mysterious death—came out of a eulogy I wrote for her for the Web magazine Salon.com shortly after her death. In response, I received hundreds of e-mails, many from strangers who confessed that this death had somehow "shattered" them to their core, to such an extreme that they were puzzled why. A few people told me that when they heard the news about her death on their car radios, they had to pull over to the side of the road to contain themselves. And this is for someone they had barely met, maybe for a minute at a reading, or never at all.

The first e-mail I received, within minutes of the article's posting, had come from a World War II history scholar at a Chicago-area university who said he felt guilty that he had been jealous of Iris for years—that she had attained the acclaim that had always eluded him, as he worked for years in obscurity on similar topics.

"Don't feel bad," I replied, simply. "*Everyone* was jealous of her."

Combing through the deluge of e-mails to come, I was startled by how symbolic Iris was to others. She wasn't just a historian of atrocities of 1930s Nanking; she was all things to all people. She represented: a working mother, a warrior for social justice, an Asian American, a voice for forgotten war victims, a suicide, a sufferer of depression, and a high-spirited person who was "too much" for others at times.

As for me, it's hard to know where to even begin to describe what she meant. In conversation, I had always referred to her as a role model, for example, with a friend a few years earlier. About a year before Iris' death, this friend, who had just had a baby, was sadly observing how all her friends and mine with high-powered careers had given them up when they became mothers. I denied that was the case, and she dared me to list someone as an example. I thought for a second, and the one person we knew who didn't fit that description was "Iris Chang." Iris represented to me what it meant to be successful, without giving up the rest of one's life. She had accomplished the feat of being an extraordinary woman who also managed to hang on to the "ordinary" parts of life, a husband and child.

Iris also resonated to me as an *openly* ambitious woman, someone who didn't act coy, the way you're supposed to, about reaching her goals. She didn't even flinch over self-promotion, which she knew was vital to success in publishing, no matter how talented one is and how just the cause being advanced. When she had met her future husband, Brett, in college, he asked her the odds of her writing a best-seller, and she answered "90 percent." No one had ever bothered to tell her that you just don't voice those things out loud; you keep them to yourself, no matter how basic they are to your being.

With her engrained high-achievement ethic, Iris also didn't seem to realize the pervasive hostility in society about openly ambitious women. I don't think she would have caught that common put-down, for instance, in referring to the most highly symbolic "modern woman" of our time, Hillary Clinton. When someone wants to insult her, all they have to say is "she is a very ambitious woman." Case closed. Even on garden-variety reality TV shows, producers know that the key to making an instant villain is to feature an ambitious woman. In such circumstances, it's a sure bet that the woman would defend herself by saying something like, "I'm not here to make friends. I'm here to win"—a statement that also tells you who you're not supposed to like. But I'm not sure that Iris would have realized that either. No one seemed to have informed Iris that when you're a woman, you're supposed to be different by being extra discreet about your appetites of all kinds, whether they're for fame, money, or food. She didn't seem to acknowledge that the risk of being indiscreet could be ridicule, shame, or rejection.

Actually, beyond addressing her ever-unfolding symbolism, much of my inspiration in preparing for this book has boiled down to a single concrete image, in a coloring book. All in black and white.

As possibly the ultimate measure of success, toward the end of her life, Iris was one of a limited number of alumni honored with their own page in a promotional publication in the form of a coloring book from her prestigious university-run laboratory high school in Urbana, Illinois. After all, you know that you've done something pretty big when you're in a coloring book.

I remember her telling me about it, how excited she was to be pictured among the likes of such luminaries as Max Beberman ("the founder of the New Math"), columnist George F. Will, and numerous Nobel Prize winners.

On Iris' page, she is portrayed as a beautiful "young historian," her long black hair cascading behind her as she looks forward and serenely smiles at us, sitting beside a book case. The caption simply reads: "Iris Chang credits her love of history and chasing down a story to the freedom she had to do so while at Uni High." Alongside that is a page-long bio listing one stellar writing achievement after another, including all three of her books.

This picture of the successful author, the one that she best projected to the public and even to me, was no understatement; her ambition and talents were central to her very being. She was a genuine scholar and an industrious worker—not a bullshitter at all. But, as her suicide revealed, much more was going on in her life than I ever had suspected, and well before the year of her death. With that two-dimensional coloring book page in mind, I saw this book project as a privileged opportunity for me to investigate beyond the public contours of this public figure, to find color, depth, and maybe even shadow.

In discussing what Iris symbolized to them, some of the respondents to my Salon article would later become partners in researching this book, mainly her friends and acquaintances. I also was guided throughout my quest for answers by circuitous trails of clues that Iris herself seemed to leave me—buried within her writing, correspondence, and hundreds of boxes of personal and professional papers that she had left to three major university archives.

Above all, in this researching and writing effort, I have tried to use her own work as an example, to basically ask the right questions—and then keep reformulating them with changing insights and circumstances. Just as historians like Iris have worked to investigate and clarify incidents obscured by the so-called fog of war, I've tried to figure out what really happened through the also-greatly-distorting fog of mental illness and family secrets. That has involved studying not only external events, but the mysteries of one person's powerful inner life, an inner life strong enough to create an explosive work of history, and also to unleash the most unforgiving type of fury and violence upon one's self.

In the meantime, in studying Iris' triumphs and struggles, I have also gained new insights into the experience of what it is like, for better and for worse, to be truly extraordinary.

CHAPTER ONE

What Did They Say Happened to Iris?

May 13, 2003, e-mail:

Dear Paula,

Thank you so much for bringing your family to my lecture yesterday—it was wonderful to reconnect with them! And seeing you last night was one of the highlights of my tour! You were an angel to introduce me to your friends and to tell Monica Eng about my new book.

(Please tell your father that my interview with Milt Rosenberg was taped last night, since the ball game ran past 10 p.m. It should air in the next few days.)

I'm now in Milwaukee, where I intend to take a long nap before my reading this evening. Thanks again for being so supportive during my stop in Chicago—I feel truly blessed to have you as my friend.

Much love,

Iris

My friendship with Iris Chang both started and ended with a single phone call from her, seventeen years apart.

In 1987, when we were both juniors in college, she was seriously considering switching her major from math and computer science to journalism. She had gotten my name from a roommate of mine who had been in one of her computer science classes, and called me for advice about taking this seemingly more risky and less traditional path. An issue was that she thought her parents, science professors at our university, had expected her to go into their field.

Even just from the sound of her voice, I felt her passion for journalism and said, "Of course, if that's what you love, go for it." Then, for about an hour, she drilled me unrelentingly with countless questions on what to expect from the journalism major, and about every aspect of my years of work on the college paper and outside freelancing. When we got off the phone, I commented to my roommate about how exhausted I was from the conversation; Iris hadn't even stopped to ask if I had to go or if I had this much time to talk to her.

Shortly after, I regretted giving Iris any encouragement to change her major. We soon became rivals. Or rather, she became my rival. I doubt she even stopped to think of anyone as her rival; that would have just slowed her down.

Iris immediately started, in seemingly systematic fashion, to frustrate all my major life ambitions. It seemed that her mission was not only to be a successful journalism student, but to be nothing short of the most successful journalist of our generation. I applied for what was considered a path-paving summer internship at a magazine in New York City, which accepted only one student per college. She got the job. I later interviewed for an internship at the *Chicago Tribune*. When I called back a week later, as instructed, the interviewer told me, "You were close, but it went to someone else from the University of Illinois. You may know her."

I was not alone in eating Iris' dust. Others on our college paper, the *Daily Illini*, openly shared my frustrations. One editor told me how Iris approached her on one of her first days on the paper during our junior year, and asked simply—without small talk or polite conversation—"How do I get your job?"

Another editor wryly said she was jealous that Iris had thought to call the *Chicago Tribune* and the *New York Times* to become a stringer from our school. She explained that she personally would have only made that move in response to some kind of overt offer or official job posting. She and her friends, who had "humorously" nicknamed Iris "Fucking Iris Chang," could only watch helplessly as Iris' stories started to run in front sections of both those national papers. And they kept appearing over the months. Iris' *New York Times* editor even told her to stop because they were getting a disproportionate amount of coverage of goings-on at the University of Illinois.

Then, after we graduated, my attitude toward her shifted again. She called me to meet up in Chicago, where she was working, and I thought about her rationally. At that point, I made a conscious decision not to hate Iris Chang.

With some distance from school, things were clearer. Any moron could see that she wasn't just getting by on her good looks. She was obviously very talented and could teach me something. As the features editor of our college paper senior year, I had edited her articles—or actually *never* edited them—because they always came in perfect. The facts, grammar, punctuation, gerunds—everything. In retrospect, I was still marveling at a lucid story she had written about recent breakthroughs in a very complicated area of artificial intelligence.

During that meeting with her in Chicago, I was immediately sorry to see that the grueling hours at her new job at the Associated Press were wearing her down. In college, she had been a steamroller of energy. But now she was frail and told me her hair was coming out. I saw then for the first time just how hard she worked, how she put a piece of herself into every story she covered.

We soon moved to lighter topics. She was happy about planning her upcoming wedding. She asked me how I was getting along. At that time, in the middle of a recession, I was fruitlessly applying for work at local suburban newspapers that wouldn't even take the time to read my ré-sumé. So I was starting to freelance. I told her of an op-ed I had written that I would try to get published. She immediately suggested that I send it to the *New York Times*. I thought she was joking. I didn't have such pretensions. I thought maybe some local alternative paper might want it.

But lo and behold, I took her advice and the piece was accepted—and a year later, on perhaps the slowest news day in history, the *Times* published it. My luck was changing. Not long before, I had signed a book contract to write on the same topic of the op-ed piece: young women and their views of feminism.

I had a revelation. So, *that* was the "Iris Code." I had finally cracked it. And it was so simple: Think big. Very big. Almost to the point of being naïve.

As I only fully realized later in looking at her letters, Iris also was very interested in learning from me, specifically about my experience with publishing a book in 1991. More than anyone I knew, she was enthusiastic and intrigued about it. Starting about the time of my first book's publication, we wrote long letters, and later, took advantage of this new thing called e-mail, in which she would batter me with detailed questions about every aspect, no matter how mundane, of writing and publishing. Throughout, she was also always available to help me work through stumbling blocks on my second book, a research project on post-boomer women's sexual attitudes, which involved analyzing overwhelming mountains of data and interview transcripts.

Meanwhile, Iris' life accelerated. She regained her old vitality and accepted an offer to write a book of her own, *Thread of the Silkworm*, which was later published in 1995, about a persecuted Chinese-American scientist and what he revealed about the paranoia of the McCarthy years toward scientists in the United States. After receiving that offer, although the money was trifling, she decided she wanted an agent to shepherd her through it. She had heard that Curtis Brown was a top agency, looked up their number, dialed it, and asked to speak to one of their best agents. A few minutes later, she had succeeded in her mission.

In 1997, with similar focus, she published her blockbuster *The Rape of Nanking*. Then, I was *really* impressed.

In China, World War II atrocities have long been a national nightmare, and they have received attention from historians and academics over the years. But it took Iris' energy, will, and engaging writing style to make the scope of the Nanking massacre come alive to a popular audience in the West. Her main contribution was her sense of outrage over Japanese war crimes, which tapped into what so many others of Asian descent were already feeling. She had also made a major historical discovery: the hidden diary of John Rabe, a "good Nazi" living in Nanking at the time, which chronicled the atrocities in China in new detail and with new authority.

From her letters, I knew how hard Iris had worked on that book. On her own, she traveled through China, Hong Kong, and Taiwan to interview survivors; she spent months researching at the National Archives in Washington, D.C., and reading records from Naval Intelligence and the State Department; she tracked down many diaries and letters from those on the scene; and pored over source materials in four languages. In an interview in 2001, the late historian Stephen Ambrose described Chang as "maybe the best young historian we've got, because she understands that to communicate history, you've got to tell the story in an interesting way."

Iris was genuinely shocked by the atrocities she had exposed, and reacted with a pure, honest rage—like someone seeing evil for the very first time. She couldn't understand the possibility of knowing about such things and *not* writing about them. Part of the power of her interviewing was that she had few filters, defense mechanisms to block out disturbing things that were said to her; I suspect she didn't even know that people came with filters.

Iris also seemed to enjoy her success, which came completely naturally to her. After the publication of *The Rape of Nanking* and all the resulting new demands on her, our e-mails became shorter and less frequent. But we still managed to talk by phone from time to time. She called me to watch her on *Nightline*, read her interview in the *New York Times*, and see her on the cover of *Reader's Digest*. Her life seemed to get more glamorous, and enviable, by the day, with reports of Hollywood meetings with filmmakers such as Oliver Stone and Stephen Spielberg, batting about names like Jeremy Irons playing John Rabe and Emma Thompson playing one of the other ill-fated Western heroes in Nanking that she had written about, American missionary Minnie Vautrin.

In the months that followed, Iris continued to make headlines. A career-defining moment was her jaw-droppingly ballsy confrontation with a top Japanese official on national television, PBS's *McNeil-Lehrer NewsHour* on December 1, 1998. For the Asian-American community, it was very notable to see a person of Chinese descent so forcefully challenge a high-ranking Japanese official. This was also startling because of traditional Japanese culture, which strongly avoids direct confrontation, especially in public.

The news peg for the interview was that the Japanese government had recently issued a formal written apology to South Korea for war crimes. The Chinese had expected their own apology to follow with the recent first-ever state visit to their country from Japan, but were now disappointed that that had not happened. The Japanese official who appeared on *NewsHour*, Ambassador Kunihiko Saito, had been a vocal critic of Iris in the past, and started off by saying that verbal apologies from Japan issued so far had been sufficient.

In response, Iris relentlessly questioned Saito, asserting that past apologies had been too limited. She said, "Well, I have to say—in all honesty—that the Chinese people are in deep pain for the fact that they don't believe that a sincere—unequivocal and sincere apology has ever been made by Japan to China. And I think that the measure really of a true apology is not what a person or a government gives grudgingly under pressure. A measure of a true apology is what one person feels in his heart when he makes an apology."

After much verbal sparring with Saito, she sprung the dare on him, which she had carefully planned in advance: "What I'm curious to know is can the ambassador, himself, say today on national TV live that he personally is profoundly sorry for the Rape of Nanking and other war crimes against China, and the Japanese responsibility for it?"

Saito responded that he "recognize[ed] that acts of cruelty and violence were committed by the members of the Japanese military, and we are very sorry for that." Then he said that the Japanese are carrying the burden and are teaching accurate history to the next generation. The conversation continued:

> [Moderator] Elizabeth Farnsworth: [to Iris] Did you hear an apology?
>
> Iris Chang: I don't know. Did you hear an apology? I really didn't hear the word "apology" that was made. And I think that if he had said genuinely, "I personally am sorry for what the Japanese military [did] during World War II," I would have considered that an apology. But it's—I think that would have been a great step in the right direction. But, again, there are words that are used such as—words like "regret," "remorse," "unfortunately things happen." It's because of these—
>
> Elizabeth Farnsworth: We have to go.
>
> Iris Chang: —these types of wording and the vagueness of these expressions that the Chinese people, I think, find infuriating.
>
> Elizabeth Farnsworth: Thank you both very much for being with us.
>
> Kunihiko Saito: Well, just one more point—

I could sympathize somewhat with Saito's frustration. Iris' relentless questioning also had often overwhelmed me. While talking with Iris usually energized me, I have to admit I needed to be prepared: I would usually wait for days to call her back because I knew a conversation with her would require a minimum of two to three hours.

Despite the typical work-related conflicts we both dished about, Iris often reminded me how lucky we were to be authors, to be able to spend our days writing about what most interests us. "Always remember how privileged you are," she told me, when I related my regular doubts as to whether my life course was one of pure folly.

At that time, I also gradually accepted, with appreciation, that she was my rival. I came to see: rivals are good. We need rivals. They raise the bar for us, to make us aspire to levels we would not have even thought of earlier. In being my rival, she was sort of a mentor.

I realized that I could also identify with her because she reminded me of myself—only much more so. I saw myself as Iris Lite. As in a typical memoir or novel of friendship, it would sound more literary to portray one of us as shy and lacking confidence and the other, bold. "And then I learned to overcome my shyness through her boldness," it would go. But, in reality, while Iris did inspire me, we were both very ambitious and likely to offend others with our directness and intensity.

And that difference in extremes did work on a practical level in a friendship, as the most basic sitcom dynamics show. Like how Will's best friend in the TV show *Will and Grace* was a zanier version of him; the same was true of Frasier's brother Niles on the TV show *Frasier*. The more extreme characters help to balance out the other ones—and make them feel more "normal."

During Iris' visits to Chicago, usually on some kind of book tour, my friends occasionally noted her quirks, sometimes humorously, and sometimes not. She was still pissing people off, always without realizing it. Once, when she was in town for a book tour, I connected her with a reporter friend at a local paper. She appalled him by calling him up and, without any foreplay involved, told him the details of what he was to cover.

I introduced her to some other friends after her first reading for *The Rape of Nanking* in Chicago. They clearly admired her, although they admitted she was a little "self-absorbed." During a conversation at a party afterward, she kept drifting to a nearby computer to check her Amazon rankings online and complained that the publisher, expecting modest sales, had not printed enough books.

Instead of being offended by such comments, I was now entertained. Partly, I appreciated these traits of directness and fearlessness, which can offend others socially, as ideal traits for a journalist. I also viewed Iris' manner as a refreshing recently-off-the-boat class thing, which we shared. While she certainly wasn't from an underprivileged background, she was someone in the position of striving, of creating all her own contacts herself. She didn't have the luxury of, or even the desire for, "coolness," or the posture of ironic detachment from achieving success. She cared about it, and was open about caring about it. One only strives when they need something, I thought, like the otherwise low-key public radio hosts who suddenly gain passion in their voices during the pledge-drive season.

Some friends wondered why Iris never wore a wedding ring, though she was married. I could understand her reasoning. She said she didn't want anything encumbering her movement—but I was surprised at her surprise at some of the results. She seemed honestly aghast and unprepared whenever a supposedly earnest intellectual type at some conference on "torture and atrocity" made a pass at her.

After these visits, I also knew what to expect from her. A week later, without fail, she'd send me a snapshot she'd taken of us, which I filed away with the letters that enclosed them. They were often written on old-fashioned homey stationery or cards, the type your immigrant grandmother would buy at Walgreen's, with simple and unsleek scenes of sparkly Christmas trees or flowers.

By that time, I was definitely a firm convert to the Iris Code, and I spread the gospel. When I occasionally spoke at universities and then was a guest at writing classes, I lectured students to "Iris Chang" it. She had become a verb to me. An action verb.

"Think big!" I told them. "That's half the battle! What do you have to lose? If someone turns you down, they turn you down, so what? And then you move on. Just get a sense of entitlement, will you? It doesn't matter if you're in the Midwest. Or if you're at a public school. Decide what you want and go get it. To the point of being naïve. Your voice is not your voice. It's the voice of your generation! Just Iris Chang it!" I explained, almost taking on her passionate tone as I spoke.

What I remember most about the morning of November 7, 2004, in Louisville after Iris' last phone call to me was the baby who was projectile vomiting.

The baby didn't make a big deal of it; she looked as angelic and sleepy as the day before. But every once in a while, she would just casually open her mouth and let out a jet stream that shot several feet straight across the room. Her father said that they had been up all night with a mop and were even considering wearing raincoats for protection.

"She picks up everything in day care," her mother explained apologetically.

Of course, my thoughts were mainly about Iris. I planned to call her right when I got to the airport late that afternoon and would have time to talk in private. I had made it a custom to return her calls whenever possible at the airport, especially in the case of long layovers and delayed flights, when I had rare stretches of unoccupied time. When I arrived at the terminal, early as planned, I first checked my home voice mail and got a disturbing message from a neighbor back in Chicago.

I learned that a former neighbor, Carole, had died. This was a surprise because she had seemed in the peak of health and happiness when she retired the year before from her receptionist job in Chicago to her storybook-cute tiny house in Florida. I called the messenger back, who told me that Carole had suddenly developed lung cancer and died only in the past several months. I was so upset I decided to wait and call Iris the next day from home.

The rest of that night I worried about Iris. In a journal entry, I simply wrote, "Iris is in danger." That night at home, I talked with a friend who called, the same one who had introduced me to Iris so long ago in college, who suggested I get on a plane right away to San Jose, where Iris lived. But I thought that was too impulsive and might make too much of a fuss.

At least my intentions to call her had been good. The next day, after fielding an unusually large number of work-related phone calls, I went for lunch at Chipotle, the Mexican food chain, and stared at myself in the reflective metal table as I ate. Halfway through the burrito, I put it down, surprised that I had no desire to finish it. I went home and did some online searches for Iris' friends.

A little later on, I suddenly sprang out of my chair, ran to the bathroom, and found that I was possessed with my own jet propulsion. The flying burrito had such force that it could not be contained; the violent force rocked my entire body, splattering the stuff from my throat beyond the toilet and all over the bathroom. I got up to try to solve the great mystery of where to find a rag for cleanup; my mind was blank. By then the room started spinning and sounds faded in and out. I carefully lowered myself to the floor, where I would have no risk of fainting, as I had done in such situations in the past. I hugged the checkered tile through that night, occasionally beset by dark thoughts. The flu was making my usual dagger-like head pain extra fierce, and I didn't feel strong enough to endure yet another long sleepless night, on top of all this nausea and dizziness. Then I thought of how much worse Carole must have felt, with an illness so bad that it had actually killed her.

The next morning, a rainy November 9, I felt even worse, now unable to eat or even drink without retching, feeling almost paralyzed by the drill behind my left eye. I knew I had to call Iris or her husband or friends, but I couldn't muster the energy. At about 11:30 a.m., my cell phone rang, and the caller ID read "anonymous call." I tried to remember if that's how Iris' number sometimes came up, and I felt a wave of guilt as I stood by and allowed the call to ring six times, waiting for it to go into voice mail. When I checked for a message, there was none. Later, I checked the log of past "received calls" on the cell phone, and it listed Iris' Saturday call as having come from her home phone. This new call from "anonymous" must have been from someone else. But then again, Iris had called me from a variety of numbers in the past.

Late that night, I felt a bit better and e-mailed Iris to say that I was sorry about how badly she was feeling and that we'd talk very soon.

I managed to get to sleep that night, and woke up to a sudden calm, like the demon of illness had done its work and then passed completely through me. It had left just as abruptly as it had come, and I was now free to go on with my life. Outside, the day was sunny and clear. I got out of bed and went to check my voice mail, while also logging on to my e-mail.

"Paula, I was so sorry to read the news in the *Tribune* this morning," said the voice of my friend, Amy Keller. "That's so sad about Iris Chang."

As I continued to hold the phone to my ear, the America Online sign-on screen appeared, and the top left corner box announced its top news story of the morning: "Best-selling author Iris Chang found dead in car on road in California."

I ran downstairs to get the *Tribune* and opened it to the obituary page. There was the one unflattering picture of Iris ever taken, of her with her mouth open as she was probably responding to a critic in debate, looking upset and wild-eyed.

The short story said that the morning before, "a motorist noticed her car parked on a side road, checked the vehicle and called police. The official cause of death has not been released, but investigators concluded that Ms. Chang, who was hospitalized recently for a breakdown, shot herself in the head. . . . In a note to her family, she asked to be remembered as the person she was before she became ill—'engaged with life, committed to her causes, her writing and her family. . . . '"

Always one step ahead of me.

I was arrested with horror, much of it directed at myself. The questions started flowing: what if it had been Iris who had called me that morning of her death, the morning before, and I had just ignored her? I was also angry at her, for her deception. That bizarre call on Saturday was meant as a good-bye. Well, actually, I thought, she was open with me on the phone, not lying at all, instead just not answering certain questions. That was what those silences were. But the larger act, planning it all out in advance, was a deception, definitely.

I remembered my last e-mail to her and, not thinking straight, wondered if she had read it. I used the America Online option that allows you to check the status of mail sent to other AOL customers. It said that it was read late last night, soon after I sent it. But Iris had died that morning. Perhaps her husband was using her e-mail?

I called my parents and some friends and then sent a mass e-mail to alumni of the *Daily Illini* from our era there. Immediately, among the other e-mails to pour in, I heard from Monica Eng, a features writer for the *Chicago Tribune*, whose work I had also edited—or also not edited—in college. She had met Iris at her 2003 Harold Washington Library speech in Chicago. Since then, Monica (whose father is Chinese) and Iris had bonded over their similar backgrounds. Iris had interned at the *Chicago Tribune*, and they both had children the same age. In her personal tribute to Iris in the *Tribune* that would follow later that week, Monica added that they both married white men they met at college and had "borne them adorable hybrid sons."

In her one-line e-mail, Monica asked me to call her as soon as I could. "What happened?" she asked me, soon after on the phone.

"I don't know," I said. "I just talked to her on Saturday. I had no idea this would happen."

Monica asked me, "I know this sounds strange, but was it the election? So many people are depressed because last week Bush got in again."

"No, definitely not," I said, surprised at the preposterousness of this notion. "She was talking about other things, and she wasn't being rational. She was clearly out of touch with reality." As an example, I told her about Iris' fears about "giving her son autism through vaccines."

She paused. "That's not so crazy," said Monica. "That's a big debate really going on, if vaccines can lead to autism. Something about the mercury content. Another reporter here from California was telling me about it."

"Oh," I said, pausing to reconsider. "Yeah, they are more worried about that kind of stuff over there."

"Maybe it was postpartum depression," she said.

"I don't know," I said, thinking back on my own research on women's health issues. I'd read that postpartum depression just lasted up to a year, and her son was going on three years old.

"What else did she tell you?" I hesitated, but still told Monica about Iris' statement that she had feared for her life because of material she had uncovered.

"It's like a Hitchcock movie!" answered Monica. "A friend calls you up, tells you she fears for her life, and three days later, she dies under mysterious circumstances."

"But it was probably a suicide," I asserted sadly. "She even talked longingly about 'wanting the lights to go out.'"

After we hung up, I lay down, feeling even more unsettled, and thought about how I hate mysteries from books and movies. Life is naturally full of enough mysteries and other people's puzzling behaviors; who has the energy to take one on for entertainment? Besides, life is not that clear-cut. Our large problems are rarely solved or explained by finding a single villain with one clear motive, like knocking off a spouse to cash in on an insurance policy. That was something simple enough to play out in an hour-long *Law and Order* TV episode or maybe in a board game, to find Mrs. Plum guilty in the drawing room with the candlestick. Here, in the case of a probable suicide, the murderer was already known, and the mystery was just beginning.

And with the self as the alleged enemy, the truth of what happened, the inner dynamics involved, could be infinitely complex. The brutality of the event, and the inner world of the victim, could be overwhelming in intensity. I thought how some of my worst moments—of anxiety, migraine, insomnia—were not inflicted by others, but originated from myself, internally.

The possibility of Iris' death by suicide was also scarier to me for purely selfish reasons than the possibility of murder. If it was a case of the Japanese right wing going after her, which many people were then guessing, then I'd be safe from the same fate. If it was suicide, then I didn't really

know how I was any different from her. If it could happen to her, someone who was so together and "perfect," then I was even more vulnerable.

That night, I started to track down Iris' far-flung friends, to get more
information. I called Amy Orfield Kohler, Iris' closest friend from grade
school. Feeling shocked and guilty herself, she tried to console me that at
least I had gotten the opportunity to say good-bye—and that Iris had
clearly made up her mind at that point to do the deed. In fact, Iris had left
her a message similar to the one she had left me, but Amy had never managed to return the call. I later e-mailed another friend of Iris', who echoed
the same regret that he had not called her recently because of the time and
energy commitment typically required for a phone conversation with her.

The next day, newspapers across the world reported the story in more
detail. The local police had confirmed that Iris' death was indeed a suicide, and they would most likely not investigate it as a murder, pending
the release of the coroner's report. However, rumors still circulated that
Iris was done in by Japanese extremists, who had hounded her personally
for years and even stopped her book from being published in Japan in
1999. Her friend, pundit Steve Clemons in Washington, D.C., commented online in *The Washington Note*:

> *It would be irresponsible for me to suggest anything more than
> the authorities are suggesting about her death, but I would
> add that I find it distressing and worrisome that two bril-
> liant change-agents, Iris Chang and the late film-maker Juzo
> Itami, who made us see our worlds differently than we other-
> wise would—each supposedly committed suicide, after bouts of
> depression. I have never bought the story of Juzo Itami, whom
> I also knew and who was at war in his films with Japan's na-
> tional right wing crowd and yakuza [criminal gangs].*

Also muddling things was the fact that many of the stories of Iris'
death—including my own that would soon follow in Salon.com—raised
more questions than they answered with their vagueness. In two *San*

Francisco Chronicle articles published online on November 12, reporter Heidi Benson wrote about an interview with Iris' husband, Brett. He had said that the root causes of her suicide were depression and exhaustion, which had developed only in the past three months. He explained that the breakdown of Iris' health was related to her relentless touring for her book, *The Chinese in America*, in the spring, and the grueling nature of doing research for her new book. "She was so driven," he said. "On top of the demands of being a working mother, she always pushed herself right to the limit. She would work until she crashed. She pushed herself far beyond what she should have done and had to be taken to the hospital." Benson added that in October, "her condition was serious enough" to send their son Christopher to live with his paternal grandparents in central Illinois. The articles still gave no time of death; was it before 9:30 a.m. PST?

Much discussion in the media also focused on the possible toll of her grisly subject matter, which seemed like the most likely trigger for her death. I pondered her emotional sensitivity to others' pain, which had both inspired her and weakened her. After her death, her peers acknowledged that she had been successful in that respect, in conveying the feelings of the massacre's victims. "Nobody voiced their pain better than Iris Chang," wrote Terry Tang in the Asian-American women's magazine *Audrey*.

I thought more about what she had been working on in those last months, the Bataan topic. At that time, I hardly knew what the Bataan Death March was. So I did some basic research, talking to a transcriber of Iris' interviews. The typist told me that she had cried all the way through the work because it was so intensely sad. The interviews covered the brutal ordeals suffered by U.S. soldiers during their time as prisoners of the Japanese in the Philippines in World War II. The Americans had surrendered to the Japanese after almost starving to death in resistance. Then, their Japanese captors starved and tortured them further, often for years, and with unimaginable cruelty. A soldier, for example, would be ordered to bury his friend alive. If he refused, they would make someone else bury them both alive. The Japanese soldiers generally believed that surrender in any circumstance was cowardly, and so they felt entitled to brutalize the American soldiers all the more.

In Iris' interviews with them, many surviving elderly U.S. soldiers also had complained that their government had turned a blind eye to them. Besides feeling abandoned while they were prisoners, the men were upset that the United States did not adequately prosecute the captured Japanese offenders. One talked about expecting finally to come home to the United States to great fanfare. However, few people at home seemed interested in what they had gone through. "'But then, there was no rockets' red glare,'" one veteran said, over and over again, referring to the celebration he had longed for.

As was the case with many of her other subjects, that interview was probably the first time that soldier had talked about his experiences in the war. A war in which his comrades had sacrificed so dearly, some with their lives, and others, with their sanity. Iris represented some of these men's last hope to get their stories told.

I realized that this material was indirectly, and directly, critical of the U.S. government. Good lord, I thought, she was waging this fight during wartime. Is this what she was referring to when she mentioned her fears of "people in high places" wanting to get her? But wouldn't the government have better things to do, to go after real enemies?

A few days passed and I dug up some of Iris' old e-mails to me. I skimmed over some short letters, including her earliest ones to me, from about the time she started researching her first book, *The Thread of the Silkworm*. It was the first of many letters in which she showed tremendous enthusiasm for my work. She also was always concerned about my health, and expressed confidence that I would feel better with the right strategy.

I found a postcard that I hadn't remembered receiving, from March 19, 2001, from her vacation to the hot springs in Calistoga, north of San Francisco. She asked me to consider joining her there months later to celebrate my finishing my last book and her finishing the last draft of *The Chinese in America*. I never took her up on it. One of her last e-mails to me, a warm one from the day after her lecture at the Harold Washington Library, also kept me up at night for how I had taken her for granted.

The most unusual memento I found was a transcript, of an hours-long interview I had done with Iris in 1993 when I had stayed with her on a research trip to Santa Barbara. One night, I had been discussing with her the interviews I had done that day on women's gender roles, and she started giving insights from her own life. I had turned my tape recorder on, in case there was anything I could use later for background in the book. Now I couldn't bring myself to read it.

To pay my condolences, I left a message with Brett. Iris' voice was still on the outgoing message. A few days later, Brett returned my call, offering a bit more information. "Thank goodness for Sominex," he said, with some irony, saying that he felt better after finally getting some sleep the night before.

While clearly devastated, he spoke with his characteristic rational and steady tone. I had gotten to know him a bit, despite his quiet and introverted ways, staying with him and Iris several times in California through the years. He explained to me his shock at waking up in the early morning of November 9 to find her gone. Soon after, to the shock of all, the police found her on Highway 17.

Brett said that in the past several months he and her parents had tried to get Iris help, which she had rejected. After many sleepless nights, she insisted in August on going alone on a research trip to Louisville—ironically, where I was visiting for the first time when she called me. "She was up all night reading Web sites, just being tormented, believing every word of them," he said. I didn't ask which Web sites they were, knowing how fragile he was feeling.

Iris had a breakdown on that trip to Louisville and was institutionalized for a few days, very involuntarily, by people she knew there. I didn't know who they were. She was so frightened that Brett wouldn't dare to commit her to a mental health facility when she returned home. He did get her to go to therapy back in California, where she would take over the sessions and then defiantly ignore medical advice. In other efforts, in the months before her death, he and Iris had methodically set up a "twenty-point plan to get Iris well." One of those points was to call friends—as a source of support. I was one of the few she had reached. He expressed his shock at all she had been doing to prepare for the suicide in the weeks leading up to it, including buying an antique gun, which was difficult to use.

While I knew the outcome, I still, irrationally, wanted to know if our conversation from the night of November 6 had helped console her at all.

"After you talked, she did seem better," Brett said, explaining that he had actually entered the room in the last few minutes or so of our conversation, despite Iris' protests to me that he had not been there. "We talked for a while about that 'standing in the fire' thing." For the next few days, she even seemed better than normal. That night, they went to see the movie *Ray*—she had always been a huge movie buff—and she went to a day spa for a massage on Sunday.

Brett told me about the visitation and funeral, which would be held in a few weeks in Los Altos, outside of San Jose, and invited me to speak there. He promised to e-mail the details. Soon after, I checked my e-mail and saw a new message from irischang@aol.com. I was startled and then remembered it was Brett using her e-mail address.

Monica and I decided to go together to California, Iris' home for the past thirteen years. The *Chicago Tribune* was sending her there to begin research on the in-depth story on Iris' death that she was writing. I was glad to have a companion for this difficult trip.

We arrived on the night of the pre-funeral "visitation service" at Spangler Mortuary in Los Altos, a center of Silicon Valley affluence—as I remembered Iris herself telling me several years before when she and Brett were planning to move there. Immediately, from outside the small funeral home, I sensed the level of public anguish about her death and how symbolic she had been as a Chinese American. Outside was a blown-up photo of Iris, looking downward, regally and beatifically, with her hands clasped.

An Asian-American activist group had set up the display. The rain spattered across the front of the photo like tears. On the altar-like table before her, surrounded by flickering rows of candles, was a long quote from Iris' third and final book, *The Chinese in America*, about how Asian Americans are often still regarded as foreigners because of the way they look, despite deep roots in this country. I went back later to find at least part of it: "'Go back to where you came from' is a taunt most new immigrants have faced at some point. As one put it, 'Asian Americans feel like we're a guest in someone else's house, that we can never really relax and put our feet up on the table.' Accents and cultural traditions may disappear, but skin tone and the shape of one's eyes do not." (390)

We entered the building and got in line behind dozens of swarming and chatting people, mostly Asian, to pass by the body and give our regrets to the family. Some reporters from Asia were on the scene. I looked ahead and saw that it was an open casket. I panicked a bit. I had not expected this. Part of my fear was rooted in my own background, which surprised me at moments like this in the strength of its hold. Jewish people customarily don't have open caskets, and I had only seen a dead body a few times in my life, and then, only with eyes partially averted. Before I had left for California, my mother had warned me about this, recalling how she as a young adult had seen the body of her aunt, who had married a Gentile, at an open-casket funeral, and then suffered the worst nightmares of her life. Unfortunately, I had mistakenly assured my mother that the manner of Iris' death would preclude an open-casket service.

As a compromise, I decided I would only look at her from a distance, but that I would look away when we got up close. From across the room, I could see that she looked like an idealized wax-doll version of herself. She was wearing her familiar cobalt blue "speaking suit." In life, Iris had two basic outfits: She either wore this suit when in public, or sweats and glasses when in private—and there wasn't much in between. That casualness is how I most remembered her, and she viewed the fancier clothes as no more than a uniform she had to put on to fit the part of serious author.

We shuffled by the wreath-covered casket and the tall, elaborate displays of flowers, many of them irises, which had been sent by Chinese-American activist groups—The Global Alliance for Preserving the History of W.W. II in Asia, the Chinese Alliance for Memorial and Justice, the St. Louis Alliance for Preserving the Truth of Sino-Japanese War. I glanced for a split second at Iris, and then had a somewhat comforting fleeting thought that she did look peaceful. She certainly wasn't being tormented by anxieties any more. Maybe that is why these goyim do this open-casket thing, I thought. Closure. And to see the person at "rest."

Later, I introduced myself to Iris' mother, whom I had never before met. Whenever I met with Iris after college, it was in Chicago or California, and until their recent move to San Jose to be nearer to family, Iris' parents had lived in Urbana. She brightened up and said in heavily accented English, "Iris talked about you a lot. She was so happy to write for the *Daily Illini*!"

I was moved to realize that the college paper, circulation twenty thousand, was actually important to Iris, even years later.

As we parted, she added, "Iris was so innocent. She was innocent."

I agreed. "She was naïve," I said, and then I worried if the word "naïve" sounded patronizing, a step more judgmental than "innocent."

A biographical display set up in the front of the mortuary overlooking the parking lot, far from the casket, revealed Iris' family's deep pride. Many childhood photos, from family trips and birthday parties. The framed *Reader's Digest* cover photo. Diplomas from the University of Illinois, Johns Hopkins (for her MA), and two honorary PhDs.

In the midst of this somber scene, I noticed a humorous picture of Brett with President Clinton in December 1998. The president's expression was one of dazed amusement. Later that afternoon I asked Brett about it, and he explained that they had been standing in a long receiving line to meet the president, the host for one of his famed celebrity-filled "Renaissance weekend" retreats in Hilton Head, South Carolina. Iris was invited because her book had been on the best-seller list for many weeks that year. While the others had just shaken hands with President Clinton and then moved on, when her turn came up, Iris stopped and gave him a three- to four-minute speech about her book and the need to get Japan to apologize. The president said he would try and took her book from her. Then she arranged a picture of him with her husband. Without any sense of self-consciousness, she spent a few minutes posing the president just right, closer to her husband, while directing the Secret Service men to step aside.

Other photos revealed Iris' truly all-American Midwestern side, such as a very innocent picture of a very young looking Brett and Iris from a sorority dance, circa 1988, titled "Peppermint Twist Social." In another picture, her proud parents waved to her as she rode in a convertible in the homecoming parade. To me it had been a seemingly unexplainable twist in her life that Iris ran for the homecoming court junior year and was chosen as one of its nine "princesses."

A few minutes later, I talked to some of Iris' friends whom I had met through the years. They were also in shock. I was the only one among them whom she had managed to contact in the days before her death. Monica soon consoled me, telling me I wasn't the only one who had a clue of the suicide to come. She had learned that Iris' mother had made Iris promise "not to hurt herself" in the week before her death. In an especially uncharacteristic move for Iris, an avowed atheist, she had called out to her neighbor the day before her suicide and said, "Pray for me."

At the end of the evening, Iris' mom invited me to stay, along with Iris' longtime friend and agent, Susan Rabiner, to take pictures. I was relieved that her mother wasn't insulted by my "naïve" comment. We stood in a line beside the open casket. Then Iris' mom asked me to turn to it and look at Iris. I peered to the side, away from her, and did the best I could.

The next day, Monica and I drove up the winding road to the mission-style chapel at the Gate of Heaven Cemetery, where the service was held. The crowd's swarming size looked like something assembled for the level of a funeral for a head of state. We had to park several blocks away because

of the fleets of cars parked ahead of us. We then walked across the daz-
zlingly beautiful grounds, whose rolling hills were full of biblical-looking
trees and flowers. When we approached the crowd overflowing from the
back of the chapel, we were greeted by a grizzled old veteran in his uniform standing resolutely with a salute. We shuffled through layers of reporters and cameras from many countries, especially from China and
Korea. We found out that that same day, services were also being held simultaneously in Washington, D.C., and in Nanjing, China, (the modern
name for Nanking) where Iris was well known.

We threaded our way to the back of the chapel, where loudspeakers
blared one of Iris' recorded speeches about social justice. Her voice was
gentle yet firm. After an introduction by Ignatius Ding, a prominent
Chinese-American activist for war reparations from Japan who conducted
the service, the family spoke.

Next were friends, including myself, who talked about how Iris inspired us. Author James Bradley, clad in a satiny Chinese warrior-type formal outfit, gave a thunderous and rapturous speech, directed at Iris' son,
Christopher (for whom the service was being taped, to watch in adulthood). Bradley also talked about how Iris had inspired him, specifically to
publish his best-selling World War II book, *Flags of Our Fathers*. In 1997,
after rejections from twenty-seven publishers, Bradley was encouraged to
see Iris' Nanking book on that era on the best-seller list. He wrote to the
author. "She responded with a picture postcard encouraging me. The picture on the postcard was a photo of her." The audience laughed a bit at
this immodest move.

"I hung the postcard photo of Iris on the wall of my study. Every day,
as I wrote through my fears, I said to myself, 'If she could do it, I can do
it,'" he said. He added that Iris later had even called him with a vital lead
to contact a specific veteran in Iowa for a story about airmen in World
War II. That contact became the basis of his second best-selling book,
Flyboys.

Next came Iris' agent (who had been the official editor of her first two
books before moving on to work as a literary agent), Susan Rabiner, who

expressed her awe at Iris' precocious talent. As an editor at Basic Books, she had connected with Iris at Johns Hopkins, where she was completing her master's degree in science writing. Susan was looking for a biographer for Dr. Hsue-Shen Tsien, the father of the Chinese missile program, who had been expelled from the United States in the 1950s. It would be a challenge for many reasons, such as the fact that Tsien, who was still alive and in China, would not cooperate; he was a very powerful Henry Kissinger–like behind-the-scenes figure surrounded by layers of protectors. And much information about him, in both China and the United States, was still apparently classified. Further, the biographer had to be able to, literally, understand rocket science. Susan thought that Iris looked too young to tackle such a project but told her to "take a flyer" about the project and follow up anyway.

Less than two months later, Iris called Susan to say that she had tracked down and had just spent four hours talking to Tsien's son. Susan signed her up, and Iris became, at the age of twenty-three, the youngest author at Basic Books.

After her first book was published, revealing her innocence, Iris asked Susan if she could pay Basic Books to publish a book on the Rape of Nanking. Susan said that was not necessary—the publisher would pay Iris—and Susan went ahead and commissioned the book. Later, Susan became her agent when Iris published her third book, *The Chinese in America*, with Viking.

By chance, as she recounted, Susan had talked to Iris the night before her death, when Iris returned a phone call about a minor publishing matter. At the end of the call, Iris told Susan, "I love you," and Susan answered the same. Later, I asked her if Iris had hinted at suicide and she said no. "We [her family and I] knew she was depressed, but never imagined that she would . . . kill herself," she said.

Finally, there were the activists for reparations for war crimes from Japan. I had to do a double take when I read the next name in the program, Iris Chang Herrera, who was described as "Iris' young protégé." Iris had inspired her as a teenager, like many young Asian women, to become an activist. By coincidence, they had the same name, with the younger Iris' mother being from Shanghai and her father from Costa Rica.

When the funeral service ended, we walked outside across the vast grounds to witness the burial. As the casket was very slowly lowered into the ground, the air was uncomfortably silent. Since Iris and Brett were atheists, no religious ceremony was planned for the occasion. So someone in the group suggested that we sing "God Bless America," and then, awkwardly, a birthday song for Iris, in advance of what would have been her thirty-seventh birthday the following March.

Iris' mom invited me to a dinner with the family afterward at a Chinese restaurant in Los Altos. She said I could bring Monica. When we arrived, I approached Brett. I had brought him some cookies, in a gift basket, to possibly bring to his home in case we would gather there. But it turned out that we were going to the restaurant instead. I had bought them at a café in Chicago. They were shaped and colored like fall leaves, and had caught my eye as something pretty and upbeat. As I handed him the cellophane-covered package, I looked down and saw that some of the deceptively fragile cookies had broken, although I thought I had packed them carefully.

"They're cracked," I said, handing them to him. "I'm sorry. I should have been more careful."

Monica and I happened to sit with some Chinese-American activists at one of the half-dozen huge round tables set up in the restaurant's private dining room. As the waiters placed lavish platters of fish, beef, chicken, and duck on the revolving lazy Susans in the centers of the tables, we all talked about our shock. One older woman activist asked if anyone had suspected that Iris was even contemplating suicide. With some uneasiness, I said that Iris had called me three days before and made that "turn the lights out" comment.

"Then why didn't you do anything about it?" the woman asked, visibly upset.

Because I had other friends and family who had made such statements through the years and had never acted on it. Because Iris had more to live for than anyone and I couldn't fathom that happening. Because I didn't want to create a big stir and panic needlessly. Because I had thought such things myself, and never came close to acting on them. Because I had assumed I was already a good friend, which had always been a point of pride and satisfaction in my life.

"I had the flu and was incapacitated," I answered.

On our way out, the woman stopped Monica and implored her to find out what really had happened to Iris.

After the funeral, I received an e-mail from Helen Zia, a well-known author and activist on Asian-American issues, who had been a friend of Iris'. We soon followed up on the phone. Helen filled me in about Iris' parents—her father was a physicist and her mother was a microbiologist— whom she also knew. That was the first time I learned how renowned Iris' parents were as scientists in China and Taiwan, and how prominent their families had been there. While in school in Taiwan, her father, Shau-jin, was *the* top scorer in the highly valued national college entrance exam, in the sections on science, engineering, and medicine.

"The top students become legendary with huge expectations that they will become future Nobel laureates, or so I'm told," Helen said.

Both of Iris' parents had come to the United States at about the same time, in the early 1960s, when both of them won science scholarships to complete their doctorates at Harvard University. Iris was born in Princeton, New Jersey, where her father had done his post-doctorate work, at the renowned Institute for Advanced Study. (They had lived on Einstein Lane, named after one of the institute's most famous teachers.) Then, when Iris was two, they received faculty appointments at the University of Illinois and moved to Urbana.

Iris' extraordinary ambition started to make more sense to me, considering her background with and influence of such acclaimed achievers. While I had known her parents were successful, I had taken it for granted; after all, my dad shared their profession, as a professor at a Big Ten university. But I didn't realize how much more intense her drive to achieve was, especially as a first-generation American, as opposed to me as a second-generation American.

Later, Iris' closest friend in California, author Barbara Masin, whose parents had immigrated to the United States from Europe, recalled to me that a common theme that Iris brought up in their conversations was how being a first-generation American affected her expectations to succeed. It was "a topic that fascinated Iris," Barbara said. In Iris' home growing up, the expectation was expressed "in an abstract sense," something not necessarily uttered directly but just understood as a given. "It [the expectation to succeed] was such a part of the environment that it didn't need to be expressed," Barbara said.

While Iris' parents did guide her into science in college, their end goal was not necessarily limited to a specific field. Their attitude was: "You can choose what you want to do, but make sure that you excel at it," Barbara said. Iris did not see this as a negative pressure, she added; Iris was grateful that she was the first-born girl, and not a girl born after a boy, who might have been less robustly encouraged "to be all you can be." (Her younger brother was also encouraged, and accomplished, but without the same intensity as Iris, according to accounts from their high school classmates.) And, on a basic level, Iris had "a tremendous amount of respect" for what her parents had done and naturally wanted to follow their lead.

As Iris had told me over the years, while she appreciated them, one of her greatest conflicts in life was to become independent of her parents, who were very protective. As I later learned from some of Iris' earlier correspondence, Iris' first choice of college had not been any of the Big Ten, but the University of Chicago, which she turned down because her parents "absolutely refused to let me go to college in Chicago," she explained to a camp friend in a letter from 1986. "As I said before, they didn't want me to get mugged. They didn't think I'd be safe in the big city when I was away from home for the first time. And Cornell and Berkeley are too far away from home. The U of I was the least expensive and the most practical place to go, so here I am!"

Brett later explained to me that her mother was influenced about safety issues by living through two wars by the time she was ten. "Her mom was born in Chung King while the Japanese were bombing the city. So that was WWII. Her mom was born in 1940, and the war went on for another five years. And then as soon as that was over, the Chinese Civil War started. It was quite a world to be born into."

But, by all accounts, Iris openly praised her parents for encouraging her abundant curiosity from the beginning. When she was little, her parents read books about raising a gifted child, and labeled nearly everything in the house with index cards to teach her vocabulary. She wrote her first story—a mystery—at age four. From an early age, she was also talking—a lot. She dominated the family conversation, barely giving her younger brother Michael a chance to talk, as he later told Monica Eng in an interview. In sixth grade, she represented her area in the state Young Authors competition. I was also there, winning a similar award from my region. I like to think that is where we may have met—and competed—for the first time.

Soon after, I got another glimpse into the pressures of Iris' world as a symbol for larger causes when the editors of Salon forwarded me a letter from one reader.

The e-mail read:

> *I'd like to be placed in contact with Paula Kamen regarding her piece on Iris Chang. I'm an attorney with the State Department, and a couple of years ago I was involved with litigation brought by former POWs of the Japanese against various Japanese companies. I don't want to see a story written about this, but if Paula is simply interested in learning a bit more about the "controversial" context in which Ms. Chang was conducting these interviews with former POWs, I'd be happy to explain to her some of the political dynamics of the lawsuits.*

This wasn't Hitchcock, I thought. With a shadowy government figure stepping forward saying mysterious things, this was more like *The X-Files*.

I e-mailed her and suggested that she, more importantly and productively, instead get in touch with Monica Eng, who could set the record straight on what she had to say in her upcoming *Tribune Magazine* cover story.

Then the lawyer answered back via e-mail, stating that Monica had already interviewed a higher-up at the State Department for her article. Her tone was very skeptical, grouping Monica with the plaintiffs' lawyers, who "want to capitalize on that suicide to once again reawaken interest in their lawsuits. . . . Since [my boss] and I have gotten really tired of being called Nazis and traitors, there doesn't seem to be much of a point engaging with her further."

Admitting to her that I was in over my head with this issue, not even understanding most of what she was talking about, I wrote back and repeated that this was likely something that Monica would be interested in for background for her story. Then the lawyer agreed to the idea to pose these questions to Monica. I forwarded this all to Monica, relieved to be leaving a paper trail and not be totally isolated with this bizarre e-mail exchange. I thought it was strange I didn't hear back right away from Monica, as was the usual case.

Instead, a bit later, I received another e-mail from the lawyer, which stated: "By the way, exactly when did I give you permission to forward our entire e-mail exchange directly to Monica Eng for use in her story? I assume she's going to quote me directly? Gee, I hope I still have a job after this comes out. Thanks a mil."

Holding my breath, I called Monica. "Oh no," she said. "I think I know what happened." She checked her e-mail and confirmed that she had sent an e-mail she had meant for me to this lawyer instead. In the e-mail, in reaction to the lawyer's hostile tone about her, Monica had gone off on this lawyer for suspecting her, primarily an ethnic food writer—"on dumplings and curries," she would say—for having an axe to grind against the government.

For a moment, I was struck with panic that this powerful person in the federal government would retaliate against me. These were very sensitive times, when the government was mobilizing against any kind of insurgent, real or imagined. I'd be sent to Gitmo, with the others—maybe locked up in a ten-square-foot cell with nothing more to protect myself than a copy of the Koran, a prayer rug, and a few moist towelettes.

Then I came to my senses, and considered how scary Iris' world was as an activist pushing for social change and questioning power. Her life was more than the glory that I had focused on when I knew her, beyond the nice hotels that she stayed in on her book tours.

I had been embroiled in Iris' hot-button public world for only a few weeks because of my Salon article, and I was exhausted and now paranoid about persecution. I couldn't wait to get back to my topic of chronic pain, which now seemed light and cheery in comparison.

I sent a calm apology to the lawyer, who responded with another angry comment about how the media didn't care about the State Department side and that there was no use talking to me again.

Still confused over what the lawyer was talking about, I got back to Monica, who tried her best with me to laugh over this incident. She described being rattled by the vehemence of some of her sources on the other side of this POW issue, who were still trying to get reparations from Japan. A few had talked to Monica about conspiracy theories related to their cause and Iris' death.

"Well, I no longer think she was murdered," Monica told me, with a tone of self-deprecation. Although the coroner's official toxicology report would not be released until after her story ran, Monica was certain that Iris had committed suicide.

After the funeral, Monica had stayed for several days in California and talked to police on the scene in Santa Clara County, and to others involved in Iris' last days.

Evidently, Iris had plotted the suicide in meticulous detail, with clear intent to be "successful." On the morning of November 8, the day before her suicide, she dropped into Reed's Gun Sport Shop in San Jose and told the clerk that she was a historian researching antique guns. Knowing that she would fail any regular background check because of her stay in a mental hospital that summer, she had found a loophole in California law that required no waiting period to buy antique firearms.

Monica wrote in her story that after purchasing the gun,

within an hour, she had jammed the weapon, which was not hard to do because loading it involves inserting a lead ball and gunpowder into the chamber and them tamping them down. She soon found a gunsmith in Santa Clara who worked out of his home, and said he could help. He said Chang seemed unfamiliar with guns and "very distracted" as he cleared the gun and, without using real gunpowder, showed her how to load. Chang wanted to go to a shooting range right away, but the gunsmith did not have time. They made an appointment for the next day. She would never show up.

Monica reported that judging by the condition of the body, which was discovered just past nine a.m. on November 9, Iris had died between three and eight a.m. that Tuesday morning. Selfishly, I felt relieved that it had not been an hour or two later when I had wondered if she had tried to call me. That morning, at least, I could not have stopped her.

But more mysteries remained, and most of my questions were still not answered. The explanation of depression as the reason for the suicide still didn't make sense, since none of her friends, including me, remembered her as especially depressed. Her defining tone was positive. And I didn't think that one could suddenly develop such an extreme case of depression in just a few months.

Monica also had trouble understanding the basis for some of Iris' fears, some of which were revealed during her breakdown in Louisville in August of 2004. Monica learned that when Iris arrived in Louisville, she refused to leave her hotel room and directed the Bataan veterans from that area with whom she'd scheduled interviews—many of whom were old and infirm—to visit her at the hotel. She panicked wildly when one of these men, a colonel, walked in her room. Noticing that she had not eaten or drunk anything for days, he offered her a bottle of water, which she refused. One of the military men who had helped Iris coordinate the interviews told Monica that Iris seemed "possessed."

Monica also had heard anecdotally from several of Iris' friends about "the *Newsweek* incident," which she couldn't yet adequately document. It involved Iris' claims that *Newsweek* had almost canceled in November of 1997 a scheduled excerpt of *The Rape of Nanking*—in response to backlash from Japanese advertisers. The significance of the *Newsweek* conflict in Iris' life was to show her the power of Japanese corporations to conspire against her and censor information.

Very tentatively, and with the worst shock behind me, I got the opportunity to start my own investigation of these matters, hoping to keep unpeeling the layers. I knew that suicide often seems unreal, but this one was particularly hard to fathom. In these first months after Iris' death, I had gotten a good idea of how to begin, mainly about which questions I needed to ask.

CHAPTER TWO

What Did She Symbolize?

*J*uly 29, 1995, postcard:

Dear Paula,

This is my first week in the city of Nanking after flying to Hong Kong and taking the train from Guangzhou. I had a HORRIBLE two-day train ride, packed in a filthy, crowded smoking compartment with soot and 100 degree F weather, screaming babies, people spitting on the floor. By the time I arrived in Nanking, I had succumbed to flu and fever and all kinds of stomach problems, forcing me to eat oatmeal and the mildest food for days. Nanking is unbelievably hot and humid (it's considered one of the "furnace cities" of China). But people here were talking about how 100 plus people died from the heat in Chicago.

Right now I'm still physically weak but I've already interviewed eight massacre survivors on videotape. Hope your health's getting better.

Love, Iris

Of all the many reasons I could think of for not doing this book, I worried most about going insane.

I couldn't even bring myself to look at Iris at her funeral. So, I thought, how would I do that day after day, metaphorically speaking, in researching a book about her over the next many months? Would it be the constant hell that my friend Paul warned me about, of "sitting with a corpse" for two years? "You deserve a break," he said, commenting on how I had spent the last few years "in a hole" writing a book on the not-so-cheery topic of chronic pain.

I had already asked all these questions of myself on my own, plus many more. I wondered if this was amoral, exploiting a friend's tragic case for a book and possibly upsetting her grieving family. But, as Janet Malcolm of the *New Yorker* has written, writers are naturally amoral. That's a part of our basic calling as book authors, to investigate these thorny and displeasing issues, beyond the surface. And with some sensitivity, maybe I could be only minimally amoral.

But, mainly, I feared being as vulnerable as Iris. Like a lot of people, in times of extreme stress, I have felt like I'm on the edge of sanity. I wasn't sure if these moments of insanity would stretch into longer periods of time with the challenge of this subject matter. And I knew there was a particular danger or challenge with writing a book that you have to immerse yourself in over months, to the point where your mind is possessed by it, as if by demons, day and night. When I was working on past books, thoughts of the writing—themes, missing information, sentence structures, word choices—invaded every possible marginal silent space in life: time in the shower, cooking, dialing a phone and waiting for someone to pick up, listening to the radio.

At that point in early 2005, I just didn't know if my brain mechanisms were all securely fixed enough for me to find my way back home again in times of extra challenge to mental equilibrium. I had just barely recovered, mentally, from the effects of about fifteen years of absurdly still-constant pain. As for many patients, that included years of fruitless invasive treatments, such as surgery and nerve block injections. Even worse than the pain were the periodic struggles to get off the mess of in-effective yet dependency-producing drugs I was prescribed. Through trial and error, I had learned, somewhat, to "make friends with the pain" and coexist with it and deal with the related anxiety of not knowing how functional I would be from day to day.

Indeed, a major reason why Iris' death had profoundly rattled me, along with my other journalist friends, was precisely this fear of toxic mental effects resulting from writing about toxic topics. At about the time of Iris' death, we were also noticing a pile-up of writer suicide obits in the news from the past year, most notably those of investigative journalist Gary Webb, introspective performer Spalding Gray, and icon Hunter S. Thompson.

Some even wrote about it. Summing up the fears of her fellow journalists prone to depression, Seattle-based author Silja Talvi, thirty-five, best known for her investigative work on women in prison such as in her new book *Women Behind Bars*, asked "If they can't make it, how can I?" in an online article titled "Writers: R.I.P." She described "social and political pathologies" that can spread from person to person like a disease.

Silja later explained to me how Iris' death, and the other writers' deaths, validated her darkest fears of the effect of her own work. Plus, the mystery around Iris' death only made her feel more confused. She told me:

> *I know what it feels like to consider suicide as the only option, and still I'd like to think that there are . . . this is actually getting very emotional for me already—I want there to be people around like Iris, like Spalding, that give me hope and allow me in a sense to keep going because I can look up to them. The "care" people who are touching on very heavy subjects, and yet they keep going.*
>
> *And when she [Iris] died, when she killed herself, I thought, "Shit—you know, what does she know that I don't know that someone like her would kill herself?" That doesn't make any sense to me. There had to have been another option. How could*

she have gotten to that point? And so I think it only added
really to my own desperation, and then I want to know why. I
just wanted to know why. What was her story? Why did she get
to that point?

But as we talked, Silja started to give me another perspective. I asked
her if writing about difficult topics can even have the opposite effect, of
being therapeutic, to give a sense of meaning to one's life.

"No one has ever asked me that question before," she answered, "but
I think it is both. I think [the writing] gives me the sense of feeling like
there's a purpose to my life and to the work that I do—and making me
feel more hopeless about the state of humanity and the incredible cruel
and brutal things that we're capable of doing to one another as human
beings. So it's both."

Later, I talked to another artist friend, Nina Paley, who happens to be a
former high school classmate of Iris, who pointed out that morose subjects actually comfort her, making her feel less alienated. Paley, an anima-
tor based in New York City, said that she finds herself drawn to dark
topics to acknowledge and work through her own pain.

"That's the human power of art, when you 'externalize the demon,'
because it's not only working for the artist but it's also working for the
viewer. It's been just a relief for me when I've seen my own demons outside of my own head. . . . It's amazing to me what a relief it is. . . . It's
only 'normal' people who are afraid of depressing things. If you're already
depressed, it's just a relief to expose it."

Later Nina said that the film she was working on at the time was keeping her going during a difficult time. "It's like I'm doing it to save myself," she said. "All this stuff is to save myself."

I also thought more about the subject of genocide, perversely, as a possibly consoling topic—in its moral certainty. Anyone arguing on behalf of
genocide victims takes the just side. Period. Who could argue that genocide is ever justified? No gray area exists there, unlike many areas of life
and politics. There can even be an aura to it. This point came up during a

discussion of a friend's book, *Holocaust Girls,* on the actual phenomenon of some American Jewish girls growing up obsessed with that era in history. In the book, author S. L. Wisenberg explains:

"We saw films about the Holocaust in Hebrew School, we spoke of it with a hush in our voices. One third of us, our people, died. There was the mystery of Death. There was the allure of the drama as well. The idea that we could have been part of a catastrophe that was historic. And we were. Just as we said every Friday in the Kiddush over the wine, when we blessed God for bringing us out of Egypt, where we were slaves." (25)

So perhaps, I concluded, while they probably weighed her down, the depressing topics Iris covered also may have been therapeutic, on some level. Her depression may have explained why she was attracted to depressing topics in the first place, which both soothed and aggravated her inner pain.

I realized that the key to working with such potentially painful subjects and effectively dealing with any ensuing mental anguish, in the long term, seemed to be actively recognizing any personal risk involved—and preparing for it. This would be my strategy, I thought, as I planned for this book project and addressed my own fears of psychological turmoil. While I knew that I could not control all of my reactions to this sad topic, perhaps I could take some precautions to limit the trauma. A *London Times* article on Iris that I had just read used another effective metaphor, comparing Iris' work as a chronicler of atrocities to someone who cleans up nuclear waste. We would expect the nuclear waste handler to be trained in taking appropriate precautions, such as wearing special gloves, the *Times* article explained. But we still don't expect that from journalists.

One precaution I would take was to start seeing a therapist again, to check in regularly. She could monitor me and let me know immediately if I was losing my mind. I also asked all my friends to let me know right away if I seemed crazy, and I'd believe them. And maybe bumping up the Prozac another 10 mg wouldn't be such a bad idea.

I also consoled myself by acknowledging that many writers regularly cover tough topics and do NOT kill themselves. Most of the people who have chronicled the Holocaust have not killed themselves. Nor do most employed in "first responder" professions, such as ER staff, fire fighters, and police, who confront the worst of life directly.

And, my therapist made the point that the great majority of people in our culture who do kill themselves have mental illness. When I asked her how I was different from Iris, she said: "You aren't mentally ill." I hoped she was right.

I also recalled the words of Amy Tan, best-selling novelist and a friend of Iris', whom I interviewed for this book. She talked about Iris' significance in telling many, many stories about Asians, to show their complexity. "My opinion has always been to really understand anybody, any one person, you need multiple stories from that person," Tan said. "You can have a story for every day of that person's life."

And now, despite lingering doubts if I was doing the right thing, it was my turn to tell many stories about Iris.

I knew I was in for some dark research after the kind, old men in Chinatown handed me a book with photographs of severed heads.

It was a beautiful spring day in 2005, and I had just said a few words about Iris at a memorial service on Chicago's South Side. As a token of their appreciation, the organizers gave gifts to all who spoke, which included the very large 1996 coffee-table book, *The Rape of Nanking: An Undeniable History in Photographs*. I randomly opened it to a page, and decided that this would not be lying on my coffee table to greet casual visitors any time soon. I was facing a photo of an ebullient Japanese soldier who was showing off to the camera a head he was holding in his hand. At his feet lay a tangled blur of bodies of those he had slaughtered. I skimmed through the rest of the book, which pictured some of the same photos that were in the photo insert in Iris' *Rape of Nanking*: rows of bodies floating in a river, mutilated rape victims, bayoneted civilians, and dead babies.

It was at that same memorial service that I had further learned how fully the unresolved history of the World War II era inhabits present politics. At one point in the memorial service we were treated to some entertainment, featuring adorable wide-eyed girls in green velvet, braids, and tights curtsying and singing.

"How sweet," I whispered to Monica, who also had been invited to speak. "What are they singing?"

"'Down with the Japanese imperialists' and 'kill all the traitors,'" she said.

A Chinese friend of hers leaned over and explained that they were singing classic songs of resistance from World War II.

Indeed, as in the California funeral service, here Iris was a martyr for a much larger cause. The service began with a moderator giving an explanation in English for her death, short enough for two translators standing by to briefly relate it to the crowd in Cantonese and Mandarin: "She was dragged down by miserable facts of history and became depressed. Because of this she committed suicide on November 9 and died that day."

At the end of the service, I walked by long card tables in the back exhibiting many of the same photos that were in the coffee-table book. But these were enlarged to poster size. I recalled that it was a similar exhibit in California that had influenced Iris to write *The Rape of Nanking* in the first place. She often described a meeting of Chinese-American activists in December 1994 in Cupertino, a suburb of San Jose. That was when this topic overcame Iris, and picked her (although she had been talking about writing it since 1989, her husband told me).

In her book, she recalled the effects of the photo display:

> *Though I had heard so much about the Nanking massacre as a child, nothing prepared me for these pictures—stark black-and-white images of decapitated heads, bellies ripped open, and nude women forced by their rapists into various pornographic poses, their faces contorted into unforgettable expressions of agony and shame. . . . I was suddenly in a panic that*

this terrifying disrespect for death and dying, this reversion in human social evolution, would be reduced to a footnote of history, treated like a harmless glitch in a computer program that might or might not again cause a problem, unless someone forced the world to remember it. (10)

The photos had especially interested Iris because she had grown up hearing stories about the massacre from her parents, and about how her maternal grandparents had escaped by boat just before it began. "They told me that The Rape of Nanking had been so intense that the Japanese were hacking even the small children into halves and thirds and that they had thrown so many bodies into the Yangtze River that the river literally ran red with blood for days," she had said in an interview in the *Chicago Tribune* in 1998. She added that, as a girl, she had gone to the library looking for information about the massacre in English and was "baffled" that none existed.

As an outsider, I, too, was baffled about why this conflict with Japan was still so unresolved in the East—and underreported in the West. I wondered why it took a twenty-nine-year-old writer from the middle of the cornfields in Illinois, at this late date, to really "break" the story. I wondered why the issue of Japanese war crimes was *still* so incendiary, underscored at that time, in early 2005, by front-page headlines of hundreds of thousands of Chinese protesting what they saw as revisionist Japanese history textbooks.

Dark subject matter was not new to me. After all, as a Jewish person, I was no stranger to the concept of atrocities against humanity being considered an appropriate topic of dining-room conversation.

The past, and our obligations to it, regularly haunted us and inhabited our imaginations. But despite the usual cast of deniers around the Internet and beyond, the Holocaust in Europe of World War II was not something we had to constantly prove anymore. Books about the Holocaust weren't labeled as having "controversial" content or being an "ideological time bomb"—as Iris' book had been typically described.

In fact, I had grown up with a body of established Holocaust scholarship and media. By the time we were adults, my friends and I had been exposed to so many stories—in children's books, films, a TV miniseries, Hebrew school classes—about the gas chambers, Zyklon B, the cattle cars, etc., that by the time we were adults, we were fatigued from trying to imagine ourselves in the role of victims. The subject followed us everywhere. At a party for Jewish young adults held at a museum, I remember looking over my cocktail and seeing that famous photo of terrified boys with their arms raised in the Warsaw Ghetto surrendering at gunpoint to the Nazis. We just couldn't get a rest from it.

I had been particularly disturbed by a documentary I saw as an adult about Anne Frank, with whom we all had identified. The film detailed the last agonizing days of the life of this sensitive soul, as she was left to die slowly of cold and disease in her camp barracks. I couldn't sleep after seeing the film; my mind flashed back to images of Anne Frank freezing to death, two weeks before the camp's liberation. After that, I decided that I couldn't bear to expose myself to anything this intense on the subject, at least for a while. I wouldn't even see the film *The Pianist*—or reruns of *Hogan's Heroes*, for that matter. Besides, I thought, the people who most need to see these images and learn from them are the descendants of the perpetrators, not the victims. We've already suffered enough, without the added torment of having to relive this madness over and over again.

In fact, I was so emotionally overloaded by the Holocaust and its crimes against humanity that I didn't even read Iris' book when it came out. I only opened it in 2005, seven years after I bought it at her first reading in Chicago and had Iris sign it for me. While I had known this was also an important episode to explore, I had limits as to what I could take.

I now also observed the difference in how we Jews related to modern-day Germany, compared to how Chinese tensions still brewed with Japan. When I have attended Holocaust memorial services, and there have been plenty of them, I've heard no one express animosity toward today's

Germany. In contrast to the Japanese government, Germany's leaders have seemed to face the Holocaust. In fact, Germany had formally apologized to Israel in 1951 (albeit with some often-forgotten qualifiers), when it expressed willingness to pay billions in reparations. In working extensively with Israel to implement its following 1952 treaty, Germany's government became further de-Nazified, and war criminals were further weeded out of high ranks. Later, as Iris herself noted in *The Rape of Nanking,* the German government made it a crime for educators to omit the Holocaust from their curricula. The German government continues to set up elaborate and artful memorials to its victims. Despite claims of defense from Japanese officials like Ambassador Saito, Japan continues to fall far shorter in consistently facing its most brutal history with full honesty and remorse.

As the weeks passed after the funeral, Iris' martyrdom status in the Asian community only intensified, to such an extreme point that it caught me off guard. In a special issue of *The Chinese American Forum* published about Iris in January 2005, one contributor, Tzy C. Peng, wrote in the issue's typically grand terms: "Alexander the Great (356–23 BC) established an empire and died at age 33. Wolfgang Amadeus Mozart (1756–91) showed his music genius and died at age 35. Iris Chang became a legend to her people at age 36." (9)

And, from the People's Republic of China came news about a nongovernmental human rights organization commissioning two bronze statues of Iris. The first would stand at the descriptively titled "Memorial Hall of the Victims in the Nanjing Massacre by Japanese Invaders," which was erected in Nanjing on one of China's many burial sites of wartime victims (also known as *wan ren ken* or a "pit of ten thousand corpses"). A bust version of the statue would be given to her parents, who donated it in early 2007 to the Hoover Archive at Stanford University, where most of Iris' papers are housed.

The immortalized life-sized bronze Iris, officially unveiled in Nanjing in September 2005, wears her typical public uniform, that business suit, and holds her book, with the title in relief on the cover in English, in one hand. She raises the other as she tells the world about the atrocities. In the tradition of socialist state-sponsored art, Iris' face in the statue looks determined and serious, despite the artist's quote in *China View* that he wanted to "present the demure beauty of oriental women."

To understand why my friend stands in bronze in Nanjing, I had to understand a lot more about the world beyond Iris Chang. As a result of this inquiry, I learned not only about the particular importance of *The Rape of Nanking* to Asians and Asian Americans, but a lot about the particular history and generally shared trauma of these cultures themselves.

A basic question was to examine why that particularly bloody episode at Nanking, then the capital of the pre-Communist nation of China, was so symbolic. As Harvard China scholar William C. Kirby wrote in the foreword to *The Rape of Nanking*, the massacre there marked a turning point in World War II: of Japan's resolve for victory, of China's resolve to resist the invasion, and of world opinion turning against Japan. As Iris then pointed out in the book, the particular brutality of the massacre, which happened over seven weeks from 1937 to 1938, was also notable. She compared the intensity of the killing in Nanking, most of which took place in just two weeks, to other slaughters of World War II, such as the European Holocaust and Stalin's atrocities, which happened over years. The Nanking death toll also surpassed what the Allies unleashed on our enemies. More civilians died in Nanking than in the American air raids on Tokyo, the combined atomic blasts at Hiroshima and Nagasaki, or the British bombings on Dresden, Germany. In her book, Iris well documented the particular joy, imagination, and cruelty that the Japanese soldiers took in the massacre, including holding killing and raping contests.

The massacre was also notable for the high numbers of civilian casualties, earning it a notorious place in history as a symbol of twentieth-century wars, which resulted in unprecedented numbers of civilian deaths. Other examples are Rwanda, Cambodia, and Bosnia, and the list continues now into the next century. Indeed, the twentieth century was the bloodiest and most violent in the history of the world; three times more civilians (169 million) were killed than soldiers (39 million). In the 1990s, Iris joined a growing number of historians studying the issue of genocide as both an end in itself and as a tool of war to terrorize populations (Iris' view of Nanking).

In her book, Iris also emphasized the universal lessons of the massacre. Despite her critics calling the book virulently anti-Japanese, she repeatedly discusses how this good and evil exists in all cultures, and that the Japanese shouldn't be singled out for such crimes of war. "Looking back upon millennia of history, it appears clear that no race or culture has a monopoly on wartime cruelty," she wrote. "The veneer of civilization seems to be exceedingly thin—one that can easily be stripped away, especially by the stresses of war." (55)

Above all, the horrors of Nanking were also symbolic to many other Asian countries of wider Japanese aggression in the 1930s and 1940s, which was never properly atoned for. In that famous debate with Japanese ambassador Saito on PBS' *NewsHour* in 1998, Iris summarized the incredible scope of the damage:

"It's not something I think is well known in this country, that [between] nineteen million to thirty-five million people perished because of Japan's invasion of China, and the fact that Japan had enslaved hundreds of thousands of women, Korean women and other Asian women, as sex slaves for their imperial army. And these war crimes have really left a deep and gaping psychic wound in China and also in other Asian countries."

Indeed, the intensity and sensitivity of this continuing tension between Japan and other Asian countries may startle some of us in the West. The tendency, stereotypically speaking, is for us to just see Asians as one group, not people with distinct cultures and histories. As a result, we can be ignorant of the deep-rooted tensions among Asian countries, and even subgroups within them.

In casual conversation, Iris would talk about these differences on a more mundane level, even in terms of complications in dating other Asians. Long ago she explained to me why she would have trouble dating someone who was the descendant of a native Taiwanese. Her parents had escaped from mainland China during the Communist revolution of 1949 to the island of Taiwan. At that time, some of those mainland Chinese who arrived slaughtered the native Taiwanese. So the native Taiwanese "would prefer their kids to marry other descendants of native Taiwanese," she told me.

A more globally recognizable example of these differences among Asians of all backgrounds—and how clueless Westerners can naïvely bump against them—was revealed in the heated controversy in China over the 2005 film *Memoirs of a Geisha*. The American producers of the film had cast two Chinese actresses in the leading roles of Japanese geishas, whom they depicted as high-class prostitutes. Much to the surprise of some Westerners, the Chinese were furious to have Chinese women playing prostitutes for Japanese men. This is a sensitive topic considering the history of Japanese domination and enslavement of Chinese "comfort women" in World War II, and Japan's longtime denials about it. (The Japanese government did not officially acknowledge the forcible recruitment of "comfort women" until 1993, and denial in high places continues today, on and off.) The resulting outrage and protests in China boiled over to such an extreme that they made international headlines. In early 2006, the Chinese government banned the film from the country.

To find out more why Iris' work hit such a nerve among Asians, I sat down with Ron Yates, a longtime Asia correspondent for the *Chicago Tribune* and now dean of the College of Communications at the University of Illinois. He had known Iris personally from his work at both posts. He also has a record of tying in what happened in World War II to contemporary history; he was the reporter who broke the story in the 1970s about how Japanese-American "Tokyo Rose" had been railroaded by the U.S. government for treason during World War II.

Yates first pointed out a deep-rooted culture of denial in Japan itself. For example, every year since the 1950s, the Japanese prime minister has made an effort to visit and pay respect to war dead at Yasukuni Shrine in Tokyo. As Iris pointed out a few times in her book, war criminals are enshrined there, making the visit "an act that one American wartime victim of the Japanese has labeled as politically equivalent to 'erecting a cathedral for Hitler in the middle of Berlin.'" (12)

As another example, Yates mentioned the 1988 movie *The Last Emperor,* which was censored in Japan.

> *There's a scene in that movie where there was a newsreel showing Japanese troops bayoneting and shooting the Chinese civilians, which was a black and white newsreel from that period. They cut that out of the version that was shown in Japan. So there's a huge sense of denial in Japan for a lot of this stuff, whereas . . . the Germans are continually reminded of what the Nazis did. The Japanese never have anybody to remind them of that, except for the Chinese every so often.*

A major reason for the relative lack of accountability from others is the obscuring influence of the Cold War against Communism. At the end of World War II, the United States and its allies needed Japan as an ally in Asia, especially against soon-to-become-Communist China, and were more interested in establishing friendship than evening scores of the past. Yates added: "The U.S. also felt that those Japanese who were probably war criminals [should be] involved in rebuilding the economy in Japan because they were the ones who built it in the first place. So a lot of these people got passes. They did hang some people considered Class-A war criminals, but a lot of them got off the hook, and then from that point forward the Japanese viewed themselves differently."

The terrible devastation of the atomic bombs, which the Allies dropped on Hiroshima and Nagasaki in 1945, also shifted the focus away from Japanese guilt. "[The Japanese] were 'victims' of World War II because they were atomic bombed and nobody else was. . . . And so whatever they did is nothing compared to what the atomic bomb did, even though there were fewer people killed during the atomic bombs than there were during the fire bombings of Tokyo," he said.

Besides, the focus of the United States after the war was mainly in Europe, drawing attention away from the Asian theater. "The big push in the Roosevelt White House was deal with Europe first, and then whatever is left over, they'll fix Asia," he said. "Because they figured for Japan it was just a matter of time for them to dry up and blow away anyway; they had no resources. Asia was the less 'important' of the two without a doubt, even though it was the Japanese that had attacked us in Pearl Harbor."

Not only did Iris' book fill such long-standing gaps of knowledge in the West about Asia in World War II, but it also tapped into major preexisting political interests in China. One vocal critic of Iris, University of Colorado-Boulder professor Peter Hays Gries, argues that such histories help build and sustain Chinese nationalism, basically creating a shared identity under a new generation of leaders. As Gries writes in his book, *China's New Nationalism: Pride, Politics and Diplomacy*, such discussions of atrocities were taboo in the past in the People's Republic of China, with the authorities' fear that it would make their past leadership look weak for not adequately protecting its citizens. For decades, under the long, harsh reign of Mao Zedong, which ended in 1976, only the most positive and triumphant parts of Chinese history were allowed to be aired. The party line was "Chinese as victors."

In fact, Nancy Tong—a coproducer of the acclaimed 1995 documentary on the Nanking massacre, *In the Name of the Emperor*—was almost arrested in 1992 in China for talking to the surviving victims of the massacre. Tong's coproducer Christine Choy, who was a friend of Iris', told me about Chinese government resistance to the topic at that time:

> *Nancy took a train to Nanking, and secretly tried to locate some of the survivors. And she got caught, because the survivors knew they were supposed to not speak to any journalists that particular year; they were warned. . . . According to Nancy, the interviews were rather strange because everyone's answer was very similar: "Yes, we were being tortured, but that was many years ago, and now we will forgive the Japanese." That was the official line in 1992, mind you.*

But, soon after that time, the narrative of "Chinese as victims" became the official party line. That was when Iris' 1997 book hit. As Gries explains, after the brutal Tiananmen Square crackdown on pro-democracy students in 1989, the Chinese government had more of a need to prove its legitimacy. Documentation of China's past victimization by Japan further became a useful populist movement. Those who were victims in Nanking were mainly poor, representing "the common man," those who could not afford to leave China when the Japanese invaded (unlike Iris' more prominent grandparents who had escaped Nanking early on).

"National identities evolve through public contestation, and are based upon recognition from both opponents and neutral parties," Gries writes. "*The Rape of Nanking* sensation provided an opportunity for a public contest between Chinese and Japanese narratives of the past before a jury of Western opinion . . . quantifying the pain and presenting the Chinese case to the world." (84) He also says that Iris' book contributed to a recent, pervasive—and politically useful for the PRC—recurring cultural image of China as a "raped woman."

The Rape of Nanking also tapped into greater political discourse in North America among those of Chinese descent. As Iris wrote in the book, vast networks of activists started forming in 1989 as a reaction to the horrors of Tiananmen Square. With the networking boost of the Internet, these groups grew and later focused more generally on Japan's need to face its crimes and pay reparations. This was the case of the Global Alliance group in the Bay Area, which had exerted a profound effect on Iris in introducing her to photos of the massacre in 1994. Such activists embraced her book upon its publication in 1997, not only for its extensive documentation of the atrocities, but for its conviction and broad appeal. Then the book sparked more dialogue of its own, including conferences at Yale, Harvard, and Princeton. A profile of Iris in *San Francisco Magazine* in March 2005 called Iris China's "one-woman version of the Holocaust movement."

The program book that we received at Iris' funeral contained many tributes from activists themselves. "It was the saddest and [most] shocking news since the movement started in the 80s. With the deepest sympathy to her family, yet no words could express our feelings of sadness and loss," wrote Sulia Chan, from the Chinese Alliance for Memorial and Justice in New York. Quoted there in a reprinted *San Francisco Chronicle* story was Julie Tang, cochair of the group, Rape of Nanking Redress Coalition: "We're pretty shaken up because we've lost someone who was for us a symbol of hope, the symbol of truth."

Journalist Helen Zia, fifty-three, who lost family members in China during World War II, added that Iris' documentation filled a gap in North American Asians' lives to help them understand their own families. "I don't think people really knew the scope of it. . . . But the lightning rod of Iris' book was that she really just put it all down in documentation. I could say, 'This happened to my grandmother and my uncle and my aunt.'"

Novelist Amy Tan also explained to me that Iris' confrontational stance was radical for an Asian-American writer. "I think what was different about Iris' groundbreaking was that she was not afraid to appear strident in public," she said.

> *[Writer] Maxine Hong Kingston is a groundbreaker in the things that she has said about the Vietnam War, for example. She's a champion for the veteran, but I think she doesn't always champion it in a way that it is quite as confrontational as Iris was.*
>
> *If you were to look at a stereotype that people have about Asian American women, it is sensed that women are reticent or modest, or we are not aggressive; we want to be polite. Iris, you would look at her in a social situation and you would say, "Oh, the way she looks she would be one of these people. She would be a very nice person." And then the fact that she would stand up there and make demands and confront a government and stand up there in front of a crowd of people and say these things, I think was groundbreaking—because it's not an expectation that people have with women. And she was fairly young.*

Helen Zia summed up that Iris symbolized "the epitome of the 'woman warrior,'" an archetype in Asian writing that has emerged from time to time to counter the traditional passive ideal. "I mean here she is this young attractive woman who fairly right out of school was taking on these immense topics and with a great sort of meticulous methodical determination. And so I think she had a dragon to slay and wasn't going to let anything get in her way. And I think she did, she succeeded, and so I think she kind of represents that to a lot of people."

But Zia, like other journalists I talked to, added that Iris basically stood out to her personally as a serious journalist, period—not just as an Asian American. Zia said she meets relatively few reporters with that drive to dig deeply beyond the surface; she meets more who take interest in "sexier" celebrity stories of the rich and famous.

> [Iris investigated] these dusty corners of history that everybody was just like "Oh let's forget that, let's move on," right? And she was willing to shine a light in those areas. . . . I thought there aren't a lot of people who go into journalism who are willing to go into the harder topics. . . . I go to journalism conventions, and if I can spot one person every few years who is dedicated to that extent I think that's a special person. And to me Iris was a special person.

Iris' book even went beyond raising awareness about the Rape of Nanking to cast attention on and understanding about other dark moments of history. Right from the start, in the foreword to her book, William C. Kirby makes the link to the Holocaust clear, quoting a poem by W. H. Auden inspired by his visit to the war in China:

> And maps can really point to places
> Where life is evil now:
> Nanking. Dachau.

The Jewish community was aware of the parallels of both experiences; both the Japanese and the Germans had highly tuned war machines, expansionist goals, and "master race" mentalities—both even performed cruel medical experiments on their prisoners. And both countries were widely considered to be among the most sophisticated and culturally refined ever to inhabit the earth.

As a result, in 1998, Iris drew standing-room-only crowds speaking at the Simon Weisenthal Center in Los Angeles—and at the Holocaust Museum in Washington, D.C., where her talk garnered the largest audience in its five-year history. Along with Asian activist networks, such Jewish groups also defended Iris when Japanese officials attacked her book. Upon Iris' death, the *Times* of London quoted a fan of hers, Dan Rose, who had heard her speak at the Holocaust Museum. "As with many speaking programs there, it was 50 percent elderly Jews, many of them war survivors, in the audience," he said. "I was overwhelmed by the warmth and immediacy with which they embraced and applauded Chang. It was an instance of bearing witness, of never forgetting, which is holy to the Jewish community. They related to her as a daughter, and vice versa." This support was strong despite some controversy over Iris' use of the word "holocaust," which Jewish groups had adopted early on to refer to their specific history.

Iris' appeal as a crusader also tapped into generational differences. She served as a career role model as an Asian-American journalist, symbolizing careers outside of the sciences explored more by the younger generation. I met University of Texas-Austin journalism student Ruth Liao, who said that her choice of a journalism career was radical in her family, compared to her sister having just entered MIT, reputed as "the gold standard" of Asian-American education. In an Asian studies class in college, she had first discovered Iris' work, along with that of journalist Helen Zia. "When it's not fiction, it's like your own history. And these experiences have happened and were recorded." After Liao read Iris' book, she said she was "bursting with curiosity"—a term that I could picture Iris using—about her own family's unspoken history in China and was emboldened to follow her writing interests.

I also learned that for younger Asian Americans, Iris came to symbolize the importance and bravery of questioning authority. This was the personal observation of eighteen-year-old University of Michigan aerospace engineering student Kan Yang. He had organized a tribute to Iris on his campus in November 2005. (This was one of several tributes held that year on college campuses, which also included UC-Berkeley and the University of Illinois.) Kan, who came to the United States from China in 1990 when he was three years old, does admit to now "following the more traditional Asian philosophy of law, medicine, and engineering being the only acceptable careers to go into (according to my parents) in choosing my major." But he still most appreciates Iris' irreverence, which went against the grain of his upbringing.

As a child, I was always taught by my parents to be submissive to authority. "Don't challenge the government, don't challenge the way things are," they would tell me. As long as I worked hard and integrated myself well into society, I would receive the redemption of success. I suppose their beliefs arose from growing up in a society that stressed long-accepted Confucian ideologies and traditions, which emphasized leading normal lives and avoiding extremes.

Furthermore, since they were raised in the 1960s in Mao's Communist China, to challenge authority often meant disgrace or physical harm to oneself or one's family. The accepted view on life at the time was that the individual was not important, but the individual's larger contribution to society, the "collective" of sorts, was. Thus, when my parents and others of their generation came to the US, they brought along these beliefs and [contributed to] my outlook on American society.

I believe that we, as Asians, became the "model minority" in the United States because we've stressed a strong work ethic

and submission even in the face of inequality and discrimina-
tion. Yet, it was this submissive silence and unwillingness to
fight for Asian rights that concealed something as large as an
Asian Holocaust from public history and knowledge.

I met other young people who described Iris' influence as life changing, such as twenty-six-year-old Olivia Cheng, an actor and journalist living in Vancouver, Canada. She was so moved by Iris' work, and her struggle with depression, that she felt compelled to take a journey to San Jose in 2006 to get to know her by reading the personal papers she left behind. Olivia visited Brett and also Stanford University to see some of Iris' research materials housed at the Hoover Archive. In an e-mail to me, Olivia said:

Hey, Paula,
I'm sitting in the AV room inside the Hoover Institution
right now. I'm watching Iris interview a number of historians
in Nanking. What a force. She's so intense and focused when
it comes to her work. Yet the few times she steps in front of the
camera to pose in front of local tourist sights, she looks shy and
girlish with her pink lipstick and round sunglasses.
It's really cool to finally "meet" her but I feel sad that this is
the closest I'll ever get.

Later on the phone, Olivia explained Iris' significance to her in broadening images of Asian women, beyond the usual fare of "prostitution, laundries and bad drivers." She grew up in a "white-bread" Canadian prairie city, where she would feel like the only Asian alive when leaving the safe confines of her Chinese grade school. She explained: "Certain experiences led me to become hyper-aware of my racial identity. It's probably why I'd be so excited and moved to see any Asian face represented in the media. It was a nod of acceptance from the mainstream. Then to read about Iris! Here was this beautiful, creative, empowered and intelligent woman who brought atrocious injustices to light."

Reflecting these same sentiments was Chinese-American broadcast journalist Nesita Kwan, forty, who anchors a local newscast in Chicago. When I met her, also in the summer of 2005, she recalled feeling proud of Iris' book when it came out.

> *I had a conversation with Mayor Daley [of Chicago] who said he was reading it. He came in one day for an interview and I asked him what he was reading, because I know he likes to read, and he said, "I'm reading* The Rape of Nanking,*" and I was thrilled, thrilled. . . . Chicago is the "ultimate American city" in some respects, and that if he's reading it when he could be reading so many other things, then it's striking a chord in someone who would be viewed as the ultimate American, in a lot of ways.*

Nesita commented that Iris' great success as a journalist, which "was so outside the realm of what is considered a respectable profession," also meant a lot to legitimize Asians as "real Americans." She continued:

> *I mean a friend of mine says to me, "You've really succeeded in the ultimate American field. This is not a field that any other country will claim as its own. Good or bad, being a media person and having some local celebrity makes you uniquely American." And I remember when he said that to me, I thought I wonder how much of my doing this and being so motivated was to prove that I am an American too.*

Reporting feeling one of the strongest and most direct influences of Iris' work was twenty-two-year-old Iris Chang Herrera, Iris' protégé whom I had met at her funeral. Herrera first met Iris Chang when she was fifteen and her parents took her to a reading about the atrocities and a Global Alliance exhibit that was held on Treasure Island, outside of San

Francisco. A friend also told her, "Iris, you have to meet this woman. She is amazing, and you guys have the same name!"

They met, and the elder Iris Chang took an immediate interest in the younger one. Herrera later told me:

> *She always takes an interest in everyone she's talking to. She*
> *was very good like that. If she was talking to you, she was talk-*
> *ing to you. She was real interested we had the exact [same]*
> *name, I mean first and last name. We couldn't believe it.*
> *. . . I remember thinking, gosh, you're so young and you al-*
> *ready wrote an international best-seller. I remember how*
> *young she was and how beautiful she was. And then I remem-*
> *ber going through the exhibit and looking at all the photos,*
> *and that's where all the questions started popping up.*

Iris Chang Herrera, whose Chinese grandmother narrowly escaped the Japanese bombing of her village, was so inspired after the talk that she did a presentation about the Nanking book at her school. Then other schools in the Bay Area asked her to speak. She soon became the youngest member in a new organization formed in reaction to Iris' book, the Rape of Nanking Redress Coalition. At the age of sixteen, Herrera attended all the coalition's meetings, including one with the Jewish community about learning from their example in encouraging education on the Holocaust. "And later on I got involved so then it was really cool. I was the other Iris Chang. She was THE Iris Chang." When Iris Chang Herrera got to college, the elder one followed through on her promise to speak for free at her university, UC-Davis, as a gesture of support for Herrera's activism on campus. Herrera concluded:

> *So much of my life is dedicated to what she was dedicated to.*
> *Truth and especially this issue of World War II in Asia. It just*
> *begs the question of: What other things in history do we not*

know about? What other truths do we not know about and how can we learn from those so that we don't repeat mistakes so that history doesn't repeat itself. And it will, it has, so it is important to know about all this.

$\mathcal{A}t$ the same time, I started to recognize that, after her death, Iris came to symbolize another issue: opening up public dialogue about the special stigma against mental illness in the Asian community—and pointing to the disproportionately high number of suicides in that group. Iris' highly publicized suicide even seemed at that point to attract unexpected converts to that cause. Iris' parents and brother spoke within their community in March of 2005 at a fundraiser for a nonprofit organization that works to raise awareness of mental health issues among Asian Americans. Iris' mother said that she wished she would have been more open about what Iris had been going through during her crisis. In the March 8 issue of *USA Today*, she said: "In Asian culture, it's considered shameful to have some mental patient in her family. But mental illness is a disease, a chemical imbalance in the brain. We should treat it just like a heart attack or diabetes."

In the article, Iris' mother also revealed a fuller diagnosis of Iris' mental illness, which doctors made only in the last weeks of her life. Iris had suffered from brief reactive psychosis and bipolar disorder, also known as manic depression. The bipolar diagnosis, of which psychosis can be part, did help make more sense of everything. Judging from the mental health basics I was learning, bipolar disorder is a more serious and possibly more life-threatening diagnosis than depression alone. When a person is manic, they lose judgment and are very likely to engage in risky and self-destructive behavior. In contrast, a depressed person may not have the energy and momentum to stop and get off the roller-coaster.

I was stunned and not stunned at the same time. During our final phone conversation that past November, Iris was paranoid as she drifted in and out of touch with reality. I knew that she had regularly stayed up several nights in a row in the final months of her life; that type of insomnia both indicates and exacerbates mania. But I still wondered if this problem was all new, only emerging in the last several months of Iris' life.

I could easily name some traits dating far back that could be considered manic. Like the marathon phone conversations. One of the quirkiest parts of these typically long conversations was that *she* didn't realize they were quirky, and never picked up on my many hints to stop talking.

Yet, I also already knew that emotional highs and lows are common among authors and other creative types. And these traits of hers were more like entertaining quirks, not pathologies. Iris mostly came off as a radiant and exuberant personality, not an out-of-control manic. In her book *Exuberance,* psychiatry professor Kay Redfield Jamison describes the desirable state of exuberance as resembling the effects of champagne and the more pathological state of mania resembling cocaine; bubbly and high-spirited Iris was more the champagne type, definitely.

More insights followed about Iris' case. On April 17, the *San Francisco Chronicle Magazine* ran a long story on Iris that touched on her psychosis and paranoia, without fully explaining it. In her article, reporter Heidi Benson cited parts of three suicide notes that were found—all dated Monday, November 8, 2004—which had not yet been made public. At that point, they best revealed her motive. The first note described the unbearable quality of her fears: "Each breath is becoming difficult for me to take—the anxiety can be compared to drowning in an open sea. I know that my actions will transfer some of this pain to others, indeed those who love me the most. Please forgive me. Forgive me because I cannot forgive myself."

The third note was a draft of the second note, which specifically described her greatest fears—not of the right-wing Japanese, as most people had assumed—but instead of the U.S. government. Her note described old-fashioned, perhaps TV-inspired stereotypes of the CIA monitoring her, not with new computer and cell-phone spy technologies, but by opening her mail and by observing her from a parked surveillance van. In that note to her family, Iris wrote:

There are aspects of my experience in Louisville [in a mental hospital in August 2004] that I will never understand. Deep down I suspect that you may have more answers about this than I do. I can never shake my belief that I was being re-cruited, and later persecuted, by forces more powerful than I could have imagined. Whether it was the CIA or some other organization, I will never know. As long as I'm alive, these forces will never stop hounding me. . . .

Days before I left for Louisville, I had a deep foreboding about my safety. I sensed suddenly threats to my own life: an eerie feeling that I was being followed in the streets, the white van parked outside my house, damaged mail arriving at my P.O. Box. I believe my detention at Norton Hospital was the government's attempt to discredit me.

As I had since the day after her death, I wondered if any of Iris' fears of the U.S. government going after her could be true—or at least based in some reality. I remembered that while Iris was working on her first book she filed numerous Freedom of Information Act (FOIA) requests for FBI and CIA documents about the scientist she was profiling.

I decided that I would follow her lead and submit a FOIA request to the government for any files compiled on Iris Chang. Making the inquiry was much easier than I had expected. I got online and instantly found the guidelines for submitting the request to the FBI.

After I'd done that, I sat back and put the request out of my mind. I knew it would be a while before I heard anything back. After all, Iris had waited years to get the formerly classified FBI files on the subject of her biography, Dr. Tsien, because of backups in the system. She had become so frustrated with the government's slowness that at one point she even enlisted the help of the American Civil Liberties Union (ACLU). Finally, the files came in the mail in 1998, six years after she had requested them and three years after the book was published. (But she had still managed to outwit the system and obtained portions of Tsien's FBI files for her book, some of which had been folded into a U.S. Customs file at the National Archives.)

But the response I received was much swifter. The following week I received a letter from the U.S. Department of Justice in my mailbox (addressed to Mr. Paul Kamen). I opened it and saw the subject line of her name. Basically, in three paragraphs, it said that the FBI had "located no records responsive" to my request. So all I could do at that point was to see what I could find myself through other sources.

To find more answers to the many questions I had, I knew I had to approach a greater and more omniscient source of intelligence than the United States government. After putting off the inevitable for a few months, I e-mailed Iris' mother, Ying-Ying, who had taken on the role of public spokesperson for Iris' family. And then I e-mailed Brett. I asked them both for interviews during my trip to the Bay Area that summer.

I knew that finding the information I needed would be a challenge, since mental illness was a sensitive issue for Iris' family. After Heidi Benson's article about Iris in the *San Francisco Chronicle Magazine*, Iris' parents, husband, and brother fired off an angry letter to the *Chronicle* for publishing the last suicide note, originally only meant for her family, which they had requested that Benson not do. I knew that her mother in particular would be guarded, although she had felt comfortable in March speaking to her own Asian community about the mental illness.

As expected, Iris' mom declined to cooperate in the preparation of this book, explaining that she was thinking of writing her own book on Iris' life and that she had to "move on" with her life. I didn't hear back immediately from Brett, whom I would reach and then interview months later.

In the meantime, I headed to Iris' original home base in central Illinois. That would be a good start. She often wrote about it with appreciation for helping to shape her into the person she had become. I also remembered her telling me personally of specific challenges she faced "as a geek" while growing up there. In central Illinois, I would certainly learn more about her transition from a "real person" to the transcendent superhuman symbol she became.

CHAPTER THREE

Were There Earlier Signs?

Quotes Iris cites under her picture in her 1985 high school yearbook:

"Imagination is more important than knowledge." Albert Einstein

"He who can, does. He who cannot, teaches." George Bernard Shaw

"Poetry is simply the most beautiful, impressive and wildly effective mode of saying things, and hence its importance." Matthew Arnold

She was talkative, idealistic, bold, passionate, tall, beautiful, with long dark hair, and she attracted much male attention. A first-generation American, she grew up in central Illinois, surrounded by a seemingly limitless expanse of cornfields. But others around her often didn't know what to make of her; she often ruffled feathers with her ambition, directness, and candor.

After she graduated from the big state university in Champaign-Urbana, she went abroad to China, and then made her name internationally. But years of exhaustion finally caught up with her. And at a time when she seemed better, when her family had assumed she was on the mend, she committed suicide. In the end, she had harshly condemned herself for not doing enough for others. Today, a bronze statue of her stands in Nanjing, where she is immortalized as a hero.

Indeed, Minnie Vautrin, who died at age fifty-four in 1941, was also an extraordinary woman who met a tragic ending.

Minnie, a missionary and the daughter of a poor French immigrant, had valiantly risked her life in confronting Japanese soldiers around the clock to save more than ten thousand Chinese women in Nanking. She sheltered them at her women's college, Ginling, which was built to accommodate no more than three hundred people. She was one of a handful of brave foreigners, including John Rabe, the "good Nazi" whose diary Iris had discovered, who bravely stayed behind in Nanking at great peril as Japanese troops advanced into the city. Together these "bookish and genteel Westerners," as Iris described them in her book, established a "safety zone" in which they sheltered tens of thousands of Nanking citizens from slaughter. At this time, Minnie had one close call after another. Once, a Japanese soldier slapped her for insolence; another time she was held at gunpoint.

Iris was well aware of Minnie's sacrifice. After all, Minnie's story was part of the intense drama that Iris lived out in her imagination as she researched her Nanking book. Calling Minnie "an American Anne Frank," Iris even used Vautrin's diary as background information for her Nanking book to describe much of the massacre. In the book, Iris herself observed the ironies in Minnie's life:

> *The Nanking massacre took a deeper psychic toll on her than any of the other zone leaders or refugees had realized at the time. Few were aware that under a legend that had grown to mythic proportions was a vulnerable, exhausted woman who never recovered either emotionally or physically from daily exposure to Japanese violence. Her last diary entry, dated April 14, 1940, reveals her state of mind: "I'm at about the end of my energy. Can no longer forge ahead and make plans for the work, for on every hand there seem to be obstacles of some kind. . . . "* (186–7)

When I read *The Rape of Nanking*, I was struck by the parallels in the lives of these two women, Minnie and Iris. And through the months afterward, I couldn't help but think of Minnie and why she captured Iris' imagination as a historian. After all, Minnie kept popping up everywhere, it seemed, in connection with Iris. In 2005, headlines in the *Chicago Tribune* announced that the Illinois governor had declared September 27, Minnie's birthday, Minnie Vautrin Day. The article also talked about the opening of a dance drama in Beijing by the China National Chinese Opera and Dance Drama Company. The plot is based on Minnie's ghost actually guiding Iris through Nanjing as she writes her book.

I was thinking about Iris' fascination with Minnie's life as I headed to Urbana. From the beginning, I decided to follow Iris' lead while researching clues from the past; she always visited library archives first—as she had done in getting to know Minnie through her diary housed in the archives of the Yale Divinity School. My first stop was the University of Illinois Library. Always proud of her hometown and alma mater, Iris often liked to point out that it is the largest public university library in the country. In 2002, at the age of thirty-four, Iris had donated her own personal and research papers there, after depositing papers related to her first book at the University of California-Santa Barbara (and before giving another collection of later papers to archives at Stanford).

The university library in Urbana, where she liked to go as a teenager, also had personal significance to Iris. It reflected some of her greatest passions growing up. "I really was maybe your quintessential geek," she told filmmaker Christine Choy in 2003 for a yet-unreleased documentary.

> *One of my great pleasures then was to read. I was a bookworm. I was constantly reading. I would spend entire weekends in the library. I think I preferred books often to parties. If I wasn't in the library I would be at Waldenbooks at the mall or in a used bookstore. I loved watching films. I would often go watch films by myself. I really was something of a*

loner. I mean I had friends, but I also needed my own space. I was extremely independent. At a very early age I started going into the library on my own. If I was curious about something, I would just start researching it on my own and would roam the stacks and look for old research journals. . . .

I was addicted to books, so if I wasn't reading on weekends, I was reading in the evenings. My parents would often force me to go to bed and they would turn off the lights, but I would often read by the crack of the light that came under the door. So I'd be reading like past 3 AM, like on my hands and knees with the book right there near the door jam. . . . Because of the reading, the constant reading, I had terrible insomnia too. Sometimes I couldn't crawl myself out of bed in the morning and I would just go through class like a zombie, and I'd be almost falling asleep in school. But at night, when my time was my own, I could read for hours. So I think I developed some very bad habits starting at an early age.

While she read all kinds of books at these times, she was always in pursuit of Asian role models. Iris continued:

There weren't many books in the library that really reflected, I felt, the Asian-American experience in a way that I could identify with, even though I searched long and hard. I remember in high school I read Maxine Hong Kingston's book, Woman Warrior. *And at the time, in fact it was probably even before high school, I think sometime in the 1970s. And while I found the book fascinating, it was still hard for me to identify with her experience, because she grew up in Chinatown, in the Stockton Chinatown, and my experience was just so radically different from that, being part of this university community in the Midwest.*

She told Christine Choy that as a teen, the library was an escape from her parents, whose presence seemed larger than life in their small community.

> *In fact when you have a town that is that isolated, often underneath the facade of friendliness you do have a lot of petty gossip. And often a lot of scrutiny into peoples' lives when there really wasn't much to scrutinize at all. I mean maybe the reason why I wasn't more rebellious was that anything I did would be immediately reported to my parents. I mean I remember later when I was in college if I went to a restaurant with friends or if I was just out having ice cream with a boy, no matter what it was, it would get back to my parents. I mean they would say, "Oh yeah, so and so saw you at this time at this particular restaurant," and we would laugh about it. But it was like there was no way you could possibly keep a secret in that town.*
>
> *And so while on one hand being in Champaign could be very nurturing, in another sense it was like being under constant surveillance. That was something I didn't like at all, and I felt that going to the library was a way to really retreat from all that, and yet it gave me ultimate freedom. See, when you're in a library it might seem really boring and dusty to most people. But for me, it was a place where I could just let my imagination roam, and you ventured into sanctuary unbounded by space or time. Anything that you would want to dream about or learn you could. . . . It was my paradise, my escape from reality.*

Iris was such a fan of archives that when Choy asked her in 2003 where she would live if she had the opportunity, she replied: "Washington, D.C., because that's where the largest library system in the world is located, the Library of Congress, and also the National Archives." In her research for her three books, she visited strings of archives across the United States—of presidential libraries, government agencies, private corporations, universities, and private citizens. Her first two books, especially, were based on primary resources, raw information, which included material from archives she had unearthed (and her own original interviews). Her specialty, even more than being a writer, was as a researcher able to dig deeply for documents that had eluded past scholars.

This was far from a chore for her. In fact, visiting archives was one of her greatest pleasures. She commonly described archives as being full of intrigue and challenge. Early on, archives were a major key to her work as an author. One of the reasons she had won over her first publisher to sign her up to write *Thread of the Silkworm* was that she had ventured on her own from Baltimore, where she was in graduate school at Johns Hopkins, to the nearby Library of Congress for research. Two weeks later, she turned in a one-hundred-page book proposal referring to documents that others had not known existed. "I spent a weekend at the Library of Congress digging and going through just about every article and book that had ever been written about Tsien," she recalled to Choy. "There weren't actually many books, but there was one book that was written by two AP reporters in the 1960s that had some information on Tsien. And so the more I dug, the more intrigued I became. Indeed I did feel as if I was a detective hot on the trail of a major mystery."

In fact, Iris became so absorbed in that research that one time she was almost locked overnight in the National Archives. This was an example of what Brett had liked to call Iris' "attention-surplus disorder," of being so focused on one thing that she lost track of all else. "She found all this exciting material on Tsien and she got onto the phone with Susan Rabiner, her editor," Brett told me later on. "She was talking to Susan so long, and she was so focused on the conversation that she didn't notice the lights were going off, and everybody was leaving. So when she hung up the phone, she was locked in the National Archives. I got this call: 'Brett! I'm locked in the National Archives!'

"She said, 'What should I do?' I told her she should call 911. So she did. And after she called 911, she started walking around and she finally found a security guard who was working his shift. He told her she was the first person he knew of who had been locked in the National Archives."

Iris' archive work took her abroad as well. In a 1991 letter to her friend Li Wen Huang, she marveled at the excitement of an upcoming research trip to Russia, where she would see

> *government archives, which are opening up to scholars for the first time in history. Isn't it thrilling that I might be among the first to learn of some of the secrets the Soviet Union, China and U.S. kept smothered during the Cold War? It's this kind of research I find so fascinating—like detective work, really—and so unlike the boring, white and grey textbooks they shoved at us in high school!*

A little later, in a letter dated March 8, 1992, Iris wrote to me about similar intrigue in searching for clues from the KGB. She specifically had been seeking names implicated in an alleged security leak to the USSR from the time Tsien was at Caltech, which would have been significant to explain why the FBI clamped down so hard on his department. She wrote:

> *And now that the Cold War is over, I may even get the chance to find out who the spy was! A professor at Georgetown University is putting me in touch with some students who can do a little research and translation for me when they visit Moscow, and I have been told that a rightly placed bribe of $5 to $10 these days may get a researcher into the archives of the KGB.*

In that letter, she described the exhaustive archival research she had done for the Tsien book, and what was still left:

Within a few months, I plan to travel to Boston—where Tsien spent his days as a student and professor at MIT—and Washington, home of the National Archives, Library of Congress, FBI, National Technical Information Service and other government repositories with which I have corresponded for months. Paula, you will not believe how much information the government has on Tsien. I have found his photographs, resumes, thumbprints, application forms, security checks on his character, actual transcriptions of telephone conversations, scrawled notes of the secret agents, detailed discussions about him between Chinese and American ambassadors, memorandum from the desk of presidents. There's still more in the files of the FBI, State Department and the Department of Defense, that has yet to be released.

In *Thread of the Silkworm*, a constant theme was the need for creative types to be alone to create—to be uninterrupted, uncompromised, and unburdened by politics. Describing her book's focus in the introduction, Iris wrote, "It's also the private story of a shy, introspective, brilliant scientist who wanted nothing more in life than to work in peace but was caught up not once, but twice, in the vortex of world politics." (xiii) That was Tsien's apparent goal, and I knew it was also Iris'—which she achieved through her work burying herself in archives around the world.

Later, she described how historical archives ended up fulfilling the greatest ambitions she had in high school for adventure, during her work on *The Rape of Nanking*. "My immediate goal at the time was to establish myself as an investigative news reporter. I wanted to travel widely, taste adventure, and expose corruption in high places. In fact, one of my dreams was to work overseas as a foreign correspondent. Nothing seemed quite as glamorous or exciting to me at the time as the idea of covering a war," she said, in an interview published in the fall 2000 issue of her sorority's alumnae magazine, *The Ellipse*. "Ironically, I did end up writing about war. Not as a journalist, but as a historian—sixty years after the

Rape of Nanking. Instead of dodging bullets, I found myself rifling through old papers in archives. Even so, it was an emotionally wrenching, psychologically draining project, one that required a great deal of investigation and research."

I thought of Iris' earlier treks as I descended the stairs way below the stacks of the university library in Urbana at the University Archives. The next day, I'd go to another building, where her papers were housed, but then I was there to talk with University Archivist William Maher. I reached a windowless basement, which certainly fit my stereotype of a secluded archive, and met the low-key Maher. Before my visit, I had asked him over the phone about Iris' papers, along with anything they had on Minnie, which was still unknown. But when I met him in person, he reported that to his surprise, he had found a file, albeit a thin one, on Minnie Vautrin that he hadn't realized was there. In paging through this long-forgotten remnant of Minnie's life, I was starting to personally identify with Iris' greatest joy, of working like a sleuth to uncover the mysteries of history in documents left behind.

Maher noted one of the items in the file, a May 16, 1941, obituary from a local paper with an Indianapolis dateline. He pointed out the indirect and discreet way a suicide was announced in those days. It read: "Miss Vautrin was found dead last night in her apartment here. The gas stove in the kitchen had been turned on and was not burning."

I leafed through the folder to see these documents, both mundane and landmark, that all reflected various sides of Minnie's personality. The folder contained an earnest note from Minnie in Nanking to the university alumni association with a five-dollar donation for a scholarship fund. The letter was dated June 24, 1937, just days before war with Japan was declared. "Am sorry my contribution can't be large, but I live in a land where elemental needs are great on every level," she wrote. Near that was a commencement program from earlier and more idyllic days at her beloved Ginling College in 1921. It described a performance in the garden of the opera *Siegfried*. These commencement ceremonies of Minnie's were very elaborate affairs, known to attract the attendance of friend Madame Chiang Kai-shek, wife of the president of China, and many prominent leaders in the reigning nationalist government.

An accompanying progress report that Minnie had written about the college described other ceremonies, which were surprisingly nonpreachy and secular:

> *The subject of the baccalaureate sermon was "Abundant Life," which is the college motto. The two Chinese characters "Hou Seng" may also mean "generous living." Surely the two meanings belong together. Where learning or religion attempt to exist as ends in themselves, they lose vitality. Where they inspire for service they transform the world.*

I found an address change form from her 1925 furlough to direct her alumni mail to where she was attending graduate classes at the University of Chicago. Then there was a clipping from a local newspaper headlined, "Minnie Vautrin Tells of Fears in Chinese War," dated May 3, 1927. It described the evacuation of her and other foreigners to a boat during this harrowing time of chaos, which included the kidnapping of a professor at a nearby university. Her concluding quoted response was characteristically brave: "Our whole experience was therefore a much less unpleasant one than most people had, and we were deeply touched by the courage and loyalty of all our Chinese friends who certainly saved us from something worse." After a short time, she was coming alive to me.

The next day, it was time to see what the archives there would yield about Iris, my real subject. Now I was undeniably stepping over the line from friend to researcher in actively digging for clues of her struggles, treating her the same way she addressed her more historically distant subjects from Nanking. To find the "Student Life and Culture Archival Program," where her papers were housed, I had to journey to the edge of the vast campus of 41,000 students, to a part where I had never before been. It was in the agricultural section of campus, on the border of the research-oriented South Farms, which I had known during my tenure there only by its smell, as modulated by shifts in the wind.

I reached the nearly century-old horticulture building, which towered over the flat horizon and stood across from the Eisenhower-era no-frills three-story modern apartment buildings for "married student housing." I walked inside and passed by a lobby display of student life through the centuries, which included artifacts from my era, flyers from a fraternity initiation from the late eighties.

Once in the Archives Research Center, I got out my copy of the papers' finding guide, or inventory, and requested the four boxes that contained the collection. It was the smallest—and first—of the three that Iris had deposited at universities. Included with the inventory were lists of other personal paper collections of alumni and associates of the university, most of whom were men and were born more than fifty years before Iris.

After a grad student returned with the boxes on a cart, I instantly remembered Iris in an apartment of hers in Santa Barbara, where she and Brett first lived in California. I had seen her filing a business letter she had just received, and I marveled openly about how organized her file cabinets were. "They have to be," she said matter-of-factly, without a trace of self-consciousness. "This is all for my biographers."

She had known that she was important and acted like it. It was still disconcerting.

But, as I now was discovering about ten years later, she was right. And I had become one of the first biographers.

Digging deeper into one of the boxes, I found a mysterious note dated from a month before, right when I had first called Mr. Maher about my visit. It briefly stated, "Photos removed by Bill Maher to security file."

The next day, I visited Mr. Maher and asked him about the note. He paused, and said that there was something else he should tell me about the collection that I might find interesting. About ten days before she died, Iris had called him in a panic. She asked him about FedExing to the archive a CD with thousands of personal photos of hers from her childhood to the present. It seems that she had e-mailed him a few weeks before, via a generic e-mail on the library Web site during a vacation period, and he said that she sounded very frustrated that she had not heard back yet. Her baffling instructions were that "no one be allowed to see the photos, ever." It seemed that while they were in a public archive, their purpose was entirely personal to her, to keep a part of herself alive there.

But, now with her family taking stewardship of the collection, I could get their permission to see them. He said he'd look into it, but I probably wouldn't be able to see them until a future visit.

I felt a chill; this was more evidence that Iris' suicide was considerably premeditated. She was obviously putting her affairs in order in the few weeks before she died, and leaving her papers behind was a major part of it. Those papers, those records of her life, could not be safer than in the hands of an archive, whose purpose for existence is to preserve the past.

When I went back to the horticulture building to further examine her boxes, I did think that they seemed to be waiting for me, or at least another biographer. The first box was like a time capsule, the kind you might see buried in the cornerstone of a building, portraying an idealized version of her high school and college life. It included the first several pages of her high school and college class notebooks, consciously presented as representative samples of what she had studied. Some were pages of very neat advanced differential equations and others of Chinese characters. Also included were background materials about her elite high school, Uni High, including a statistical profile on the classes of 1987 to 1989, which were a few years behind hers. It revealed what I was learning about the school, that it boasted an unusually high number of Ivy League acceptances and National Merit Scholar finalists. The average ACT and SAT scores were through the roof.

A résumé, which she probably used to seek a job after her college graduation, cataloged her achievements, which included the 1988 internship at *Newsweek*, stringing for several national newspapers, working on the *Daily Illini*, and freelancing for technical computer publications.

Next were piles and piles of her college articles, including unusually light ones from when she started at the *Daily Illini* junior year (the year before I was her editor), such as a review of a Whitney Houston concert and a story on Pop Rocks candy, complete with a scientific explanation of their inner chemical workings. She reviewed some light books, such as one about handling criticism, *When Words Hurt*, reflecting what I would later find to be a lifelong interest in popular self-improvement guides. She also included another review of a book entitled *Mortal Fear*, a mystery about a Harvard medical student stripper, which she panned: "Anyone interested in reading a hot, feverish thriller should avoid *Mortal Fear* like the plague." Later *Daily Illini* stories, for which I had served as editor, were more serious and had a scientific bent—stories on genome maps and new technology in reading brain waves.

I found a *Chicago Tribune* story with headlines that I had otherwise forgotten about, until that second. Iris had contributed to the report from Urbana as a stringer. The headline read, "Slain U. of I. Student Had a World to Live For." It was about a straight-A veterinary student from a prominent family who had been mysteriously murdered one night in her Urbana apartment, without leaving any trail of clues. The case was never solved. I remembered that story alarming me a bit, when I lived a few blocks away in an old house with friends. I was the one stuck in the downstairs bedroom. Whenever I heard the old house rattle at night, I never knew if it was someone coming for me. But then I made myself forget about it after someone told me, judging by the "professional" way the murder had been executed, that it was probably a mob killing to get revenge on the victim's rich father for something—and I knew the mob didn't have a bone to pick with me.

There were also letters of reference, including one from her favorite journalism professor, Bob Reid. I then remembered making an appointment to see him—as he was the one who chose who would go from our college—to ask about my applying for that magazine internship in New York City junior year, which I had seen posted on the bulletin board. He had looked at me a bit aghast, and more embarrassed, and stammered, "That slot has already been filled." It had been a done deal for weeks.

I saw some articles from the national magazine *Campus Voice* that Iris had freelanced, and started to feel an inner twinge of annoyance toward her, like I did in the old days. I then remembered that I had been the one to first get that gig as a stringer reporting from our university to that magazine. Then she found out about it, somehow, and applied. I had already reserved the beat of our university, but she somehow talked her way into covering some events at colleges on the West Coast. I vaguely remembered why I didn't like her much in college: that she had achieved with such intensity, that she seemed to be achieving for the sake of achieving, meanwhile being oblivious to others in her path.

I opened the second box, which demanded an entirely different and nobler response from my gut. Any bad feelings for Iris immediately dissolved. One of the first papers I saw was a copy of a letter addressed to "Mein Führer!" in German, dated from June 8, 1938. It was German businessman John Rabe's letter to Hitler naïvely telling him about Japanese atrocities going on in Nanking, with a plea to put pressure on the Japanese to stop.

That letter, which he sent upon arriving back in Germany from where he had been based in Nanking, turned out to be a terrible mistake. To make matters worse, he sent it right after publicly showing a film by American John Magee, which someone else had smuggled out of the country, documenting the atrocities. Two days later, the Gestapo showed up at Rabe's door to arrest him. They only released him when his employer, the Siemens Company, which would soon demote him, vouched for him. The Gestapo sent him away with a stern warning not to talk about the atrocities again, especially via that film. Like Minnie Vautrin, his fate was not a happy one. His family suffered from great deprivation in Berlin after World War II. During that time he was banned from working because of his prior Nazi affiliation. He died in 1950 of broken health.

This copy of Rabe's collection of papers represented probably Iris' greatest research discovery. As I saw by that huge box, what she had labeled as a "diary" of his was actually a large archive of books of notes and correspondence. They included more than two thousand documents on the massacre "that he had meticulously typed, numbered, bound and even illustrated," as Iris had described in her Nanking book. "These documents included his and other foreigners' eyewitness reports, newspaper articles, radio broadcasts, telegrams and photographs of the atrocities. No doubt Rabe recognized the historical value of this record; perhaps he even predicted its future publication." (194)

There she had also explained her amazing resourcefulness in finding these papers, which were later published in a book and gave new "outsider" documentation of the extent of the massacre at Nanking. In researching Rabe, she suspected he might have left some kind of journal behind, as was the case with Minnie Vautrin and several other Westerners who together helped establish their "safety zone" of refuge in Nanking.

Iris knew that Rabe had apprenticed in Hamburg around the turn of the twentieth century. With that clue, she contacted her friend John Taylor, the noted expert on World War II intelligence at the National Archives in Washington, D.C. He referred her to a professor in California, who directed her personally to his friend, the city historian of Hamburg. That historian sent out letters to track down Rabe's granddaughter, Ursula Reinhardt, in Berlin, who then dug up from storage the historical treasure that her family possessed. Until then, Reinhardt had not realized its value. Iris was the first researcher to see it.

Finally, during that visit in Urbana, I skimmed through the last two boxes, which were long and flat and contained dozens and dozens of full-page clips from newspapers across the world in 1998 reporting about Iris' book, *The Rape of Nanking*. At first glance, they did not reveal much, quoting Iris saying similar things in different interviews about why she wrote the book and what it was about. But occasionally they revealed the extreme pressures she was under at that time—which I hadn't noticed during all the heady times when the book first came out.

A theme of the articles, often stated as an afterthought at the end, was the mental and physical toll the dark material took on her. She talked about being sick throughout the two years she worked on the book. Among other articles, the *Washington Post*, which described her as a "rapid-fire talk machine," mentioned her reports of her hair falling out while writing the book. "I couldn't sleep," Iris described in that "Style" section interview. "I couldn't eat. Even my editor lost 10 pounds from the stress of dealing with all this, even secondhand. . . . You think you know what evil is, how bad things can be. But nothing prepared me for what I found. Even stories and films of the Holocaust." In another interview published in a "Style" section, this one in the *San Francisco Chronicle*, Iris described the images still tormenting her. "To this day, you think there's no pain left to feel, but when I saw a film on the rape of Nanking (last year), I started crying," she said. "Sometimes you think you're numb, but you're not." The *Baltimore Sun* quoted her talking about times writing the book "when I'd start shaking all over and I felt this tremendous pain inside me." The reporter continued: "Which is why Ying-Ying Chang has told her daughter to pick a 'light topic' for her next book. 'You don't want to dwell on this for so long,' her mother had said. 'I'm very concerned for her health, but I'm so proud of her.'" Iris told Terry Tang of the UCLA student newspaper: "Sometimes I would be shopping or walking through the park, and without any warning, some image from *The Rape of Nanking* would just float in front of me. I would tell myself, 'Put it out of your mind.' I didn't want the events to spill over and poison the rest of my life."

I was most struck by a comment Iris made in an article in the *Champaign News-Gazette* about her experiences dealing with the success of her book: "I guess I've gone from hell to heaven, haven't I? But that's not an entirely correct analogy. It's more like being strapped to a roller coaster and not being able to get off."

Iris talked about pressures to always be on, such as after a speech to hundreds at the Holocaust Museum in Washington, D.C. Afterward, a friend asked her to a party, where she expected only a few others and would finally get a chance to relax. It turned out that it was a reception for six hundred people, where she was expected to make another speech.

That speech was taped by a Taiwanese TV station and broadcast several times internationally. The odds were that she had been in another city that morning and was going to another the next day.

Iris also talked about her experiences on the road constantly hearing stories of torture from readers. "Strangers approached her to talk about their sufferings, sometimes decades in the past," the article said. It then quoted her comment: "This is why I often find it so physically and psychologically draining. . . . I've literally had people come up to me and break down in tears as they recounted their own stories."

Soon she was dogged by some of the most noxious types of people to roam the earth, Holocaust deniers. Iris herself recognized this denial as a part of the territory in writing about genocide of any kind. She told the *New York Times* that for those who commit genocide, it is standard that: "First you kill, and then the memory of killing is killed." She noted the time-tested tactic to find errors in minor details in order to discredit the larger argument that a greater massacre had really happened.

Iris also was confronted with the particular sensitivities of conservatives in Japan to facing war history. The assault on her book from Japan started when her nemesis, the ambassador from Japan, publicly denounced her book in April of 1998. "While I expected to be attacked by the right wing groups in Japan," Iris said afterward, in an interview with the liberal Japanese journal *Ronza*, "I certainly did not expect that somebody from the Japanese government would risk his reputation to declare that my book is 'one-sided,' 'erroneous,' and filled with 'historical inaccuracies.' He failed to come up with a single example to prove his serious allegation, and when I challenged him to a nationally televised debate, he declined to participate." (She would later get that chance for debate on PBS' *NewsHour*.) A few months later, six Japanese academics called a press conference in Tokyo against her book. Later that year, Japan's consul general called the book a "preposterous fable." Political cartoons in conservative magazines appeared showing her as a mannish, fang-toothed, and hysterical monster inciting mobs of angry Westerners to violence against Japan.

Much of the criticism she faced revolved around death-toll numbers and photo captions. In interviews, she stressed that she had cited a full range of figures about those killed in the massacre, not just the most disputed larger one of three hundred thousand. She had taken the three hundred thousand from the records of the International Military Tribunal of the Far East (IMTFE), which prosecuted Japanese war criminals. Also known as the Tokyo War Crimes Trial, it went on for two and a half years and achieved a record as the longest war crimes trial in history. It lasted three times as long as the Nuremberg trials in Germany.

In a syndicated Associated Press article published in the *Boston Globe*, Iris dismantled the Japanese right wing's arguments against her book, one by one. Her critics had said that Iris' figure (which is the standard figure given in every country but Japan) of three hundred thousand was impossible because the population of Nanking at the time was only two hundred thousand. She countered that Chinese government archives cited about six hundred thousand citizens remaining in the city at the time of the invasion; once again her archival research was a foundation of her argument. The Japanese historians had said that some of the Chinese soldiers were to blame for the massacre of civilians for disguising themselves as such. Iris responded: "To commit widespread massacres of civilians because there are some soldiers hiding among them is a clear violation of human rights laws and established laws of war." She also denied manipulating any of the photos, which had been in the public domain for decades and undoubtedly still showed Japanese soldiers committing atrocities against Chinese citizens during wartime, even if some of the dates were off slightly.

When asked if she was a pawn of the government of the People's Republic of China, Iris advised such critics to read her first book, *Thread of the Silkworm*, which had been banned in the PRC "because of its exposure of some corruption in the Communist party," she told Japan's *Ronza* in its October 1998 issue. She also stuck by her statement that while the Japanese had not recently banned mention of the massacre from textbooks, they had indeed "whitewashed" or "minimized it." Recognizing that the Japanese had made "vague" apologies to China in the past, she still demanded a specific apology about the Rape of Nanking.

Another series of articles traced the impact of the far right in Japan in stopping her book's publication there. It happened with Iris' rejection of her Japanese publisher's terms in publishing the book, which responded to right-wing pressures. Iris had agreed to the correction of ten errors, mainly involving misspelled names and erroneous dates in describing Japan's military history. But she would not follow the publisher's request to "correct" sixty-five other facts that she did not see as mistaken. The publisher also wanted to release a companion volume giving the "other side" to the story, denying the Nanking massacre. Iris objected to this mishmash of mixed information.

Ironically, as a result of minor errors with name spellings and dates, despite getting the major part of the story right, her book lost credibility across the political spectrum in Japan. The far right used the cancellation of her book there as "evidence" of its falsehoods. At the same time, liberal groups criticized errors in *The Rape of Nanking* as setting back their cause. (Traditional Japanese culture is more likely than that of the West to put extreme value on precision and less on the "big picture.")

And then there were the death threats. Articles reported how Iris' former Japanese publisher received a faxed threat and was visited by right-wing groups making protests. While Iris said she never received any death threats directly, she did regularly receive hostile e-mails and phone calls. She was openly worried, citing the history of intimidation from the far right in Japan regarding this topic. In her book, she wrote about Azuma Shiro, the first Japanese veteran to "admit openly his crimes in Nanking," who has received numerous death threats. She also covered the fate of the past mayor of Nagasaki, who had made comments condemning the emperor's wartime guilt, and then was assassinated. As a result of these concerns, she never did visit Japan, and was known to be secretive about her home address, using a post office box for all mail, even from friends.

These documents of her achievements—and struggles with the immense fallout from her book—were a good start in understanding Iris' internal life. But while I was in Urbana, where she had grown up, I knew I had to take advantage of personal witnesses, to go beyond the résumés, class notes, and newspaper clippings. Those people with whom she had studied and worked would give me greater insight into her early challenges and motivations to take on the world.

CHAPTER FOUR

Why in the World Did She Run for Homecoming Court?

*F*rom Iris' fiction story "The Halloween Prince," published in spring 1988 in her college literary journal, *Open Wide*:

> *What was worse, she wondered. Dangerous, short life threat-ened by a million things, one of which included bad boys with baseball bats, or a secluded long one, year after year, same rocks, same food, same water, able to see the world on the other side but never able to reach it.*

In the early fall of 1988, in the offices of our college paper, Iris asked me to vote for her for homecoming queen. She was one of ten "princesses" running for that position. Most, like her, were in sororities. She had applied to a special committee to be selected for the race, and now was awaiting the final outcome of the campus-wide popular vote. Her bio and picture were posted in the Illini Union with the others, if I wanted to see them, she said. I politely demurred, wondering what would possess someone to do such a thing. With my limited time, the last thing I would do was take time to vote for something I considered as backward and frivolous as homecoming queen.

Indeed, I was aware of the fraternities and sororities on our campus, representing the largest Greek system in existence, and I tried my best to avoid them. At best, I saw the Greek system as a quaint anachronism, a holdout from the era of *Animal House*, when women named Babs sported bouffant hairdos and skintight girdles, then the most conventional deterrent to date rape.

As it turned out, Iris didn't make that top spot as queen, but seemed to enjoy her reign as one of the princesses. The court was a central focus of the homecoming parade, where the royalty and their dates waved to the crowds. The high point was the homecoming game's halftime show, when the court members lined up for the announcement of their titles on the fifty-yard line, as their names each flashed on the giant scoreboard above. They all wore the type of ceremonial sashes that contestants in beauty pageants don diagonally across their chests. The ribbons listed the names of Big Ten Schools; Iris represented Purdue.

Years later, I was still confused about Iris' gambit to be queen, along with her motivation for joining a sorority her junior year. Indeed, of all the questions about Iris' life that I asked during this investigation—regarding conspiracy theories, right-wing Japanese enemies, the fog of mental illness, "the model minority" expectation—these stood out as particularly vexing. As I perused the national Web site of her sorority, Phi Beta Chi, I wondered how irreverent atheist Iris, future chronicler of atrocity, fit in. The official mascot was a "white lamb," the flower was the "white rose of Sharon," and the motto, reflecting the religious origins of the sorority, was *Amor Via Vitae In Christo,* or "Love through life in Christ." It just didn't add up.

But, after getting to know Iris more through those who had known her early on, her choice, her desire to be a part of this scene, made more sense. Through the sorority Web site, I tracked down some of Iris' sorority sisters from her era and learned that their sorority (now closed on the Urbana campus) was relatively small and low profile, known as a "sorority for those who don't like sororities." I already knew that not every sorority member fit the stereotype of being a huge partier, which Iris never was. Moreover, many sororities have Christian roots but allow secular behavior, just like many private colleges, which make attending services optional and membership open to those of all faiths. Also, Iris matured physically in college, becoming quite a beauty, which doesn't hurt one's chances of success in a sorority. Like a lot of late bloomers, she went from being an awkward kid in high school to a decidedly glamorous woman.

Above all, it seems clear now that, like so many, in college Iris was finding herself, trying on a lot of different roles for size. One basic role, among many, that she aimed to fill throughout her life was of "real American," something a homecoming queen epitomizes. As Chicago has been called "the most American of cities," the University of Illinois during homecoming week is probably "the most American of universities." That is where the tradition reputedly started, as well as the first halftime show. The university was also among the first schools to have a marching band, which still regularly plays John Philip Sousa's original composition for the university.

Plus, success of all kinds was important to Iris. A friend of hers from high school, Kathy Szoke, persuasively argued that this run for queen wasn't entirely inconsistent with Iris' character. In an interview with Monica Eng for Eng's 2005 *Chicago Tribune Magazine* article on Iris, Szoke explained that it appealed to Iris' competitive and crusading side: "I think she looked at it as a challenge. She looked at the court as this certain clique of girls and thought, why shouldn't a shy little Chinese bookworm be able to break into it too?"

That sense of rising to meet challenges did make sense, considering the contrasting "shy little Chinese bookworm" that she had been earlier in high school. After learning more about her difficult social life in high school and beyond, I could understand that underlying need for acceptance, championing the underdog—and personal transformation. Although Iris had told me about her early alienation, repeatedly, during our friendship, I was late in realizing its intensity. In preparing for this book, I discovered in my own journal an entry from December of 2000 that mentioned my surprise at a recent conversation with Iris in which she told me that she "always felt alienated from other people." I now do not remember that conversation at all.

Indeed, a theme, and a major source of pain, in her early life was being constantly misunderstood by the larger group of her peers, who judged her typically long-term focus as being "calculating" and her ambition as being "selfish." (However, she always managed to find close friends at every stage who were genuine kindred spirits.)

It was now clear that although Iris had extraordinary talents as a writer and thinker from an early age, like a lot of "sensitive types," she lacked some of the most ordinary skills for picking up social cues and "playing by the rules." Usually marching to her own drummer, for better and for worse, she was always more advanced than peers and coworkers in some ways, and much less in others.

Those who knew Iris in high school gave me a better sense of this awkwardness. Nina Paley, a high school classmate, said that she was not surprised that Iris had been depressed later in life, remembering her as "withdrawn." Another classmate, Dan Shapiro, said that she was "somewhat socially awkward" and "quite shy." (But he added, "In my mind's eye, I can also picture her in normal conversation, laughing at jokes, and an occasional temper.") Her history teacher Dr. Chris Butler recalled Iris as "awkward, quiet and not real sociable. I mean, she always struck me as . . . ill at ease. She seemed kind of spacey, but that could be because she was thinking about all sorts of other stuff, you just don't know."

Iris' creative writing from that time reveals an unusual amount of sensitivity, despite still being very much a kid. In the many short stories and poems published in her high school literary magazine, and later in college, a common theme was the fleeting nature of life. At a memorial service in Urbana in late 2004, her English teacher Adele Suslick made this observation and read parts of what may have been Iris' first published poem, which appeared in a 1980–81 issue of the high school literary magazine *Unique*. Iris was thirteen:

> *Time*
> *Moving steadily*
> *Destroys, mystifies, conquers*
> *Absolutely impossible to stop*
> *Eternity*

Like other poems she wrote then, one from the 1984–85 issue, "Fire on Water," talks about conflicts of reconciling opposing internal forces:

> *And I see different emotions*
> *And aspects of mind like*
> *Excitement and calm,*
> *Fantasy and abstract thought,*
> *Creativity and logic*
> *Fire on water*
> *This turmoil and beauty is* [sic] *deep within everyone,*
> *Always in conflict with each other,__*
> *Yet one is never able to destroy the other.*
> *They coexist forever.*

But then again, I thought, it could just be about opposites, nothing more. What writer type was NOT awkward and alienated and moody in high school? Revealing a lighter side, she also wrote poems that were completely positive, in a dreamy way, like one that described a sunrise heralding the possibilities of a new day; an early issue featured her full-page illustration of a unicorn.

I also remembered her talking numerous times about the pain she felt in high school as a special target of bullies, which was a defining experience in her life. In 1998, during a stop in Chicago, she went on and on to me about how hard it was for her to go back to Uni High at that time to collect an award. "Paula," she said. "If it weren't for this award, I'd be happy to never go back there."

Another friend, Li Wen Huang, whom Iris met later in graduate school, noticed this obsession with those bullying experiences. In their playwriting class at Johns Hopkins, she noted that a constant theme in Iris' writing was high school bullying. Even after Iris became successful, she still talked about it, especially while agonizing about attending her ten-year reunion. "She seemed to be very traumatized about kind of being the nerd in high school and . . . I think she wanted to belong, and she didn't. And you know, they made sure that she felt that she didn't belong. She's very successful, and yet she's still very . . . sensitive," said Li Wen.

As I later learned in interviews, Iris' class at Uni High was particularly known for its merciless taunting. "It was the worst situation I've seen this school in," said history teacher Dr. Butler, who has taught there for about thirty years.

Other graduates of Uni High confirmed that while that type of problem happens at every school, Iris' class was especially bad. "There are about forty students in a class, so each class has a really distinct personality," said Nina Paley. "It's like what [cartoonist] Matt Groening said: junior high is the deepest pit in hell, and high school is the second deepest pit in hell."

Iris' coeditor of the school literary magazine, Daniel Kolodziej, remembered Iris' especially extreme daily torments by bullies in high school. He was also a victim of it himself, to the point of getting into a serious brawl to stop it. He described the problem as mainly verbal, the result of very articulate kids who "knew how to get under your skin." The verbal teasing, usually in the form of constantly repeated name-calling and imitation of the person's mannerisms, was "malicious" and ever-present, he said. To escape teacher scrutiny, often the bullies coded insults, choosing seemingly innocuous words that only their victim might understand. Dr. Butler recalled that teasers imitated Iris' high-pitched voice and called her names (among them, "Iris the Virus").

While Iris got teased worse than most, she was not unusual in being "teasable." In fact, Daniel Kolodziej said students there would make fun of someone for *anything* that stood out, including his "funky" last name. Iris' friend Amy Kohler said that others would tease her for being a dancer by walking beside her with their feet turned out.

"The teasing was pervasive," Daniel said. "I'd say if you were in a job and people were like that, people would get sued, you know, and people would get fired."

"So it wasn't just like normal teasing everybody has in high school?" I asked. Daniel replied:

> *It was daily if not hourly. . . . Imagine that for five years. There really was no one to turn to. I mean we had school counselors and stuff but we really didn't know to talk to those people, and there was nobody observing. . . . Anytime you had any bad feelings about it, someone would just chalk it up to teenager angst or something. No one really recognized this as a phenomenon, and certainly not at that time.*
>
> *I think more so now, you hear about news reports, and certainly with Columbine and stuff like that, people are a lot more in tune with that. For me, and for Iris, and I know for my brother, and I know for some other people, it was a severe and constant problem. And to this day I still feel badly about it; I still feel bitter about it.*

Then he added, "I know why she would be a target," saying that Iris came off as "grating" to some people.

> *She was not afraid to speak her mind. At least that's my recollection of her, that she was never really afraid, but she was very, I'd say . . . she was difficult. . . . It sounds like a harsh word, I think, to say someone is "difficult." But some people kind of know how to speak their mind, and get along with people at the same time, be diplomatic. I would not say she was diplomatic. She was not someone who knew how to get her way*

without rubbing someone the wrong way. . . . She wouldn't be
someone who would say, "Well, that's a good opinion, but have
you thought about this?" She was not a diplomat.

He added that "it was a geeky school, but I guess as geeky schools go she was one of the more geeky. . . . As I recall she wore slacks and a dress shirt every day, kind of like a button-down oxford shirt. She looked kind of boyish in that sense, so she wasn't wearing the latest clothing."

Like Daniel, Iris was not able to simply ignore the bullies, which made things worse. "The point of a bully was to get under your skin. When they know they're under your skin, then they're going to keep doing it. And the only way they really know is if you react to it, and the more you react the more they do it. . . . I mean she was insecure like a lot of people, I'm sure, but she wasn't afraid to say what was on her mind," he said.

Others told me that her open ambition and achievements exacerbated the situation. For example, she didn't hesitate talking about her membership in children's Mensa, an organization for those with high IQs. She had written for an application and was accepted. Her classmate Amy Kohler shared the insight that other students didn't understand Iris' basic underlying nonadversarial attitude in such discussions. In talking about her own achievements, she didn't mean to put anyone down: "She never felt like there was limited success out there in the world. There was enough for everybody. Her success wouldn't hurt anybody else's. . . .

"I remember, she was very serious about 'I'm going to be someone and I'm going to do something' and college, and next, and next. I mean I guess she was similar to me in that way. Some kids at that age are just thinking about being kids," Amy said, laughing a bit. "She would have fit in much better in college than she did in high school. And that was always one of my problems in high school, too. I remember when I got to college and I said, 'Wow, this feels really much better.' And I think it was the same thing with her. It's just that she was just too mature to really know how to be social with kids in a high school situation."

Amy added that Iris also was completely unprepared to deal with teasing because there was absolutely none of it in her home. She didn't know how to handle teasing, and was not interested in teasing others. While others bonded this way, she refused to take part, even with the easiest targets, such as a more persecuted girl at their school, a child genius who was years behind the rest of them in age. Iris also did not share the socially bonding experience of knowing about popular culture, especially music (beyond classical), which was not a topic of attention in her academically focused and serious immigrant family, said Amy.

But, despite Iris' typically serious personality, Amy reported silly times together as kids, like telling ghost stories together and scaring each other. Daniel said he appreciated working with her on the literary magazine, where he saw some lighter sides. "She . . . had a good sense of humor, and we always had a good time in the way we put together the magazine. We had to meet weekly and read other peoples' poetry and make fun of it," he said laughing, "and read our own stuff. She was very expressive. She had a lot of good writing and we would talk about each others' writing. She had a lot to say about a lot of things."

In tribute to Iris, and to his brother, who died at about the same time, Daniel set up a literary prize at their high school. "I was very moved when I found out she had died. It made me very sad, sadder than I would have maybe objectively expected," he said, echoing the words of many of his classmates. Nina Paley said this was the defining tone on their alumni LISTSERV after the death. Classmate Dan Shapiro, who had seen her speak at the Holocaust Museum in Washington, D.C., said, "In part because of her shyness in high school, a lot of us who knew her casually were deeply impressed by her professional successes. Her death seemed particularly tragic, most of all for her family and friends of course, but also because of the sense that she had a lot of wonderful writing left in her that the world will not get to enjoy."

Iris' high school English teacher Adele Suslick remembered both Iris' stubbornness and "sparkle." She described her drive as a matter of being focused, very focused, about what she had to accomplish, like a "bullet train." This was the beginning of a long dialogue I would have about Iris' habit of planning her life strategically, which some would see as positive (focused) and others as negative (calculating). Suslick said:

> *That is one thing about Iris, she was very goal oriented. She always knew where she wanted to be. Nothing was done accidentally. She had thought about the outcomes and where they would put her. It was almost . . . "intellectual chess" degrades it somehow, because that means game playing. I don't think she was game playing at all, but she had strategies in mind and was very directed in that sense.*

She said Iris was a natural crusader, facing harsh opposition when she was the only girl to join the math team. She was aided by her expert debating skills, being very prepared for any possible argument. And she led a drive to revive the literary magazine *Unique*, which she coedited for two years, after it had lain dormant for a few years.

> *Adele Suslick echoed the words of others I talked to who said that Iris was motivated not by grades, but more personally to make her own mark. I think she was most into getting her projects done, and to some extent that involved grades, but she wanted to see things completed. The finished poem, the finished short story, the finished debate, the finished note cards. Getting the project done mattered a lot to her. So again, it was almost like building a trail of accomplishment. Yeah—grades, I mean she always earned A's; it wasn't an issue, I don't think. It was to make sure that the work was done and done well and was noticed.*

Suslick noticed that Iris identified herself as a writer early on, and lived according to how she had defined that role. "It's almost as if she programmed herself. . . . She defined the role, and then stepped into it."

I asked Suslick about the bullying problem, and she answered, chuckling, "I never saw her as a weakling. I honestly didn't. She was so able to do verbal judo, and she was not shy. She was straightforward, up-front, honest, and she may have been feeling that she was bullied. But she did not act as if she was fearful, and in fact she often times looked to be the stronger of the two in any altercation."

Suslick had an altercation of her own with Iris. She had served as the faculty sponsor for the literary magazine during a year when Iris was an editor. One time, before the magazine went to press, she saw that a large part of the content of the issue was by Iris herself. (Her work had gone through all proper channels to be accepted; Daniel Kolodziej remembers that the editorial board likely voted on everything anonymously, with a few levels of committee review required. Iris had no authority to just publish whatever she wanted as editor.) So, to Iris' extreme displeasure, Suslick informed her that she would make her long "short story" anonymous in the journal.

"I said, 'Iris, is this a school magazine or is it your publication?' The next year Iris had somebody else be the sponsor."

Later I returned to Iris' high school library, in a drafty old three-story building on the university campus, to find that anonymous story. I knew that "anonymous" was not something that Iris would have liked being, ever, and I hoped to put the record straight. This story seemed at first to be childish because of the subject matter: a dialogue between a young curious dandelion and an older wise tree. But, as with another story of hers from college (about a frog) that I later found, the treatment was surprisingly philosophical. In both cases, the very innocent subject goes through a struggle to leave the comfort and safety of home to satisfy a deep longing for knowledge and discovery. Among other deep subjects investigated, the dandelion asks about the purpose of philosophy. He worries that it has been put to bad use, such as by Hitler in his ideology of the "master race." The tree agrees but also argues that philosophy can be helpful:

> *It gives us a chance to step outside our own existence and ask "Why?" It allows us to provide an answer to that question.*

*The dandelion was still for a long time. When he spoke at
last, his voice was quiet and thoughtful. "That's what I'm
looking for, what I have always been looking for. An answer."*

Indeed, even as a teen, Iris was always aware of—and preoccupied
with—the bigger picture in life. This awareness resurfaced later on, in
July of 2003, as she reflected on her upbringing with filmmaker Christine
Choy. At one point in that footage, Iris described an innocent and almost
idyllic childhood of faculty barbecues, piano lessons, and music concerts.

Christine, a tiny, fast-talking, chain-smoking woman known to swear a
blue streak, boisterously replied from off camera: "You're so normal it's
absurd!" she said.

Iris laughed.

"You know, most people rebel and go shoplifting or listen to rock and
roll music, popular music. You were not rebellious," Christine said.

"No," replied Iris.

*I feel there are many different ways of rebelling. I didn't want
to rebel in a conventional way. I feel like if you're going to
rebel, you write a book or produce a movie that will shock the
world. That's a real rebellion. I don't believe in small rebel-
lions that are going to waste your time, like shoplifting. What
does that mean? That doesn't mean anything, right? Or going
and puking after a rock concert. You know, time is limited;
life is short.*

Later in college, despite some stumbling, Iris blossomed on many levels to become more outgoing. Her Santa Barbara friend Barbara Masin
remembers Iris and her joking about them being "ex-shy people" who
had forced themselves to change against the grain later in life. Brett later
told me that Iris felt freer at that time in her life to start breaking away
from her parents, living away from home for the first time. "I think that's
why she did so much better when she went to college too, that she was

basically on her own and she got to exert herself and sort of develop a lot," he said.

After majoring in science during her first two years, Iris became very focused on her career as a journalist. "From the time I started dating her that's what she cared about more than anything else," said Brett, who met her during her senior year. "She was strategizing about what she should do to help to maximize her probability of winning a Pulitzer Prize."

"She was talking about a Pulitzer Prize?" I said.

"Yes. I never really encountered anybody like her before."

But, to Iris' confusion and disappointment, her sorority sisters and others didn't take as kindly as Brett to her eccentricities. Her longtime social struggles to "fit in" with the larger "popular" crowd remained. In fact, when she first went through sorority rush as a freshman, she did not get into a sorority. "She was only like sixteen years old," Brett explained, "and she didn't have the right clothes, she didn't have the right background. And so the sororities weren't all that interested in having her join. She was sixteen and she probably looked like she was about thirteen.

"So then something happened."

"What was that?" I asked.

"For her first two years she lived in the dorms. . . . She had fun there, but I think she was thinking about getting an apartment. But there was some girl who was killed in an apartment right around that time, and Iris decided it was safer to live in the sorority. So she just went through sorority rush and she joined that sorority. It was very unusual. Almost nobody joins a sorority when you're a junior."

I was a bit surprised that this would even be a motivation to join a sorority, wondering if this was a sign that her strong anxieties and safety fears had started earlier in life than others had supposed. But, then again, it was a scary case and she was especially familiar with it because she covered the murder as a stringer for the *Chicago Tribune*.

If fear was a motivator, Iris didn't say so publicly. She explained her motivation to join a sorority in a later interview for the national sorority

alumnae magazine: "I was looking for a more intimate social environment. Also, I wanted to try something new, to enjoy another aspect of the
collegiate experience."

Iris was always positive about that time, but I still wondered how she
really fit in. I tracked down a few of her former sorority sisters and asked
them.

I first met a woman—whom I'll call Jennifer—who had been on a
committee that had selected Iris for the sorority. I asked her first impression of Iris: "She was well liked. I mean, I hate to sound superficial as a
sorority girl, but [Iris] was beautiful. She was successful academically. She
had her act together, and you could tell right away. So she was well liked
from the start. I don't think there was any question that we wanted her to
be part of the house."

Jennifer lived with Iris for a semester, along with about seven other
women, in the basement of the sorority house. There, in that basement,
which was termed "the dungeon," new members "did their time" until
they got to take one of the more desirable and more private bedrooms
upstairs. Jennifer did recall conflicts between Iris and other members regarding neglecting her cleaning chores because of her preoccupation with
her work—to the point of "hyperactivity." And she said that she and
other members always wondered what Iris was writing about them in the
journal that she fastidiously kept.

But she said Iris "was a dedicated member in terms of full participa-
tion." And that their small house of about fifty women total, which was a
fraction of the size of other sororities on campus, was proud when she
made it to the homecoming court. Jennifer even remembered lending Iris
the more professional-looking suit she wore that day, persuading her to
wear it instead of the flouncy dress Iris had picked out.

"I would have never thought of her being depressed. If anything, she
generally seemed happy. In fact, not only happy but happy and content
with her life," she said.

I later found out more of the real story of what her sorority sisters
thought of Iris from another sister, Vicki Wagner, now a manager at an Illi-

nois-based agricultural company. She likely had been on the selection committee to choose Iris for membership (she couldn't be sure), and was Iris'
closest friend in the house. They had spent hours on the house's front
steps, during which Iris would grill Vicki about her blue-collar small-town
upbringing, which fascinated her as being very different from her own. Iris
also asked Vicki about her rationale in choosing a boyfriend, almost in a
scientific way. "With her there were always a thousand and one questions.
The wheels in her head were always turning constantly, and I supposed
that's what made her an author and a reporter and everything else."

At first, Vicki gave the same basic description of Iris' life at the sorority
as Jennifer. But then, late into a second interview, late in the conversation, after I asked more about Iris fitting in, she added: "I never thought
she had a lot of common sense. There's things she would do that were
just odd to the rest of us."

I asked her to name specific incidents. "She would come into the room
very late at night, and there's eight of us, I think, or six of us that shared
that room, and she would hum. She would hum the whole time and half
of us were trying to get to sleep, and we're like are you kidding me? But
she always, always hummed, I mean always."

"Did anybody talk to her about that?"

"I don't remember. I don't know if we talked to her about it or made
fun of her. I'm not going to tell you that the eight of us always got along,
and I'm not going to tell you that we were always the nicest people in the
world, because frankly we weren't. . . . That's just age and immaturity
and that type of thing."

"Not even talking about yourself, could you just say generally were
people talking about her behind her back a lot?" I asked.

"Oh yes, yeah. Her nickname was Iris Changalang."

"What does that mean?"

"Kind of like a dingaling . . . That's what we called her and . . . that
was certainly behind her back. . . . I'm telling you we weren't the nicest
people and we talked about her, and I do feel bad because I was always
really nice . . . to her face, but boy, behind her back we called her Iris

Changalang. And, of the six or eight of us that were in the dungeon, I was probably the nicest to her because I just always felt sorry for her."

Part of that sympathy was a result of Iris' regular phone calls to her parents, which Vicki thought upset her greatly. "I vividly remember several phone calls or conversations that she had with her parents. And I'd walk in the bathroom, and she'd been crying. And I asked her what's wrong. . . . Then you just stop asking, because it's kind of pushy. She always just kind of brushed it off like it was nothing."

Vicki also tried to console Iris after her fellow sorority sisters, including Jennifer, read her mysterious diary and confronted her about it (which may have been a major source of her crying with her parents). They were upset about some unflattering portrayals and "were pretty mean to her, to Iris. And Iris was like, 'I didn't do anything.' And I remember her crying about it once when we were sitting on the steps. She was like 'I just need to know what I did.' And then you try to explain, and I think—now that we're talking about it—I had that conversation about that quirky behavior that she exhibits. And I was like, 'You just have to be more normal.'"

I asked if the overall feeling toward Iris in the sorority was negative or positive.

"Overall, negative probably."

Later, Vicki continued: "I don't think she ever knew that I didn't really care for her. I mean, honestly, I don't think—and it wasn't that I didn't care for her, because I did like her uniqueness. I just thought she was Changalang."

I asked about homecoming, if that status as princess changed how people perceived her.

"No. I think everybody was really, really surprised, like they were surprised that she achieved that. But everybody thought it was odd."

"Why was that?"

"Just because of how she was in the house, how odd and different she was in the house comparatively. Not that we didn't all have our quirks, but everybody couldn't believe it, they couldn't believe it."

I said I knew this sounded like a strange question, but did it matter to everyone that she was good looking?

"No, and it wasn't even a big discussion in the house. We discussed it amongst ourselves at how surprised we were that she was on the court, but that was it. I mean that was like very minor in the house altogether."

"I know there were just ten people on the court, and you were a small sorority, so. . . . "

"It should have been a huge deal but it wasn't," she said.

But Vicki added that she was deeply impressed by Iris' achievements and enjoyed corresponding with her over e-mail later in life, when Iris seemed "more levelheaded" as a mother. Vicki said she appreciated Iris sending her photos of her family and was impressed by the description of "author" on her business card. Iris exposed Vicki to a level of success she could not imagine while she was growing up. She described her emotion when she saw Iris on public television one night confronting the Japanese ambassador.

"Of the people that I was surrounded by in life, there's not many that are going to be on TV for positive reasons," she joked, laughing a bit. "Occasionally an arrest photo or something might show up there, but not usually for positive reasons. In fact, I woke my husband up and said, 'You will not believe who's on TV!' . . . And looking back I shouldn't have been nearly surprised as what I was, because I always thought that she would be that anyway. I just always thought she was the smartest person I knew."

I would like to say that these social clashes were limited to her college sorority, but they weren't. Such conflicts were typical of her interactions with her fellow journalists, at every stage—that is, until she got famous. Mike Mettler, one of her fellow magazine interns from the summer of 1988 in New York City, recalled to me via e-mail: "I think the group opinion of Iris that summer was of someone who was superintelligent and incredibly driven, but also someone who was a bit green when it came to social situations." As an example, Mettler, now a magazine editor in New York City, gave the example of a group outing to Central Park on Earth

Day. "It was a scorching-hot day, so most of us were decked out in shorts and T-shirts, but Iris was dressed like we were going to a social—patent-leather shoes, dress skirt and panty hose, the whole nine. At one point, she took off her panty hose in front of everyone, which became a bit of a running joke that summer. (Somewhere in my photo archives is a pic of her smiling/laughing after she put panty hose on the head of another fellow intern during one of our in-dorm parties.)"

Some of our classmates from the *Daily Illini* told me after Iris' death that jealousy had been behind any conflict with Iris. When I became friends with Iris after college, I remember feeling I should hide that fact from my past colleagues there, who scowled whenever I mentioned her name. Ironically, I found out more about the source of their feelings at an alumni event *honoring* Iris in the fall of 2006. As a part of a ribbon cutting to open a spectacular new media building, organizers held a ceremony to induct an Illini Media Company "Hall of Fame." That list included mainly older men who did their time there in the fifties and sixties, such as film critic Roger Ebert and likable pornographer Hugh Hefner (not present). Iris was the only woman of the seventeen inductees, and the only one who had graduated college after the early 1970s. She was also the only one pictured in the accompanying slides who was unwrinkled; she was frozen in time from when she died at age thirty-six. And she had always looked young for her age.

Throughout that alumni weekend, our own sort of "homecoming," I asked people point-blank why they hadn't liked her. Summing it up best was a fellow editor, who now, like most of the alumni, has reached a respectable level of success at a national newspaper after more than a decade of dues-paying at a smaller paper. She said that while she respects what Iris did with her career, "I don't have to like her personally." She explained that what she respected and appreciated best about the *Daily Illini* was the sense of community, of working together with others. She herself had started working there in the first week of freshman year and was there almost every day until graduation. In contrast, she saw Iris purely as a "self-promoter" who only did the minimum work at the paper to get bylines and suit her career goals. The work that Iris published her senior year, like a lot of our features contributors, was mainly from her journalism class assignments. This editor was particularly annoyed on a daily basis in their journalism law class, when Iris would sit in the front row and dare to argue with the scholarly professor, a renowned national expert on these issues.

Once again, Iris' outspokenness, individualism, and ultimate focus on the big picture turned off others as "selfish." And, to some extent, they were right. When one fixes on such high goals, relating to the community isn't necessarily the first priority.

I would like to be able to say that clashes were limited to those who knew her from high school and college, when people were at an age where they didn't know any better, and when the stakes—sorority popularity and school paper assignments—weren't very high. But this pattern continued, with even more punishing intensity, when she was an intern at the *Chicago Tribune* (after an intense stint at the Associated Press in the summer of 1989), with full-grown adults. One of her fellow interns for that year, Christie Parsons, who is now a Washington correspondent for the paper, recalled to me how Iris did not fit in—not knowing or caring to follow rules there. As a result, editors at the city desk, where they started, kept talking about Iris negatively even years beyond her time there. In later notes of hers I found, Iris expressed disappointments with politics in the *Tribune* newsroom and with the limits of daily journalism in general to go more in-depth with a story. But she added that the experience was proving useful in shaping her, since, for example, she was learning to not be intimidated by famous people she interviewed.

I remembered Iris talking a lot about clashes with editors there, but also about her much-valued friendship with Christie that started on their first day as interns. Christie recalled: "She [Iris] really was the first friend and the first friendly person" at the newspaper when she started.

An interesting contrast between the two was adapting to the old-school macho hard-edged newsroom culture on the city desk. While Iris was clearly driven, she still stuck to her own rules, even if it meant less "success" at the paper. This counters the stereotype of the superachiever as a "brownnoser" or "kiss up"—someone who will do *anything* to get ahead. Ultimately what mattered were her own voice and her bigger vision for her career.

Christie recalled their different reactions to a routine type of intern assignment to call family members of trauma victims to get comments for a story: "I just remember this one time that I called this grieving family three times in a row after they had hung up on me. I mean I called a third time after they had hung up on me. It was just despicable behavior, really. But all I was thinking was I'm not walking back out to that desk without a quote from the family. . . . I was trying so hard to internalize all the rules and expectations because I really wanted to excel there," she said.

In contrast, Christie said, Iris "walked in there and was more skeptical of people on the desk. Like people that I automatically respected because they were *Tribune* editors. She had strong opinions about who they were and what they were all about."

Christie recalled how Iris absolutely stunned others in the newsroom one day by refusing to call one family of a trauma victim a second time after he or she had told her once that they didn't want to talk.

When the editor protested, Iris handed him the phone: "Iris just said, 'Here, ask them yourself.' And she walked away from the desk, which was just unheard of. I mean, God, it was just not heard of. I never would have done that in a hundred years."

"I'm sure she had a bigger agenda for herself," I said.

"Yeah, she clearly did. I showed up and most interns showed up and were going to do whatever they were asked and to do it just so well."

"Because they wanted to stay at the *Tribune*?"

"Because they wanted to stay at the *Tribune*. That didn't seem to be her goal. . . . She wanted to do her own kinds of stories and after a time that's what she did," Christie said, referring to Iris' later work in the features department.

Perhaps for this reason, a few editors at the city desk seemed to want to put Iris in her place. One of the most oft-repeated anecdotes about Iris was about the time she was sent to Chinatown for a story. There had been a major political incident in China, and since she said she spoke Mandarin, they sent her there to get local commentary. Christie related:

> *The way the story came back to the city desk was from a photographer who was with her. She walked up to somebody on the street and said something in Chinese. And he just looked at her blankly. And then she said something again in another dialect or phrasing it differently—I don't know. And he shook his head. And she tried a third time. And the person just was not responding. The photographer then said, "Do you speak English?" And the guy in a perfectly American accent said, "Yes, of course I do. This is Chicago."*

People in the newsroom liked to tell that story over and over, embellishing it over the years. That all stopped when Iris got famous.

At that time, Iris herself was critical of these editors, especially a few of the older men's condescensions to her as a young woman. While she later became friends with these men and grew to respect them, Christie agreed that the city desk was not the most reflective atmosphere at that time. "I mean people don't go home and read [feminist theorist] Catharine McKinnon at the end of the day and reflect upon why they were condescending. . . . People go home, and they have a beer at the Billy Goat [tavern], and then they smoke a couple of cigarettes and get up early so they can do it again the next day."

Iris had clashed with *Tribune* editors from the interns' first day there. At that time, Christie, Iris, and one other intern, John Fountain, were invited to the office of the editor of the paper, Jim Squires. Squires, who is from the South, started the meeting by talking about college football in that region. Christie, who attended the University of Alabama and is from that state, went along and joined the conversation.

But Iris kept interrupting and trying to change the topic. "She wanted to know how the *Tribune* was put together and how and who was making what decisions and all this, you know. And I understood this was like a BS session. . . . I just remember that John and I were leaning back in our chairs just kind of chit-chatting, and Iris was leaned forward asking questions. And when we walked out, I was going to turn to her and say, 'Iris, why were you going over the [personnel] flow chart with the guy?'" she recalled, laughing. "But she turned to me and, 'Why were *you* asking him about football? Who cares about football?'

"The point was Jim Squires did. As I look back on it, I think that was when I got hired, that moment."

(The other intern, John Fountain, also went on for a long-term career at the *Tribune*, and then later at the *New York Times*.)

While she appreciated Iris' company, after work Christie did occasionally become frustrated with Iris' inability to take a hint and relax. When they went out for pizza after work, Christie would signal that she just wanted to rest, but Iris still wouldn't turn down her intensity. "So I would actually just say to her: 'Could you chill out? I need *not* to talk about the *Tribune* for five minutes.'"

Like Vicki Wagner, Iris' former sorority sister, Christie recalled conversations to convince Iris to act "more normal" to get along with others.

> *I did have that time . . . when I wished for her sake that she would just try to follow the rules a little bit more, try to get in the game a little bit more. And I felt frustrated with her a little bit as a friend because she wouldn't internalize, she wouldn't play by the rules. She wasn't trying to win the game. She wasn't playing the game well.*

She also recalled, "and at the very end I just remember this conversation where I said, for example, 'Iris your hair is down to here,'" she said, pointing to her upper thigh. "It really was that long. I said, 'Look at the professional women in the newsroom. They don't look like that.' I just remember her brushing off the comment, because she wasn't trying to be that."

Then, when Iris published her best-seller, Christie finally understood what Iris' bigger agenda was—and all that nonconforming behavior made sense. "My reaction was yeah, okay, now I get it," she said.

In fall of 1990, Iris soon moved onto her next goal, pursuing a graduate degree in science writing from Johns Hopkins, where she had won a scholarship. From Baltimore she continued a long-distance relationship with Brett, as he headed for Santa Barbara, where his graduate advisor had moved. Iris fared better socially at Johns Hopkins, surrounded by other introspective writer types. But Brett recalled that some of the writers were so sensitive there that she had the opposite problem she'd had with some of the veteran male editors at the city desk of the *Tribune*. She was actually *too* hard-edged for some. Brett said:

> *There was a bar where they would all hang out, and one time this poet made a statement, and Iris disagreed with him. And she just focused her attention on something else, and she looked back and he was crying because she disagreed with him. So Iris is very kind hearted, you know, and she tried to apologize to him for disagreeing with him, but it was certainly a different crowd. So she went from the* Chicago Tribune *newsroom, right, with these tougher reporters, to dealing with poets who would cry if you disagreed with them.*

Iris also had misadventures trying to find a mentor at Hopkins, someone who "got" her, like her prized journalism mentor Professor Bob Reid at the University of Illinois. In fact, she made a point of "collecting" mentors, evidenced by the table full of them at her wedding, as Professor Reid's widow Marilyn told me.

But at Hopkins, the nonfiction writers were in the minority on the faculty; most focused on fiction and poetry. While Iris did manage to befriend a few, she was very disappointed that some "tried to blow her off," said Li Wen Huang, her classmate there. Part of it could have been rivalry; some of the faculty members were making extreme efforts to find a small publisher, and Iris had already landed a book contract with a major publisher (for *Thread of the Silkworm*). An interview with Iris in the Johns Hopkins alumni magazine from November of 1997 even made the point, saying she had landed her first book contract in 1991 at the age of twenty-three "to the envy of more experienced writers who have spent years trying to get their first book published."

Li Wen added that it didn't help her popularity with the faculty that Iris came on so strong. "She was very direct, very aggressive and she would definitely put people off by that. It's like who is this person?" She added that another trait that faculty members may have interpreted as arrogance was her arguing style in class; she would like to save a "trump card" point, and then brandish it triumphantly at the last minute to claim victory. "It's kind of like, 'hah!' And that really would put people off even if she was right, because 'she showed them.'"

As a graduate student, such tactics wore thin. But when Iris was a crusading celebrity journalist—such as when she was on national television nailing the Japanese ambassador, they were considered admirable traits. Indeed, everything changed in late 1997, with the incredible success of *The Rape of Nanking*. Iris' supposedly superior "big picture" and "arrogant" attitude now made sense to those from her past, with them often reacting privately with guilt and shame over past doubt of her. And her international best-seller status gave her a new aura of success and confidence. While she did continue to confuse and alarm some with her directness, most were now much more likely to excuse her.

A woman who worked for Iris' publisher at the time, Basic Books, recalled similar mixed reaction to Iris. Some were taken aback by her aggressiveness in dealing with them, but ultimately they greatly appreciated her for her work. In response to my Salon article, she e-mailed me:

Iris was our first, our only! best-selling author. Everyone heard from Iris—she had advice and thoughts on every aspect of her book, and would call every day to find out 'the [sales] numbers.' Reactions to her were mixed, again, just as you described, but tempered by this book that we were all involved in from the earliest stages. God, we were all so horrified and floored by every line in that book, and when it took off the way it did—it really did seem that she was embarking on a MISSION—that she had the power to confront GOVERNMENTS.

Ironically, now mixing regularly in elite circles, Iris never fit in better in her life. Hanging out with celebrities was natural for her. While author Amy Tan described Iris as "in awe" at such events, I did not get the sense that Iris was intimidated. After all, she was with her kind. No one thought she was too ambitious; no one thought she was "weird"; and no one was jealous—because they were as successful as she was.

In fact, Iris made a particularly big hit at one of the most exclusive events she attended, the White House's Renaissance weekends in Hilton Head, South Carolina. She and Brett went together once in 1998, when her book became a best-seller, and then again in 1999. "Iris really wowed a lot of people because most of the people there at Renaissance Weekend were older," said Brett. "They were in their forties and fifties, and they built up their careers over a period of time. And here's this woman who was thirty, and she looked like she was twenty-five. She was beautiful and articulate, and so they actually had her speaking at the closing speeches. They'd have a Nobel Prize winner, and a TV personality, and then Iris. She was a big hit. I mean her book was on the best-seller list almost that whole year."

"So there was no one she was scared to talk to because they were so famous?" I asked.

"Not at all. Actually she loved it because there were a lot of best-selling authors there. Even when she was just starting she had no qualms at all about calling a best-selling author and asking advice. And so that's one of the reasons why I think she succeeded is she went right to successful people and asked them for advice. And so she loved the opportunity to schmooze with all the famous authors."

Brett talked about a quick friendship that Iris struck up with Arianna Huffington, a major celebrity in Santa Barbara, where they had first lived in California, before moving to the San Jose area.

> *Michael Huffington had been elected to Congress, and then later he ran for the senate, so they were THE glamour couple in Santa Barbara. And so in the first or second Renaissance Weekend, Iris went to the beauty shop and Arianna Huffington was sitting in the chair next to her. And they just hit it off; they just got along great. So later that day Arianna Huffington was waving at her, and she was waving at Arianna Huffington.*

That said, Iris always being true to herself, she still managed to ruffle feathers at the Renaissance weekends. Along with the few other Chinese women attending, including Amy Tan, Iris was often invited to speak at break-out discussion sessions on racism, one of many social issues addressed there. As in other situations, she spoke her mind, either ignoring or ignorant of expected political correctness. When her turn came to testify about racism in her life, Brett recalled, "Iris would always say, 'I've never experienced any racism in my life; I think this is silly. People should just move on and not worry about it.'

"And of course a lot of the other people there made their living worrying about it, so they were really hostile towards her. And she was like, 'I don't want to participate in this. I'm not that interested in it, and these people are hostile towards me.'"

It turned out that while she recognized prejudice against Chinese Americans in her first book on the scientist, and in the third, *The Chinese in America,* she didn't see it as a problem she had personally. She grew up in a community with a significant Asian population. In *The Chinese in*

America, she described herself as descended from a wave of intellectuals, such as her parents, who came to the United States in the 1960s and flourished in university towns, which she called "the first outposts of multiculturalism, and Chinese scholars were able to particulate in university town life without being self-conscious about their non-Caucasian appearance and speech patterns." (262)

One of my favorite stories about her during that period was when, with a similar down-to-earth attitude, she dumbfounded—to the point of speechlessness—a prominent *New York Times* food critic. The two had just spoken at the *L.A. Times* Book Fair. A mutual friend asked them to join a group for dinner. Brett just remembers the critic's name as "Jeffrey," and he labeled the following story, an e-mail, to me as: "You really shouldn't have said that to Jeffrey." Brett recalled:

> *So they all went out to dinner together at Wolfgang Puck's restaurant, and Wolfgang Puck was there. And he saw that the food critic for the* New York Times *was there. So they put them at the best table. And [Puck] came over, and his wife came over. And they were trying to charm them and serve them the best dishes in the whole restaurant because Wolfgang Puck wanted a good review in the* New York Times *for his restaurant. And so that was nice, Iris got a real kick out of that. But then [the food critic] started asking Iris about where she lived, and Iris said she lived in Sunnyvale. And he said, "Sunnyvale?" And she said, "Yeah," and he said, "There aren't any good restaurants in Sunnyvale; why don't you live in San Francisco?" Iris said, "Oh, there are plenty of good restaurants," and she started to name them. He said, "But none of those restaurants have a good wine list." And Iris said, "I actually prefer grape juice to wine."*
>
> *And he just didn't know how to respond. And I think he just got up and walked away. One of his friends said, "You really shouldn't have said that to Jeffrey."*

This continual rendezvous with celebrities is what I remember best from Iris' life as a best-selling author. But, of course, it turned out that her celebrity status, this role she had assiduously studied and then purposefully stepped into, was a double-edged sword. As her behavior became more quirky in the late 1990s, those who knew her, including myself, were more likely to let it go. Her fame also brought difficult new pressures to perform and dazzle at higher and higher levels—and made her some new enemies, ones that were more shadowy and harder to track than the most mystified of high school bullies, sorority sisters, crime reporters, sensitive poets, or wine snobs.

CHAPTER FIVE

Who Inspired Her?

*F*rom a December 18, 1991, letter from Iris to friend Li Wen Huang:

> *Publishing is the weirdest business I have ever encountered. It slides somewhere in the crack between art and commercialism, between high ideals and outright manipulation.*

From a September 23, 1995, e-mail to me:

> *When you're not too busy, I would love to know how you promoted your first book. . . .*

> 1. *Are there any mistakes that you made with your publisher or matters of promotion that I should watch out for? Can you offer me any tips or advice?*
> 2. *How soon should the media in every city be contacted about the book before a scheduled booksigning? A month before? A week before?*
> 3. *What can you tell me about the following agents: Mitch Douglas at International Creative Management in*

*New York City and Sandra Dijkstra Literary Agency
in Del Mar?*

*. . . Dijkskra and I have never spoken, but her office mailed
me her press kit. . . . She's transformed a number of unknown
writers into stars. Tan was a struggling technical writer with
just one short story published in some literary journal when
Dijkstra approached her and nagged her for more (pardon,
the short story was in* Seventeen *magazine). Anchee Min was
too poor to afford envelopes when she mailed her material to
Dijkstra. . . . While she is determined to build the careers of
Asian women writers, I wonder if she might put some in the
shadows in order to spotlight her more famous Asian clients,
like Tan or Kingston.*

*Information is power, so anything you can send me on those
two agents would be scrutinized and carefully weighed. The
Nexis Lexis articles can indicate for us at a glance which of
the two is getting more press.*

Before she got famous, Iris wasn't misunderstood by everyone. She always still attracted more than her share of friends and mentors. As she inspired them, in turn, they influenced her, helping her to develop and articulate her most basic ideals and hone her powerful writing skills. To understand Iris, one has to meet her allies.

Notably, in college, one of them did stand out in his steadfast support. He was a respected man of substance who proved to be an especially loyal lifelong supporter. That was her mentor, journalism professor Bob Reid.

Iris talked about him constantly, even after graduation, quoting his wisdom about journalism here and there, for example, about the role of the free press or the privileges of being an author. To comfort me when I was discouraged, such as when I was exhausted after finally finishing my second book, she e-mailed in July of 2000: "You should be proud of everything you've accomplished so far. Professor Robert Reid once told me that writing two books is equivalent to the work of an entire career. So you've already achieved more than what most people do in a lifetime." Her advice to me about outlining one's writing in advance with questions had been his to her as well, and she'd followed it: all of her book outlines primarily consisted of pages and pages of questions. Another major influence for her was his advice to reporters to "leave our comfort zone," or push ourselves to interview and get perspectives from people we wouldn't normally face in our regular lives.

Reid, an old-time newspaper man, was legendary for his high ideals—and resulting toughness. He would customarily give a student an "F" if they turned in an assignment a second late or misspelled one name. I knew about that reputation for greatness at all costs—and, therefore, I avoided him almost completely.

Besides being extreme idealists, a major trait that Iris and Professor Reid shared was the propensity to talk, a lot. As one journalism department member told me recently, other faculty sometimes saw Professor Reid as "a bother," often extending their meetings for hours to debate before any vote. After he retired, their meetings shortened considerably.

As a student, Iris would spend hours talking to Reid about journalism and personal issues. With remarkable openness, they discussed her emotional fallout from the dark topics she was researching in college and beyond. In media interviews before and after her death, he described an episode during which she had broken down in tears in front of his class while describing her experiences writing about a man who had died of AIDS. "She put her head on the table and started sobbing," he recalled in the January/February 1998 *Illinois Alumni* magazine. "She sobbed for five minutes. Everybody sat respectfully, nobody was uncomfortable. Then she lifted her head up and began talking." He added that she also called him for support when she was working on *The Rape of Nanking* and once "ended up crying for an hour on the phone. She said she didn't know how she could go on, knowing that human nature was capable of such cruelty. It took more than an hour, but she worked herself through it."

Taking the podium at an Urbana memorial service for Iris in December of 2004—a service I could not attend, but that I later watched on DVD—the sixty-four-year-old Reid admitted holding back his deep grief; he was under doctor's orders not to excite himself because of his serious heart condition. In an effort to be upbeat, he commented about their typically marathon-length phone calls. He remembered happy ones, such as "when she had done something with *Thread of the Silkworm* that she was particularly proud of, the reporting coup she had made that day. And she wanted to call and have somebody to share it with."

Professor Reid recalled an especially intense period when Iris judiciously took advantage of a one-time-only deal with a phone company, U.S. Sprint, which somehow had offered her free long distance for a month, up to ten thousand dollars worth. (She even made the phone company put it down in writing, because—especially as a researcher calling China regularly—she knew she would exploit the deal to its fullest.) One day, she called Reid at the start of his office hours, which she knew began right at 4:30 p.m. "She got me when I had been drinking iced tea most of the afternoon, and we just talked and talked and talked. And Iris was a very interesting conversationalist," he recalled.

"I finally got to the point where my kidneys were about to burst, and I had to say, 'Iris, I'd love to continue this conversation.' By this time it was 6:30, and my wife was waiting outside to pick me up. 'But I have to go to the bathroom. I just have to go.' And Iris says, 'How long will it take?'

"I said, 'I don't know.'

"And she said, 'Well, I'll call you back in ten minutes.' And she did that, twice."

He also spoke of how she fit his longtime ideal of a journalist as being part scholar

> *with the spirit of a poet thrown in. . . . I've never seen anybody who put together those traits the way that Iris did. I mean, that was my model of what you ought to be. And Iris managed to live it out and I'm very, very proud of that. And I think she*

did it largely on her own with a little bit of me basically say-
ing, "It's okay. Even if the other kids think you're weird be-
cause you're so passionate about important things, it's okay to
be that way." And I think she developed a kind of sense of
honor about that.

In turn, Professor Reid clearly inspired Iris. He shared parts of a letter that Iris had written in 2002 to nominate him for a teaching award. As he pointed out, it says as much about his mission as about hers:

More than a decade has elapsed since J–380, and now as an
author, holding people accountable has become a vital part of
my life. His words still echo in my memory. His fierce moor-
ings of preparing students for battle: without an independent
press or an educated citizenry, democracy cannot long sur-
vive.

Watching the recording of that memorial service, I was most struck by Professor Reid's stark admission how Iris had helped to inspire him to keep him going through dark times. Referring to Iris' letter about his idealism, he said:

I tried to live my professional life and my personal life, to some
extent, that way. But I, too, sometimes felt a little bit left out
as journalism started changing to more of a business and less
of a profession. . . . [And] the campus started changing from
a place where we want to run the university like a business,
which it's not, instead of like a social institution, which it is.
And it's easy for a teacher who believes what I believe to be-
come discouraged in the face of that kind of opposition in the
profession and on much of the campus.
    And I've got to say that Iris, more than any other student
I've had—I've had some others who were really helpful in this

respect—inspired me. And that is really what Iris gave to my life and enriched me and kept me going. . . . I think I would have quit teaching much sooner if it hadn't been [this way]. Iris was the first one to really blossom where I could see there was some effect from [my efforts].

Perhaps he was so candid because he knew he was at the end of his life. He died within days of that service. At the end of the DVD, the camera focuses on him, flickers, and then fades away.

I regretted that I was never able to interview Professor Reid. I also was not able to get insights from Iris' other major life mentor, her friend and editor Susan Rabiner, who decided not to be interviewed. In my e-mail request to her, I had acknowledged that I knew that she was representing Iris' mother who was working on her own book on Iris. She responded that this was the case, but: "more important is my own feeling that the author/editor relationship is best kept private."

While speaking to her would have been helpful, I did not need any convincing about how strongly Susan had influenced Iris. She was the one who "discovered" Iris when she was in graduate school, to write *Thread of the Silkworm*. Susan officially edited Iris' first two books, worked on editing the third as a freelancer, and became Iris' agent at the end of her career. A powerhouse in her own right, Susan is well known as both an editor and agent: as the former editorial director of Basic Books, and as now representing many major authors in the literary agency she runs with her husband. "Iris owes her success to Susan," Brett told me, adding that "Susan was a second mom to Iris."

Iris talked often about Susan through the years. Just as she did in citing Professor Reid's journalistic wisdom, she would also often quote Susan about the art of suspenseful book writing. She would say: "Susan Rabiner says that a book proposal should answer these five key questions." Or "Susan Rabiner says that a book's introduction should be written last, but not first." In a blurb for Susan and her husband's 2002 writing and publishing guide, *Thinking Like Your Editor*, Iris expressed similar praise for Susan's idealism. She compared Susan to "a modern-day Maxwell Perkins," the legendary book editor of F. Scott Fitzgerald and Ernest Hemingway. She also described Susan's "blend of practical and intellectual advice with true Renaissance spirit—an idealistic urge to elevate books to the highest standards of literature, without sacrificing any integrity of scholarship."

While by all accounts Iris never joked at all about the subject matter of her writing, Iris did reap material from her first superficial impressions of the fast-talking publishing world. In a letter dated December 18, 1991, she wrote to Li Wen about off-the-cuff conversations with her soon-to-be editor, Susan:

> *The relationship I have with Susan is a very strange one. In some ways, it approaches the intimacy of a mentor and student, of mother and daughter, especially when the aesthetic side of the book is being discussed. She is constantly petting and stroking me with little comments like, "This book can transform you from an unknown writer into a rising star!" or "This is a BIG book—I'd be surprised if it isn't played up on the front page of the* New York Times*" or "Iris, I love working with you because you're so smart, you're exceptionally talented for your age, you're a person with dreams, you're a fantastic interviewer, you're sensitive, etc. etc. etc."*
>
> *But when the topic is money, Susan becomes quite a different person entirely. The conversation goes something like this:*
>
> *"I can't get you a bigger advance, Iris, because of a number of reasons: your age, the recession, and the fact that your book has a liberal slant as we enter a conservative age. You're only twenty-three years old! Iris, I'm old enough to be your MOTHER! How many other twenty-three-year-olds do you know who have an offer from a major publishing house? Forget*

twenty-three-year-old first-time authors. . . . Do you know how
much Carl Drassy [sic], the inventor of the birth control pill,
got as an advance for HIS book? Do you know how much
Robert Gallo got? Do you know what MOST authors get here
at Basic Books—and we're talking about world-famous Nobel
Prize winners here! . . ."

Susan Rabiner has the rapid-fire rat-a-tat speech of a
used-car salesman who flings out numbers, facts and names
over the telephone so fast it leaves me sputtering. It pays to say
absolutely nothing, because nothing seems to unnerve her more
than dead silence—"Iris, are you still there?"

Iris went on to describe challenges with her agent search. She made light of one agent that Susan, with whom she had an unusually harmonious relationship overall, had suggested to her. In that same 1991 letter to Li Wen, Iris recalled a phone conversation she had with that agent. Iris was disappointed to find out that his "agency, I must add, specialized in selling what he called 'non-books,' one of which was entitled *How to Shit in the Woods.*"
Iris described her follow-up questions to him:

'How to,' I asked hesitantly, 'SIT in the woods?'
'NO!' he bellowed. 'How to SHIT in the Woods! The author
was thinking of changing it to When Nature Calls, *but I felt*
the original title was so wonderful we couldn't discard it.
And let me tell you, Iris, one of the reviewers liked the book so
much he compared it to Thoreau!!! And when you're an
agent, and one of the clients you represent is on the same level
as Thoreau. . . . Well! What more is there to say?'

There was nothing more to say. I hung up and called Cur-
tis Brown.

We had many conversations about her first agent, from Curtis Brown, with whom she ultimately had a fallout. In fact, the topic of relationships with agents was probably what we talked about most during that period, even more than romantic relationships. As one classic author was quoted as saying, when bankers get together, they talk about literature. And when writers get together, they talk about money.

Then, Iris spent weeks considering her next step. She asked for my help in this case, as with others, in researching two particular agents with my special access to the then-typically-restricted (and expensive) Lexis Nexis newspaper database (available at a university at which I was affili-ated as a visiting scholar). After much agonizing thought, she ultimately decided to go instead with an agent at a big organization, the William Morris Agency, with whom she was ultimately displeased for not return-ing her phone calls and giving her enough attention. In her opinion, he considered her too small-fry for him. Finally, she was satisfied joining Su-san's new literary agency.

Despite her confusion in the beginning in figuring it all out, Iris ulti-mately had no complaints about how the publishing world had treated her. "My experience with publishing has been quite good, and I've never seen any kind of dirty politics or anything negative really in the decade I've spent there," she told Christine Choy for her documentary in July 2003. "I've been very fortunate that the publishers that I've worked for are very high-minded, and they are almost academic, I think, often in their thinking. I've heard horror stories with other people, but I've been very fortunate. I haven't experienced any of that."

Besides her allies in writing, when Iris and I talked over the years, a fa-vorite topic was her friends. I talked to many of them, who all gave me distinct insights into her personal evolution of becoming an author and the accompanying stresses. To my surprise, some even gave me perspec-tive into my own friendship with Iris, from Iris' point of view, showing me what she wrote about me in letters to them.

As for me, Iris had served as an inspiration for them in her success. These friends also all were shocked by her suicide and were grasping to find concrete clues from the past. Ironically, most said that they had also held back in discussing with Iris their own toughest times, including struggles with depression, fearing that Iris' world was "too perfect" for her to understand such problems. They used the word "perfect" a lot.

One of Iris' favorite people of all time was her childhood friend Amy Orfield Kohler. I met up with Amy for an interview in Raleigh, North Carolina. She looked both fragile and strong, like the lifelong dancer she is. She was now a college dance instructor in Asheville, North Carolina, from where she had driven to meet me. I had met Amy only once before, at a dinner in Chinatown for Iris' friends during one of her Chicago stops years before.

As Amy took out piles of photos and letters, we started talking about how she and Iris met the summer before high school. "They had this kind of lab summer program where we all did physical fitness all day, and then we had been measured on body fat at the beginning of the program."

"These skinny little girls, yeah," I said, looking at a photo of her and Iris sitting at a birthday party around a table at the Chang house. "She didn't look so happy there, sort of a little intense."

"She was always very serious."

We looked through other photos; in all of them, Iris was not smiling. Then we came to one of her joking as she brushed her teeth.

"Brushing the teeth, a little less serious," I said.

Amy continued, sharing some of her experiences with Iris:

> *We'd spend the night at each other's houses a lot, and I re-member one of our favorite things to do when I would spend the night is scare each other to death. She loved watching* The Twilight Zone. *We'd watch* The Twilight Zone, *and we'd get each other totally spooked out telling ghost stories. . . . I don't know if you ever did this when you were a little girl, but there used to be this thing, she'd tell me the story about if you said, "Bloody Mary," and turned your back to a mirror a certain number of times, a hand would come out and just grab you.*

About the atmosphere at the Chang home, she said: "It was very welcoming, and her parents seemed genuine and caring, very loving people and very successful people. There was that air in the atmosphere. . . . I mean, I could just tell. I mean, my father's a professor. . . . So there was that academic atmosphere that I recognized, and it was familiar to me."

Amy also felt she understood Iris' drive for justice because her father, Gary Orfield, was a controversial and vocal civil rights activist. He cofounded and now directs the Civil Rights Project at Harvard University. "My dad was similar to Iris in a lot of ways. He stirs things up. He always had people mad at him. So I think Iris and I understood each other really well because of our families."

After Amy moved away with her family freshman year because of her father's new job, she and Iris kept in touch mainly because of Iris' initiative in always writing her. Amy also didn't find it strange that even in high school, Iris wrote a lot about her career in her letters. "When you're a dancer you have to think at a young age about your profession, unlike most people. Even though we had different goals or aims, there was very similar thinking about a career at that age," she said.

We went on to look at pictures of both of their very traditional big weddings, from about fifteen years before (which I didn't attend; Iris and I only became close friends shortly thereafter). Both of them served as bridesmaids for the other. The photos showed each of them as brides in big white dresses, flanked by rows of bridesmaids in long and bright gowns carrying bouquets.

I looked through more photos and said, "I never saw this one. It's one of Iris holding Christopher, and she's laughing. It's a very exuberant picture. He's reaching up to the chandelier in their home. Wow, that's the happiest picture yet."

"Yeah, it is. She does look really happy, doesn't she?"

Near that was a more familiar and equally upbeat 1999 Christmas card letter that Iris had copied and sent to friends. The next letter was handwritten on flowery stationary I had also seen before. But at first reading, I immediately saw that this was not stereotypical frivolous post-adolescent girlfriend conversation. In a letter from April 15, 1992, a twenty-four-year-old Iris updates Amy on her strenuous scientific research for *Thread of the Silkworm:*

> *At the moment, I am feverishly trying to read everything that was ever published about the Chinese ICBM [Intercontinental Ballistic Missile] program before I go to Washington and conduct research in military archives and talk to the major military experts and Air Force generals and CIA historians. I have to understand the basics before I can ask intelligent questions and it's not easy: there's a lot to learn about uranium and plutonium and polonium—beryllium and dimethylhydrozone and whatnot. Unfortunately, chemistry was not my strong suit in high school or college, but it's a lot more interesting now that it's being put into practical application.... (You would not believe how many Chinese miners died of radiation poisoning, cave-ins and disease in their search for uranium.)*

I went on to a later letter from July 27, 1993, also detailing her research in China. Like the ones I had from her from that period, Iris described nonstop activity, which I only now in retrospect could see as a possible sign of mania or a low-grade form of it. She wrote:

> *The entire trip was so packed with interviews and trips to archives that I was booked to the limit—mornings, afternoons and evenings. Sometimes even the mealtimes were booked with appointments. There was this constant rush of exhilaration, of jumping in and out of taxis, as if I was working for the Associated Press again (except for the fact that all the interviews were conducted in Chinese). Yes, the Associ-*

ated Press—only I was the assignment editor, the reporter,
and the photographer.

She went on to talk about how she felt "so lazy, it's embarrassing" as she recovered from the weeks-long trip to China: "I'm in vacation mode now and will stay in that mode for at least a week longer, because my parents and Brett's parents and my friend Paula Kamen will be visiting during the next two weeks."

I stopped and read her enthusiastic description of our meeting in college and my subsequent book work. She asked Amy if I could interview her for my book on young women's sexual attitudes, in a part on interracial relationships (which I never followed up on). Here Iris was advocating for me and talking positively about me behind my back, in a letter she probably thought I'd never see. I thought of my other friends and how we typically tease each other and sometimes talk not as flatteringly about them when they're not around. Iris never said anything negative about any of her friends to me; here I was seeing that as her pattern with others, too.

I asked Amy more about their typically long phone conversations, mostly from when they were young through the end of the 1990s, when they drifted more apart, as was the case with most of Iris' friends, particularly those living outside of California. Amy brought up two major conflicts Iris was having through that time. First, Iris was passionate about writing a book about the problem of the biological clock in women's careers, and the potential of science to overcome it. She sent Amy, as well as me and many other friends, her proposal for it in 1996. But no matter how hard her agents tried, even after Iris became famous, she couldn't sell it. Iris told me that editors had thought that women were returning to the home and wouldn't want to have kids that late in life anyway.

Amy added: "And then the other big thing I remember is around *The Rape of Nanking*, how upset she was when the Japanese started pulling ads out of. . . ."

"*Newsweek?*" I asked, remembering talking with Iris about that incident myself in 1997.

"Yeah, yeah. That whole time period where . . . and I think that's the time period where she felt, to me it seemed like she felt most threatened from the outside world."

Amy was referring to a life-defining conflict that Iris had with *Newsweek*, which she saw as an attempt by Japanese corporations to censor an excerpt of *The Rape of Nanking* in a fall 1997 issue. I only vaguely knew about that conflict from when Iris had called me and expressed her anger about it. "It felt like a whole new world, that someone could dislike something so much that they might want to hurt her in any sort of way," Amy said. She added that this incident from the past, which I had yet to research in detail, exacerbated Iris' more irrational fears later in life of organized Japanese and U.S. government conspiracies against her. "I didn't necessarily think there was a plot [at the end of] her life. But I thought she had a lot of real reasons why things that had happened in the past could contribute to her feelings later."

Amy added that Iris was also caught off guard by the huge outpouring of grief from victims of the Japanese at her readings. "I think she was somewhat overwhelmed sometimes by the amount of emotion that would come out," Amy said. ". . . I think she liked the fact that it was such a healing thing, but I think it was more profound than she ever imagined."

In the remaining years of Iris' life, Amy distanced herself more from Iris. Amy was going through some difficult problems with her health and marriage that she did not think Iris would understand. "I often thought wow, my life is really just really always a mess, and Iris' is always perfect. And if I had had any idea. . . . I mean her life to me from the outset was almost too perfect and I felt, 'Well if I just talk to her about this it's going to be a drag because she's got it all together.'"

This hesitation to talk to Iris continued until the very end, to Amy's deep regret. She never returned Iris' phone message/good-bye call—almost identical to mine—that she received days before her death in November of 2004. "I think the irony is that I think I didn't call her back because I was in so much pain myself with something in my life. And I'm like I can't call her when I'm feeling like this. I thought I'm going to get in a better place, and call her tomorrow. So that taught me a great lesson to never make those kinds of assumptions," she said.

Back in Chicago, I spoke with another close friend of Iris', Li Wen Huang. With her large cache of letters she had saved from Iris, Li Wen was able to fill in the gaps for me about Iris' life at Johns Hopkins from 1990 to 1991, as well discuss Iris' early ventures into publishing and her marriage.

The two had bonded at Johns Hopkins with their similar backgrounds, as Chinese Americans from the Midwest. Li Wen grew up in Sioux City, Iowa, the daughter of, "what else," she said, a Chinese restaurant owner. Hers was one of the few Chinese families in that small city. "It's just kind of that Midwestern sensibility that you get," she said. "It's practical, it's straightforward, there's not a lot of pretension."

Despite finding Iris "exhausting," Li Wen was attracted to her intelligence and her strong curiosity. Like others, she drifted in and out of the present tense when she spoke about Iris.

> *That was one of the things I always said about Iris is that she's always going one hundred miles an hour. You can tell she was a really bright person. Things are flying around in her head, so many things, and she was also very articulate. But sometimes it was such a stream of consciousness, and it was just a rapid fire that if you didn't jump in there and just cut her off, you weren't going to be part of the conversation. She's just so intense about different things. We didn't always agree, but it was always interesting to have that kind of debate and that discussion with her, because she was really engaged, was really intelligent and also had a good sense of humor. And we could sit there and laugh about things.*

When asked to describe Iris, Li Wen said the one word she would use would be "anxious." Iris was always worrying about anything that could possibly go wrong. But then again, she always ultimately managed to make herself look at situations more positively to fend off those thoughts. "There was a lot of anxiety in her, but even though she had all these anxieties, it didn't stop her from going and doing whatever she felt she needed to do," Li Wen said.

Li Wen noticed how in graduate school Iris' continuing relationship with Brett was a source of grounding—and some needed lightness—for Iris. "She seemed to be calmer and at ease around Brett. That was one thing I noticed about it, and there was definitely a kind of a glow between the two of them when they were together. . . . They were playful. And they really did love each other, and they really did care about each other. It was definitely, I think, a special relationship.

"I remember her telling me the story of how she met Brett and she would always talk about his being this 'fresh-faced farm boy'; that was the phrase that really stuck. She was like, 'Isn't he wonderful, just a fresh-faced farm boy?'"

In 1991, when Li Wen visited the couple in Santa Barbara and then the San Jose area, where they moved in 1996, she witnessed Iris' trust for Brett endure. "I remember going out for sushi with them and you know it's funny, because she would always turn to Brett like, 'Brett what's my favorite thing? Is this my favorite thing?' He was kind of there to tell her, 'Yes, you like this; no, you don't like that.' She was always flying around in so many directions that sometimes she [needed a]. . . .

"Grounding influence?" I said. Li Wen responded:

Exactly. In fact I remember we had this conversation about how she didn't understand the need for caffeine or soda, like coffee. . . . And it's funny because as she was saying that, I looked at Brett, and Brett looked at me, and we shared this knowing smile like we know why Iris doesn't need caffeine. Because she's

*just an intense and high-spirited person, she definitely doesn't
need caffeine at all. In fact she would often ask at restaurants
for chamomile tea to calm her down or relax her.*

Her letters from Iris at that time also showed that Brett influenced Iris
to take time off. "A couple weeks ago Brett and I were tired, irritable and
pretty burnt out from work," she wrote to Li Wen on March 8, 1992.
"We were working seven days a week, often past midnight, and suffered
from terrible headaches that didn't make us any more productive. So we
decided to do absolutely no work on Saturdays, and our lives have improved considerably since then. We dined at Chinese restaurants and
bought ice cream cones and took long walks on the beach. This weekend,
we did nothing but eat, sleep and watch movies on the VCR."

Iris always described Brett positively to her friends, despite some ongoing struggles.

*I think there was a lot of stress because both of them were
really, really focused and very intense people, very focused
people, very ambitious people. Brett was spending a lot of time
at work. He was really focused on work, and Iris was also very
focused on her work, so I think . . . there were parts of their
marriage where they didn't get to spend a lot of quality time
together because they were so focused on their own things. And
I'm sure there's some conflicts that came out of that. I mean
she didn't really go into detail with any of that, but sometimes
you could sense that.*

A challenge of Iris' move to California was that she found it socially
isolating, with people seeming less reliable than before. "This is how it is
in California," I recall her telling me. "People make plans with you, such
as to meet for lunch, and they don't show up. You just can't make that
plan without calling them that day to remind them."

But, Iris still kept positive and greeted the move as a new adventure. She thought that the California focus on fitness and the outdoors encouraged her to be more physically healthy. And, as she also told me, she was glad to break away from her past and redefine herself, following a long and honored tradition of those who move West. She was also following a tradition of children of immigrants to break away and find themselves—before they are able to reintegrate themselves with their culture. Brett said that since she always had a hard time saying no to her parents, the distance was helpful to her growth.

In a letter to Li Wen dated October 22, 1991, Iris enthusiastically recounted her recent move with Brett to Santa Barbara. One of her first actions was to enthusiastically seek out a visit from the Welcome Wagon. As with the homecoming court, Iris was utterly fascinated by "all-American" traditions. She wrote:

> As a child, I always wanted a Welcome Wagon Lady to come to our door, showering our new home with gifts, but my parents never called for one every time we moved, either because they didn't know they could or because they just didn't care. So I grew up feeling a little cheated when I read children's stories about the Welcome Wagon Lady handing out free gifts to some family just because they were the new family on the block. The Welcome Wagon Lady showed up with a wad of coupons and free stuff like bookmarks and refrigerator magnets bearing the names of local businesses. I was entitled to attend a Newcomer's Coffee Hour, a Mary Kay party and a Tupperware party. She also handed me a Welcome Wagon newsletter, which contained a calendar of events: Bridge Night, Coupon Exchanges and Elections for the Kid's Carpool Committee. "We'll teach you how to play Bunko," she said, smiling. "Bunko?" It was, according to the Welcome Wagon Lady, "a wonderfully, wonderfully fun card game."

At that time, Iris wrote many long letters seeking publishing advice from Li Wen, who was working as an acquisitions editor for a Chicago medical publisher. Iris wrote in an October 22, 1991, letter:

> *Tell me what you do in acquisitions. Do you shuffle through the slush pile every day? I read once that the editorial assistant, usually a young graduate from some Ivy League college, is plopped next to a heap of unsolicited manuscripts on the first day of work. Plowing through it is like excavating for gold and ancient relics. As you sift your fingers through your bucket of earth, eager for a piece of Indian pottery, you find stones, twigs and bottle caps instead. Maybe an occasional dry bone. And dirt. Lots and lots and LOTS of dirt. (Is that why [your] work-study student quit after only one day)?*

Iris specifically asked Li Wen for advice about dealing with her publisher, Basic Books, which she felt did not at first recognize the potential for *The Rape of Nanking*. Despite Iris' stated expectations that the book would sell modestly, she also did sense its possibilities for success. "She really believed this book was going to be big, and obviously the publisher didn't or didn't think it was going to be as big as it became," Li Wen said. ". . . She would be confused about why the publicist isn't doing this or that or the other thing. It's like, 'Well Iris, not everybody goes 150 percent all the time.'"

Li Wen witnessed the evolving pressures Iris had with her first two books. The first one, *Thread of the Silkworm*, was stressful because of a low advance and large amount of money needed for years of research and international travel. Iris' letters at the time, to me and to Li Wen, are filled with anxieties over money and discussions of applications for grants, which she asked us to review. Despite the grants she did receive—most notably from the National Science Foundation—she often talked about a frenzy of activity to make money: signing up at temp agencies, teaching a few classes at a local college, and even enlisting with "Entertainment Casting Company in Oxnard as an extra and bit actress." To get free photos of her for her book publicity, she modeled for a student at the Brooks Institute of Photography.

Some stresses in completing *The Rape of Nanking*, for which she also got paid a relatively small advance, were also financial. But there, she suffered greatly with the darkness of the subject matter. As she had told reporters after the book's publication, Iris let Li Wen know that the grisly material was having an effect on her, and interrupting her sleep. "That's one of the things I noticed about Iris is that, especially when she was intent in writing a book, she would be pretty much an insomniac," said Li Wen. "She'd be really stressed out because she couldn't stop thinking about things. Because I mean that's the thing about Iris, that focus becomes an obsession and she's so obsessed about it that she can't let go."

Like her other friends, Li Wen was taken completely by surprise at the suicide, not suspecting bipolar disorder, nor even depression. She and others at Hopkins saw Iris as an "extreme" and "really smart and quirky" personality, not a troubled one. If anything, Li Wen said that she had some jealousy over Iris' apparently perfect life. "Yes, definitely you were wishing you were her or you wish you were like her. I certainly did. I was like, I can't compare to her. My life will never get like that," she said laughing.

That "public persona" of perfection was a reason why Li Wen avoided discussing her own depression with Iris, although Li Wen was very open about it to her other friends. Plus, the typically hours-long phone conversations with Iris were a disincentive to getting in touch more often. Li Wen explained Iris' intensity on the phone by her extreme focus, which would distract her from any hints, or even direct pleas, to end the conversation. "She'd call me at work and I'd be like, 'I have to go!'" Li Wen said, imitating her old desperation in her voice. "She would say, 'One more thing.' And so you're trying to get things done and it's like, 'Iris I have to go! My boss is standing in front of me!'"

After our meeting in Chicago, Li Wen mailed me copies of letters that she had since unearthed from Iris over the years. In one, she wrote a note to me that I would find "quite a bit" on myself. There, Iris wrote about me for more than a page, first telling Li Wen how we knew each other from college. Then she went on in detail about my first book. "I'm really impressed with Paula. *Feminist Fatale* is the first book about women in their twenties written by a woman in her twenties. It's fascinating—you should get a copy if you can. She interviewed hundreds of young men and women across the nation and wrote a three-hundred-page book. And do you know how long it took her to do all of it? Only six short months! Incredible!"

Again, like when Amy showed me Iris' mention of me in her letter, I was moved. Maybe to her I was a bit of a "verb," an example for getting stuff done. At least for those five minutes when I was more famous than her, when my first book came out, right around the time when she got her first book contract. But that was also a long-lost time when I actually seemed to get away with pushing myself to extremes, and before I had to resign myself to a more balanced—and less immediately "productive"—schedule.

I read on about more serious observations: "That was when Paula started getting the headaches. They were horrible migraine headaches, starting from her left eyeball and arching over her skull in a long burning streak to the back of her neck. I believe the pain is caused by stress, as well as those hours of staring at a computer screen."

Here she was, acting like me now, and trying to figure out the cause of a mysterious and invisible health problem. I stopped and remembered that I had, at first, thought her breakdown in Kentucky in August 2004 was due to stress—not neurobiology. In my book, I'd make a point of the need to avoid "blaming the victim" for causing an essentially genetic and neurological problem and adding to her misery. Yet, I'd failed to have that insight with Iris.

In her letter, Iris went on to chronicle the good reviews of my first book that happened "despite the headaches." She mentioned that I was asked to lecture at Northwestern University, and she said "that alone was probably nerve-wracking, because Paula stutters very badly, but she says her speech is gradually improving from all of this exposure."

At first I was horrified, as this problem has been an extreme source of insecurity for me since childhood. When I've worried about it, I've tried to assure myself that it's probably not very noticeable. And she said: "Very badly." I didn't think it was that bad. But maybe it was.

Then again, she certainly was not maligning me; she was recording her observations and sincere concern. Compared to what I'm doing now, that was a modest observation.

In the end, I was also touched seeing her positive mentions of me in several other letters and postcards from Li Wen and from other friends, all in the spirit of being happy for my writing achievements. For example, she told two Chicago friends about a quote of mine about my book in *Time* magazine, and asked them to congratulate me in person if they saw me. Yes, she did think "there was enough success to go around," as Amy had described earlier.

Iris' enduring optimism was the overwhelming observation of her closest friend for the last decade of her life, Barbara Masin, who described Iris as one of the most "positive and energetic" people she ever met. "I really didn't notice any negativity in her approach. Even if there were obstacles, it was about how to overcome them. It wasn't, 'Oh this is terrible, here's an obstacle; help me commiserate.' It was, 'Okay, I have this issue; here's what I'm thinking of doing. What do you think? Do you have other ideas? Let's brainstorm.' It was that kind of a thing, and definitely not depressive at all."

They also found they had a similar style in focusing on work. Neither would have made a good chick lit heroine. Like ours, their conversations centered on work, and specific steps to take to get it done. "I think often when women are together they kind of go, 'Oh'. . . You know, everyone moans a little bit about what's going wrong in their lives and you kind of listen and say, 'Oh I understand.' That wasn't us," she said, laughing. "You might almost say we had almost 'masculine' conversations, at the risk of stereotyping, because it was all about projects. It was about doing stuff. It was about getting things done."

Barbara, who was a year older than Iris, met her through a friend in a writers' group in Santa Barbara in about 1994, when Iris was getting ready to publish her first book. They bonded immediately as "ex-shy people," she observed. Immediately, bursting with questions, Iris sought Barbara's advice about public speaking, which Barbara did professionally in her job and which Iris was also learning in classes in nearby Los Angeles. "You know how Iris was, asking lots and lots of questions on every angle, every conceivable angle of a particular topic," Barbara laughed. That included Iris asking Barbara about hypothetical situations of how she would answer specific questions.

> *It was interesting because she seemed focused and scattered at the same time. . . . But very high energy and she knew what she wanted, and I like that in people. . . . The fact that she set goals for herself, and she didn't think small, because people often are very self-limiting in their goal setting and so forth. And Iris was not that way. And so to me that just connected with something within myself because, yes, I think we both felt the same way.*

Iris was "fascinated" that Barbara, a tech executive just in her twenties, was already traveling the world and speaking before high-ranking government officials for her work. That involved speaking in at least three other languages—German, French, and Spanish—in which she is fluent. One of her jobs has been serving as a delegate from the United States to the International Standards Organization, and another has been promoting new manufacturing technology internationally for an electronics firm.

When I first met the tall and worldly Barbara at the funeral—and then in Santa Barbara a year later to talk specifically about Iris for this book—I could see that Barbara was a good match for Iris. She is clearly independent-minded, unpretentious, curious, and fascinated with the written word. But she is much calmer, with a greater sense of ease than

Iris. At one point, when I asked her if she "freaked out" over something that had happened with Iris, she just said, "I don't freak out."

I hoped that she would not only tell me about her friendship with Iris, but also fill in some of the blanks of her final years. Barbara was the only one of Iris' friends who had known about the mental illness. However, she had stipulated at the start of the interview that she didn't want to talk about it directly.

She did talk fondly about their friendship. Barbara witnessed Iris' dramatic personal transformation from where she started out, as a nervous unknown author with her first book.

> *I remember her first book signing which was at the Barnes &*
> *Noble here in Santa Barbara on State Street. In fact it is still in*
> *the same location, and she had a table set up there right by the*
> *entrance with her books on it. She was wearing the red, I think*
> *it was, the Jones New York suit. . . . She was there and I came by*
> *just to offer general support and buy a book and have it signed*
> *because traffic was kind of sparse at the time. Of course, in her*
> *later book signings that was absolutely not the case.*

"So she was actually nervous?"

"Oh, very nervous."

"In what way? Just knowing what to say?"

"Very high . . . you know like a thoroughbred racehorse at the starting gate of a race, that sort of high-energy nervousness."

"That's an interesting analogy. She was all ready to go."

"Yeah, raring to go. She wasn't exactly sure, you know, what to expect and how to go about it. Even if people tell you umpteen gazillion times, until you actually do it yourself, there's still that factor of the unknown, so I think that's really what it was."

In turn, Iris inspired Barbara in very concrete ways, specifically encouraging her to write her book, *Gauntlet,* which traces her intriguing and prominent family history of resistance to Nazism, and then to Communism in the former Czechoslovakia. Iris also advised Barbara to get her facts from archives abroad, and to broaden the story beyond her family to telling a bigger one about Communist oppression in Central Europe.

"She [Iris] was the one who said, 'You need to write this.' [The book] has given me a lot, you know. It taught me a lot about my family. It also opened my eyes to how certain things in this world worked still, and that history is not always dead and gone but history informs the present and the future. I kind of understood it in an intellectual way, but now I really understand it," she said laughing, "Because I've lived through it; I've seen it."

Barbara added that Iris was attracted to the *Spartacus* element of her story—"the individual standing up against this all powerful, almost overwhelming might of the state. Because I think she saw herself as someone who did that. And she admired it in other people."

We talked about Barbara's grandfather, the famous general Josef Masin, who was executed by the Nazis. That was before he had left a secret note to his family, tucked between bricks of his prison walls, encouraging them to always speak out against oppression.

I said: "So it was not exaggerating saying that you came from a family that has a tradition of standing up for things, or going against the grain?"

"Fighting for freedom was my grandfather's testimony. He lived by that creed. He believed that a human being is defined by his or her principles. You can make compromises, but every time you do, a part of yourself dies."

Because of Iris' muckraking style, Barbara described Iris' sensibility as more journalist than historian.

> *She was out there digging up the facts, however unpalatable they might be, and holding them up and sticking them in peoples' faces and saying, "Here, look at this. This may be ugly. It's not pretty, but you must take notice." She did that to the world at large, and that's a journalist's sensibility. . . . Whereas a journalist deals with contemporary issues, she was looking at*

past issues. But I think her journalistic training and her sensibility informed what she did.

In fact, Barbara made a point of describing Iris' basic independence as that of a *"freelance"* journalist, not tethered to any media organization or university.

She didn't want to work within academia and be a historian with the "publish or perish" dictum, and whatever group think might be imposed on you by your department or your peers if you go to conferences and you depend on them to get your accreditation to further your career in the profession. She wanted no part of that. She was always a lone ranger, like a freelance journalist out there digging up stuff and thrusting it into the limelight for people to take notice. She was a real crusader, and I liked that about her.

And that was something that I could kind of empathize with, as well. We discussed it on quite a few occasions that neither one of us wanted to become part of a large organization.

Sharing Iris' love for research, Barbara also worked closely with her on *The Rape of Nanking.* Guiding her correspondence with German officials Barbara helped Iris track down the diaries of John Rabe, which graphically detailed the massacre. She also translated them out loud for her, which was always difficult for Iris to handle.

She [Iris] always got very distressed when she was dealing with atrocity-type situations. She took it very personally. . . . For me it was you read it, and it's not nice stuff, but there's a part of yourself you can kind of shut off. You kill that part of you just to get through that material. And I don't think Iris ever did that. She really was viscerally as shocked for the last atrocity as for the first one.

Like most of Iris' friends, Barbara did not see clear signs of Iris' serious mental illness until the very end of her life. She wrote off her quirks as quirks. Barbara didn't even question that Iris hardly talked about her son, whom she was taking pains to shelter from much-feared harm. Iris' habit of working all night was a sign to Barbara that she was "an extreme night person," not a manic.

> *You know, some people are day people and some are night. I just thought here was a very extreme night person, you know, someone who thrives on working late simply because there are no external environmental influences. And I can understand that because when I started writing my book, I did a lot of writing between the hours of nine and midnight. Nine p.m. and midnight. It's very quiet, kind of a focused time, so I could see that.*

Regarding the long phone conversations, she commented:

> *I thought that was an Iris quirk. It was interesting because sometimes when we were talking, I would hear her typing along to things that I was saying. She would type things up, kind of like notes to herself. Or I would suggest a certain book to read, if I was talking about something that I had done or something along those lines. Click, click, click—I'd hear the keyboard.*

With the suicide, Barbara was left with a tremendous void in her life, with Iris as both a rare colleague and personal supporter.

> *I think about Iris every day. She took a vibrant interest in anything that I did. . . . I miss her example also, that she was out there doing these things. . . . Just knowing that when I got back from a trip X, we could compare notes about whatever*

happened. . . . She was someone who I respected a great deal
for what she did, what she stood for, and I was proud to have
her as a friend.

Like Barbara, of course, I also felt this loss. In the months after Iris'
death, when something good happened to me, when I had an accomplishment to share, I found myself seized with the impulse to let Iris
know—before, of course, quickly realizing that this was not possible.

In interviewing her friends, I also continued to wonder how much I
had really known her, how close a friend *I* had really been. I had been
woefully ignorant of *the major conflict of her life*, the one that ended it:
her mental illness.

As I realized later while studying more about bipolar disorder, these
problems likely went on for a long time, years before her death. While I
blamed myself for not being sharper, I also acknowledged that I was not
alone in my ignorance. She was probably both actively hiding the mental
illness and denying it, a common combination. And, uneducated in bipolar disorder, we didn't know what to look for.

Her condition had most notably deteriorated in her last years, when I
had the least contact with her, when I happened not to visit California
and stay with her for days, immersed in her world, as I had regularly done
during the previous decade. I hoped that some of her other friends from
California, especially from her later years in the Silicon Valley, to whom I
would speak soon, could give me a better idea of the signs I missed.

In the meantime, I thought I'd look more to my own "primary
sources"—letters, documents, and tapes that I had kept of her expressing
herself in her own words—which I had accumulated through the years, to
tell me more about Iris' inner demons. For some time after her death,
looking at them was still too painful for me. In them, her voice speaks to
me intimately and directly—so much that I can hear her voice in my head
as I read—making it harder to detach myself from her as my journalistic
subject. But I knew I had to face them to begin to figure out my nagging
question of what clues I personally had missed for so long.

CHAPTER SIX

What Did She Tell Me,
As a Primary Source?

*F*rom a handwritten note, March 7, 1993:

Dear Paula,

I'm so glad we had a chance to get together at Medici's, although I'm sorry we couldn't have a one-on-one discussion about books, boys and bank notes. When do you think you might be in California again? . . .

As per your phone call from the airport, don't hesitate to call me if you want to talk about relationships and how Brett and I have handled some of our own problems, etc. That's something you should mention in your next book—relationships between spouses or lovers who both work in highly competitive or high-profile careers.

Keep in touch!

Love, Iris

Quote cited by Iris in her 1996 never-sold book proposal on the biological clock:

A man, though gray-haired, can always get a wife, but a woman's time is short.

—Aristophanes

With Iris, there was no small talk, even first thing in the morning. During one of my visits in 1994, I woke up at about nine a.m. and saw her staring at me across the living room from another futon. (She often slept in the living room because her tossing and turning disturbed Brett.) Seeing I was finally awake, she asked: "Why do you think poverty exists?"— and continued this line of inquiry almost nonstop until late that night.

After several days with her, I decided to go to a hotel, which I would fund from the honorarium from a speech that had brought me there in the first place the week before. As I truthfully explained to her, I wanted to stay weeks longer in Santa Barbara, where I felt like I was discovering some of the good parts of alternative medicine and could further benefit in mind and spirit from hours-long daily walks along the beach. But, what I kept to myself was that I couldn't bear another minute with her. So when I bid her good-bye and arrived in my low-rent hotel room with the torn bedspread and stale smoke smell, I remember almost sobbing with relief. After months and months of nonstop struggling with my chronic pain disorder and book deadlines, I finally was able to truly rest and have a vacation, something I could never do in her presence.

This was one of many moments with Iris that I recalled as I was combing through my old journals after her death. I was looking for clues of what was going on in her mind, and also in mine. Had I ever really known her? Of course, the planning of a suicide, which does indeed reveal a secret life, doesn't mean that all else in the relationship was a lie. I do see that our sharing about our inner lives was intense, as revealed by the "paper trail" of our own friendship. That was mainly in the form of journals and letters from the 1990s, when we were closest. While I certainly did not know all there was to know about her, and certainly never will, this material does offer a window into the major issues, mainly regarding motherhood, that she was pondering at the time. Ironically, as I went through this most personal "archive," I became more detached, probably as a mechanism for understanding it all and not letting sentimentality cloud my view.

My main "collection" of letters from Iris was a special group that I had, years ago, made a distinct effort to save in a folder in my apartment. Those were the most "notable" ones, the most eloquent and expressive. But then, in 2006, I found a surprise stash—in my scary dark old apartment-building basement storage space. In the midst of a move, I had ventured down there to look through several boxes of non-crucial papers, the ones not requiring special preservation in the limited confines of my apartment. I found that most of these papers, which I had left there a decade earlier, were now molded together into papier-mâché-like bricks and were largely unreadable. As I reached for hunks to throw into garbage bags, I glanced at one with familiar handwriting on the top. It was Iris'.

I peeled the thin paper off the wedge of letters. It came off perfectly, without a tear. Then I went through the boxes and salvaged many more letters from her. In contrast to most letters from other friends of that period—which were mostly handwritten—nearly all of hers were typewritten and therefore completely legible without the problem of smearing.

Now, after a decade, these more "mundane" letters from Iris did seem extraordinary, after all. They gave me a view of our more typical correspondence, which was more frequent than I had remembered. While I certainly had been jealous in her seeming effortlessness in attaining what she had, I did appreciate her generosity toward me. As the letters revealed, and as I only now fully realized, she was always trying to help me. This was the case before my trip to Santa Barbara in 1992 to promote my first book. She sent me pages of bookstore, university lecture, and media leads, many of whom she had called for me in advance. In turn, I cheered her on, like she was a member of my home team. We had come from the same place, and she made *all of us* look good. Indeed, in my journals from the time, I repeatedly noted that unlike many people one meets who "make you feel small," she always "made me feel big." That was the type of person I had to hang around more, I told myself, not so-and-so and so-and-so.

The most unusual document I had on our friendship was one of the most revealing. I retrieved a twenty-five-page transcript of an interview, which in form and function fit our worldviews as journalists. I had conducted this with her on August 4, 1993, when she was twenty-seven, about issues related to my second book on women's sexual attitudes. She had already been married for two years. I did this on the fly, late at night in her apartment as we audibly tore through Chinese take-out. At the start of the meal, she had started giving her opinions on what I had interviewed others about that day, and I thought it wouldn't hurt to turn the tape recorder on. I ended up not wanting to use my friends as sources for that book, but still kept the transcript stashed away. Now I look at it with new eyes to see her overarching drive for independence and self-transformation early in life. Some of her thoughts on specific issues, from intermarriage to the biological clock, also do reveal some of her most driving personal concerns over transcending limits.

As the dinner discussion turned into an interview, my first question to her was general, how our generation differs from past ones in relationships. She said she thought that we have more tolerance in interracial dating, especially among whites and Asians. I asked if she was "surprised that you married a white man."

"In my heart, I knew I always would," she said.

Iris explained that she was influenced by American culture as a child, as a "voracious" reader of novels, from Sidney Sheldon to Charles Dickens, and as a viewer of films. Growing up in a white culture, she admitted that she thought like a white woman when it came to men.

> *All the heroes and heroines were white, so I guess without quite realizing it, I always identified myself as Caucasian, although I also identified myself as an Asian woman. But the images of the man I would marry was always white. . . . I think if I had grown up in China or Taiwan, the image that I would have of my future husband would be much different. I remember distinctly when I was a child I used to dream in Chinese before I went to school, because my parents spoke Chinese. But when I attended kindergarten and first grade, there was an abrupt change. I suddenly started dreaming in English. The friends in my dreams would be Caucasian. Some would be Asian, of course. But when I started dreaming about my future husband, I mean literally my dream would be that he would be blonde and blue-eyed.*

I asked what her parents thought about that. "They couldn't control my fantasies," she answered.

While both her and Brett's parents were surprised at the choices the other had made in a mate, they soon came around. Brett's parents had expected him to marry someone more traditional and from a small town, like his mother, a kindergarten teacher. In her, they got quite the opposite, as Iris liked to joke to me.

Iris also described her own parents' earlier preference, before she met Brett, for her marrying someone who was Chinese American. "They [my parents] would cite statistics, and they would cut out all these articles and put them on the refrigerator and show me statistically that marriages between people of similar backgrounds were statistically more successful than people who came from different backgrounds," she said.

But ever the debater, Iris argued that dating another Chinese American would involve more family "biases" and other baggage. "It was more of an honest and open way of doing things," she said, describing her relationship with Brett.

Iris explained the greater cultural complications with a Taiwanese-American student at the University of Chicago whom she had met at summer camp and briefly dated in college, who represented her typical experiences with such men. She said:

> *He was completely unable to relate to me at all. I mean this was a guy who was involved in all the Asian activities on campus, who hung out with only Asians. They were really locked into the Taiwanese-American community in Chicago where all the parents lived; the fathers tended to be doctors and the mothers tended to be housewives. It was very incestuous. This was a closed community, and the kids all hung out with each other.*
>
> *And so when I went out with this guy, he was a complete jerk. We were talking about racial matters, and I made a point of saying that I would hope that one day there would be more intermarriage between the races, and there wouldn't be as much trouble. And then he said, "You're a complete hypocrite." And I said, "Why?" He said, "Would you let your daughter marry a white man?"*
>
> *I said, "How do you know that I'm not going to marry someone white myself?"*
>
> *He was shocked. . . . I realized I was not going to go out with anybody who is so cliquey and not open-minded. I don't like going out with people who are so fixated on race.*

Iris made this argument to her parents, and, she noted, "they soon agreed with me. They didn't care who I dated anymore. They just wanted me to date someone who was kind to me, who was intellectual, whose parents would be just as cool as they were with it."

Besides being accepting of interracial marriage and children, Iris actually was a staunch advocate of it. She did research on the topic and cited statistics that the children of such marriages are known to be more intelligent and healthy. "Plus, they're gorgeous," she said. She also noticed them in her school, having no trouble fitting in. "Genetically, if two different strains come in together, sometimes you have the best of both strains. It's kind of like in China when they have two different strains of silkworms mating. The more different the strain, often the healthier the offspring.

"It's so funny because I mentioned this to my husband, and he comes from a farm family. And so he says it's sort of like hybrid sweet corn."

She also supported intermarriage as a way to make society more tolerant of other races, having everyone eventually blend together. She recalled bringing that point up to some friends from Hopkins who challenged her on this view, saying "it's a pity that a minority has to lose its cultural identity in order to be accepted by this country." Her partly humorous response was: "There is no shortage of Chinese people on this planet. I don't think we're in any danger of disappearing off the planet."

But she agreed that this might be different for me, since the number of Jewish people is relatively few. Her advice to me then, and through the years, about men was as scientific and logical as her views on antiballistic missile systems. She repeatedly advised me to attend computer conferences, where the men were diverse and outnumbered women. That was way too extreme a step for me, although, I have to admit, it was pretty logical.

In our interview, Iris remembered how she had found she had a surprising amount in common with Brett, who had a "background hauntingly similar to mine." Both were from central Illinois, had "traditional" backgrounds, and had "worrywart" mothers, both of whom sent their children warnings in the forms of newspaper clippings on AIDS in their letters after college. They both were each other's first long-term relationship.

Always struggling to find her own voice and get out of the shadow of her parents, Iris greatly appreciated Brett for giving her ample space. He always allowed her the independence she needed, even to the point that others skeptically observed that she acted like she was NOT married. He did not seem to protest that Iris did not wear a wedding ring, kept her last name, and often stayed with male friends for weeks at a time when traveling. This laissez-faire attitude was also the case during their three years of dating, and even when she announced that she was moving to the East Coast in fall of 1990 to attend Johns Hopkins, instead of joining him immediately in Santa Barbara, before marrying in 1991.

"If he had said, 'No, you can't go to Johns Hopkins, you can't do this, you have to be with me all the time, I probably would not have married him," Iris said. "But he was just like, 'Well, you know, I have to let Iris do what she wants to do.' And so people were saying [to him], friends and relatives, not many, but a couple of them said, 'I think you should wear your pants in the family.' But I was marrying him, not them."

Another theme of the conversation was her need, from an early age, for commitment in any relationship with a man, to "not be taken advantage of." She said that this was the result of her "obsessive" personality. "Just [because of] the intensity of emotions," she said. "And I knew that if I completely focused all these emotions on a single individual and he dropped me, that would just be enough to just send me over the edge. I mean I could not, I could not give another man that much power over me."

"It's about losing control?" I asked.

"Yes. And so I couldn't even talk coherently when I was with boys. I'm afraid they thought I was hopelessly shy and awkward and dorky. I don't think I was perceived as an attractive teenage girl, to be honest with you."

I asked her how much of that restraint with men was due to her career ambitions. "I had a lot of career ambitions," she said. "It was very much a factor."

Her reasoning was power dynamics, not prudery. While she could only approach it with a committed partner, she saw sex as natural and healthy, a view she said was ultimately championed by her scientist parents. She talked about them openly discussing the biological aspects with her from a young age, even drawing pictures of the sperm and the egg.

Iris was clearly the most passionate during this interview—and indeed the most passionate I had ever seen her—when we talked about children. Specifically about ambitious women's sacrifices as mothers. Very aware of women's power dynamics in relationships since she was young, she expressed her anger that women have to give up so much for their families. In fact, trying to reconcile these two needs, for children and for a career, would be a major cause for the rest of her life. As she lamented to all her close friends, she was frustrated for years by her inability to get a contract for her book proposal on outwitting the biological clock through science. This was despite her laser-like focus and aggressiveness, the consecutive work of two high-powered agents, and a mighty international sales track record.

The issue went right to the heart of her characteristic desire for control and to overcome limits in life. And both of these needs, for children and for career, were absolutely vital to her, essential to her being.

"I must have children," she told me. "I would have to have that, my children. Marriage is not that important. . . . The children are actually, ultimately. . . .

> *It's a piece of eternity. It's important that somebody lives on after me with a piece of me. . . . You know, men come and go, but your children are always going to be your children. They're part of you, they're your flesh and blood. I think the bond between mother and child is maybe even greater than that of the mother and father. My mother has said that herself. My editor, who is also a mother of several children, has told me, "You don't understand, Iris, because you haven't had children yet. But you will one day. The worst thing you could do to hurt a woman is to take her children away from her. That's even worse than having her husband killed. That's the worst thing that could ever happen to you." . . . She is a career woman and very family oriented. She said, "I don't even know what I would do. I don't even want to think about it."*

But Iris expressed fear, and even rage, about the sacrifices involved with motherhood, including losing control of one's life.

That's what worries me. I get resentful about this sometimes because I think, I'm going to be so, so powerless with my love for my children. Do you understand? I'm going to be, my, my life is going to be so dominated by these people who I've never even met. I don't even know what they're going to be like. But I'll shape them. They are my children, even though they're people.

But it's just that these people will demand so much of your time. Once you have a child you can't get rid of that child. I mean that's why, I mean the whole issue of children's still so . . . it's so frightening to me in a way. . . .

Now it's just me and Brett and ideally it's like having a honeymoon every night. Yeah, I have my work and I have my freedom. Yeah, I want children. But, this is what angers me Paula, I mean. Again, as you'll remember, I mentioned this over a lunch months ago in Chicago. I mean, I would like to have children, but I'd like to wait maybe a few decades before I have them, after I've accomplished everything.

I laugh here in the background at the audacious length of this desired delay.

"And as women you can't," she quickly responded, quite seriously. "It's not the same for women as it is for men. You have to have children before forty, whereas as a man you can have them in your eighties or nineties, or your sixties. . . .

Do you know why it makes me mad? Because it puts me in a powerless situation, is that the men know that they can wait forever. And you, you can't wait. Then they've got power over you. They might even, like I read, remember that "marriage myth" thing? I mean like a few years ago everyone was going just nuts, like bonkers, over this marriage survey or marriage study done by that Harvard professor? Because they said if

you're a woman and you're over forty, you have a better
chance of getting killed by a terrorist.

Remember that? Well, I was reading in Newsweek *like*
these men were sometimes taunting the women with that and
just making them feel insecure."

I mean I was so angry because it's like they have all this
power. Don't you see?! Do you ever get this mad sometimes
when you think about it? I'm like how dare they??!! And, if
[women] had a longer biological clock, then they could say,
"Fine, I can do that when I want, too," and men wouldn't
have power if they had a shorter biological clock. Men would be
frantic to commit because they can't have babies by themselves.
So we would actually have more power over them. And like
they would be desperate to get married and there wouldn't be
this problem. But they have this longer biological clock and we
have the shorter one. And it's like no matter what—like you
might want to save up enough money then maybe—but if
you're over a certain age and you can't have children any-
more, no one would want to marry you and that just makes
me so mad. I realized this at an early age.

She started to pound her fist on the table for emphasis, as she said:
"That the biology of a woman's body limited her. Not her intelligence,
but just that her *body* did."

Iris' strong resistance to women's traditional powerlessness, at least the
part based in biology, is reflected in her original 1996 book proposal,
"Turning Back the Biological Clock: The Fertility Revolution that Is Re-
defining Power between Men and Women."

In it, she described the biological clock as "the chief source of eternal
injustice of power relationships between men and women." It was a no-
win situation. "The aging woman" who puts off marriage and family suffers with anxiety noticing her ever-decreasing "opportunities for love and
companionship," she wrote.

"Among unmarried women friends of mine in this particular age group, I sense signs of real desperation."

I paused a bit before reading on.

Later I came across some of the notes she made for the proposal explaining how influenced she was in particular during her 1988 internship at *Newsweek*. While she had looked forward to entering "the glamorous world of magazine publishing," the reality, she wrote, was closer to "Sylvia Plath's *Bell Jar*" novel from the 1950s, in which "brilliant women who were pigeonholed and trapped by corporate world sacrificed family life or marriage.

"Suspicion and hatred of other women creep into their conversations, as well as complaints that the men they date don't want to commit," she said in the proposal.

She goes on to point out that other women, who do have kids earlier, still can't win. She describes "the supermom," as ending up with "exhaustion, frustration and health problems. The stay-at-home mom fares no better, making extreme financial and career sacrifices."

However, this dismal tone soon shifts to optimism with a discussion of her great hope, science, to enhance fertility later in life. "Given the current speed of medical innovation, I predict that the *battle of the sexes* during the *feminist revolution will be a mere skirmish compared to the global power struggles provoked by the biological revolution in the near future*," she writes [emphasis hers]. She goes on to demonstrate that "fertility research in just the last few years has dazzled the public with techniques that seem to burst right out of the realm of science-fiction. A grandmother gave birth to her own daughter's baby. Postmenopausal women became pregnant with the donated eggs of younger women. Women without uteruses rented the wombs of others for their embryos. Women began to deliver babies at ever older, unprecedented ages."

At the end of the proposal, Iris does recognize possible conflicts, about which she would interview ethicists and scientists. For example, "Can unforeseen biological problems await the human products of this infant technology? The fertility methods, after all, are so new we have not yet experienced long-term, adverse effects on human lives."

While progressively recognizing women's right to careers, this proposal would still get mixed reviews from feminists today. Part of what would give these critics pause is that Iris seems like a throwback to earlier writings of the "Second Wave" feminism of the 1960s and 1970s. Like radical feminists of that earlier generation, she analyzes reproduction in terms of stark power dynamics and sexual politics. Reflecting the heated battles of the time, when women had yet to prove their capacities and seize significant power, her proposal shares a combative "battle of the sexes" thrust.

At the same time, Iris' proposal reflects very traditional views, that the woman must bear the burden of child care alone. She never proposes that the man share the load, nor that corporations or the government help to supply child care. She assumed that all change needed would have to take place in the individual, not the society. She also assumes that no man would want to marry a woman who is older and not fertile; love and fertility were synonymous in her world. Even a decade ago, her views of singledom were also dated, reflected by the old-fashioned words she used such as "career woman," and, on a harsher level, the constant and entirely unironic mention of the word "spinster."

And her overarching faith in doctors as solving women's problems by "engineering" women goes against much of the grain of the women's health movement, a separate branch of feminism that arose in the 1970s to question doctors as absolute "experts." In fact, Iris directly criticizes books such as *The Change: Women, Aging and the Menopause*, by Germaine Greer, which discouraged scientific "tampering" with menopause, like with hormone replacement therapy. Greer advocated seeing menopause as a natural and desirable fact of life, not a "medical problem." Iris quoted Greer as saying: "Let younger people anxiously inquire, let researchers tie themselves in knots with definitions that refuse to stick, the middle-aged woman is about her own business, which is none of theirs."

Iris then countered:

*Perhaps I am one of those "younger people" who "anxiously in-
quires," but I cannot blindly ignore the results of biomedical research that is bound to have severe repercussions on me, the lives
of my children, and the rest of womankind. I want to know
what is causing the biological clock and what options women
have under the current level of technology. What are our risks to
our individual lives and to the future of our society?*

While this proposal may be easy to criticize for these reasons, it's also
poignant for its idealism and hopes for women to achieve their highest
potential. As Iris states in the beginning, she is investigating this topic for
women seeking "stellar" careers. She was concerned about making
women's biggest dreams come true by systematically and scientifically
breaking the barriers involved.

All my sources show that a "stellar" career, followed by children, was
Iris' own personal plan. She did put off having children for years to attend
to her books, and then, at age thirty, finally felt ready to try after the success of her best-seller in 1998. Then, when she didn't have a child as fast
as she expected, she optimistically told me that she would solve the problem with infertility treatments. Her belief in science as overcoming obstacles still reigned.

That next year, when she was thirty-one, I saw her briefly during my
visit to California. I asked her how that effort was going, and she answered abruptly that she didn't want to go into it, that it was very difficult, but that she was confident a child would happen soon. By the
defensiveness of her reply, I knew not to ask again. This was the first sign
of struggle in her life, and of keeping something major from me.

While I didn't realize it, I can see now that this is when our friendship
got more distant. My own archive's letter and e-mail volume, which decreased after that, proves the point to me. Her e-mails got shorter. I
blamed her work schedule, as well as mine. I also saw, realistically, that e-

mails were inherently quicker and more casual than our original long letters, and correspondence with *all* my married friends, who had gotten busy with families, had slowed.

It wasn't until after her death, when I interviewed her closest friends from her last years of life, that I realized I had not been the only one from whom she was beginning to distance herself.

CHAPTER SEVEN

What Did Her Friends Observe in Those Last Years?

*F*rom December 1999 Christmas card letter:

Dear Friends,

It's hard to believe that we are fast approaching the end of a millennium! When I was a child, I knew I would be thirty-one years old on Near Year's Eve, December 31, 1999, but at the time 31 seemed terribly old—so, well adult—and 1999 belonged in the realm of science fiction, not real life! But here we are. . . .

This year, Brett and I will attend the Renaissance Weekend New Year's party at Hilton Head Island. My brother Mike, who started his own internet company in San Jose, will join us at the end of the celebration as well. To avoid a potential Y2K disaster, Brett and I have decided to spend a few extra days vacationing in nearby Savannah, Georgia. In the last few weeks, I've been shooing Brett away from my stash of "Y2K food"—extra water, canned tuna, etc.—but I recognize the silliness of it all because we're going to be in the South, anyway, where the rations won't make a difference.

1998 was a giddy year for me—one of the most exciting years ever! Even now I'm still reeling from a book tour that spanned 70+ cities and hundreds of interviews. The success of The Rape of Nanking *spilled into 1999, and forced me to take steps to reclaim my life. Earlier this year I resolved to remove myself from the lecture circuit completely, in order to focus on my third book,* The Chinese in America, *scheduled for publication by Viking Penguin after the year 2001. It wasn't until summer, however, that I managed to close out every single one of my lecture commitments.*

During the first half of this year, I spent weeks rummaging through libraries and archives in New York City, Chicago, Washington D.C., Los Angeles and the San Francisco Bay area. This gave me the opportunity to visit many beloved friends across the country. Then, after a summer vacation in Europe (first in Switzerland as a guest of the American-Swiss Young Leaders conference, and then in Rome for a romantic getaway with Brett), I stopped traveling entirely and buried myself with work. . . .

This fall, we almost bought a house in the Los Gatos mountains area. It was a lovely A-frame with floor-to-ceiling windows and a spectacular, breathtaking view of hills and trees. The commute, however, would have been terrible for Brett (30 minutes to Cisco, even without traffic) and also for me (at least ten minutes of winding down a mountain pass just to get to downtown Los Gatos.) There also lurked the ever-present danger of mud slides, forest fires, etc. In the end, the decision came down to a choice between convenience and beauty—and convenience won, hands down. (In our present location, we can walk to a park, a video store or supermarket within minutes!) Next year, we'll probably rent a house near Cisco, that way Brett will enjoy an even shorter commute, and I can join him occasionally for lunch in the Cisco cafeteria.

There were sad moments in our year. One was the death of Tash, our tiger-striped family cat. She died of natural causes at the ripe old age of 20—equivalent to 140 human years, I've been told! . . .

Another low point this year was the cancellation of the Japanese edition of The Rape of Nanking. *As reported in the news, my ex-Japanese publisher, the Kashiwa Shobo Company in Tokyo, suspended publication of my book after receiving death threats from Japanese right-wing extremists. However, my agent and I are now exploring the possibility of getting* The Rape of Nanking *translated and published outside of Japan, such as in Hawaii or Singapore, and then shipped into Japan by progressive-minded distributors.*

I hope you'll stay in touch with us via email, or visit us when you come through the San Francisco Bay area. May you have a wonderful holiday season, and a fabulous year 2000!

Love, Iris

Certainly, I thought, Iris' obsession with the biological clock, in her own life and as a book topic, revealed a strong consciousness of her own mortality. I'd later find some of her note cards that she had used to put together the biological-clock book proposal, which included her own personal thoughts: "At 20, inner voice whispered: hurry! 1/4 of your life is already over, could not relax. Could I establish myself in 6 years? Impossible." "I got an acute sense of time running out."

Iris' friend Dale Maharidge made that point right away when we talked. He had always seen Iris as "oscillating," his word for describing someone with a palpable sense of urgency to achieve. "I tend to gravitate towards very intense, super-wired, oscillating people. I like oscillators," said Dale, who now teaches at Columbia University, where he is associate professor of journalism. "One of the common things of the personality type of the oscillators, we'll call them the overachieving oscillators . . . is an acute awareness of mortality. Iris was aware of mortality. *I* was always aware of mortality. I have a young student who is stunning; she's at the *New York Observer* right now, she is so openly aware of mortality and she's like twenty-six, you know. You look at life—'how many books do I have in me?'"

As with her other friends, I had been very interested to meet Dale, after hearing Iris rave about him through the years. She had talked about the Pulitzer Prize for nonfiction that he won in 1990, when he was only thirty-four. A self-proclaimed oscillator himself, Dale is the author of seven books and is a big talker. He is also very hard-driving in his work. In fact, he champions "method journalism," or getting emotionally involved and immersed in one's story. For one of his books on the homeless, he said, "I spent a couple of years riding the rails off and on across America. The last chunk I was doing it for five months and I never stayed in a hotel. We slept under bridges, in hobo camps."

His friendship with Iris started quickly. After being introduced in the early 1990s by their mutual editor at the time, Dale and Iris started hanging out all night talking about writing in cafés in Santa Barbara. He was often passing through doing research for his book *The Coming White Minority: California, Multiculturalism & the Nation's Future.* When Iris moved to the San Jose area in 1996, they also saw each other because he was teaching nearby at Stanford. Part of their bonding was over their mutual choices of dark subject matter. Dale's were extreme poverty and racial tensions. He said: "We became fast friends. We were doing a special kind of work. We were in a dark place. Not many people dwell there and it's lonely; it's really fucking lonely."

But Dale said Iris alarmed him by becoming increasingly eccentric in her views. He pointed to about 1999 as when Iris "got weird," a time when he consciously distanced himself from her.

He recalled one time that December when she had asked to meet him at his office at Stanford. "So I'm in my third-floor office in McClatchy

Hall and Iris is coming down the hall and she looks so stressed out. She comes in and she's oscillating. She says, 'Dale, I'm worried. Y2K. I'm losing my money.'

"I said, 'Iris sit down.' 'I'm going to lose my money.' She was totally freaked out. When the year 2000 hit, the banks were going to erase her money and she would be broke. She was serious. I wanted to slap her, like 'Iris sit down, you're not going to lose anything. At worse case scenario there will be a day there'll be some glitches. You're not going to lose your money.' 'I'm going to lose it.'"

Dale added that

> *she was getting weird before this. The conversation before that was, "I'm moving to Nevada." "Why, Iris?" "They don't have a sales tax there. I will save on the state tax. I'll save money on my taxes." I said, "Iris, California has like nothing. We have nothing on state taxes. If you make fifty- or sixty-grand you're paying three or four thousand dollars, nothing. Not like New York State, not like other states."...*
>
> *But she became obsessed. I said, "Iris, you want to live in a shithole in Nevada?" That's the word I used. "A shithole in Nevada so you can save ten thousand dollars a year, eight thousand dollars a year?"*
>
> *Then, the Y2K conversation. I swear I sat there for an hour and a half calming her down. It exhausted me. I found my conversations with Iris were exhausting me.*

Dale pointed out that a lot of her fears were about money, which was strange since he knew, as was common knowledge, that she had received a sizable advance for her third book, *The Chinese in America*. One of Iris' transcribers of her interviews, for the third book and the next one on Bataan, told me she was shocked to hear that Iris was rich. Iris had made a special effort to call her, sounding desperate to get a discount on the transcription work.

But, then again, it's hard to know when quirks have crossed a line to become bona fide mental illness. After all, these fears could be rationalized, could be explained. Dale said that he wondered if her obsession with money was cultural, a result of insecurity her parents had in Taiwan and China. Dale even chuckled about this, saying that he once interviewed one of Iris' cousins for his book on race patterns in California, *The White Minority*. "He says, 'Dale, the Chinese, we're the Jews of Asia. We are worried about money, we have weird moms.' I put it in the book. . . . Iris and I used to joke about that. But she was obsessed with money. And not in the way of like I want more and more; she wanted security. She was really worried and I guess again with the cultural—what happened with the Japanese invasion and to Jewish people—I don't have that experience."

Obscuring matters, he also pointed out that quirky behavior by an author is not unusual. "[Susan] says, 'Dale, I know a dozen authors just like her—hyper, tense, we're all crazy.' I have thirty or forty students who have that oscillating caliber. They are clones of Iris."

By other accounts, Iris "got weird" starting most noticeably in 1999. Iris' longtime friend from her *Tribune* internship, Christie Parsons, told me that she did notice a change when Iris last visited her in Springfield, Illinois, in 1999, when she seemed "preoccupied." But I myself thought she was fine that year when I saw her in Santa Cruz, where I was visiting another friend. She seemed quirky, as usual; she suggested that we go to a day spa but wouldn't go into the whirlpool because of a fear of bacteria. Even though the day was supposed to be light, she monopolized the conversation at an outdoor café afterward with talk of American war veterans, which I mostly tuned out in favor of reclining and absorbing the sun.

A few years after that, I wrote down my first blatantly negative words about Iris in a journal, in an entry for Labor Day in 2001. I had just returned from a "fatiguing" lunch with her in Chicago, where she had stopped on business at the last minute. I had expected to be drained afterward, but not to the extent that I was.

Part of the problem was that even before I saw her I had already never felt worse, mentally or physically. I was getting off a very addictive pain drug, which, ironically, had been prescribed to me by a doctor at a "holistic center." The withdrawal was making my usual chronic pain much more intense, and created an overwhelming undercurrent of anxiety, which at the time I didn't know was necessarily tied to the drug or whether it would ever diminish; hence, even more anxiety. In this time of struggle and uncertainly, I was conducting my own detox program and taking temporary refuge at my parents' house in the suburbs, where I felt more grounded, emotionally and spiritually. It also gave me some structure, to have meals with them and wake up and go to sleep at the same time. It turned out that I was doing exactly the right thing, that I later felt better and saner and more independent than ever.

Needless to say, I was not in an ideal frame of mind to meet with someone who enjoyed the "perfect" life, as I felt Iris had portrayed herself in her e-mails and Christmas cards. Furthermore, she seemed more removed from me than ever, to the point of being oblivious to my plight. When we first met at her Michigan Avenue hotel, I was holding back from her, not telling her the extent of my crisis at the time, because I thought she wouldn't understand.

But, as we started eating lunch, she said, "You seem depressed." I acknowledged that much and hoped to go on about another topic. But then, intensely focused on my problem, she talked for a few hours about ways I should remedy it. I see now that she was indeed perceptive of what I was going through and that this was her best effort to help me, by giving me concrete suggestions of what to do. But at the time it came off as ludicrous and superficial advice.

"She says such dumb things that take a lot of energy to discuss," I wrote in my journal that night, explaining why I was so wiped out. An example was that she repeatedly insisted that I move to a foreign country, to experience another culture, as a remedy. "That would take too much effort," I had explained to her. "Like with learning a new language, finding

someplace to live. Right now I just need the most familiar place possible."
As usual, her advice to me mainly was to separate myself from my parents,
which had helped her. The farther away she went from them, starting
when she moved out of their house in college, the more she seemed to
find herself.

After a few hours, I impatiently waved at the waiter to get us the check.
As I was distracted, she asked me, "Do you have to be anywhere now?"

"No, not really."

"Do the trains run at a special hour today?"

"Not really," I said, counting my bills.

"Good, then you can stay another hour, when Terry comes," she said,
referring to the other friend she was meeting there at the restaurant, before going someplace else for dinner. Then I actually panicked, not knowing how to get out of it. I braced myself for another hour of outlandish
suggestions, and my fruitless explanations of why they wouldn't work.
The following sixty minutes went by like hours. When her friend finally
came to meet us, Iris asked me to stay on with them for dinner.

"Um, I just realized that the trains are actually *not* running much today because of Labor Day," I lied, very badly. "I'd better go."

Once on the train, I collapsed into my seat. I staggered back to my
parents' house and managed to write a page in a journal: "She reminded
me of my old self," I criticized, now understanding the depth of my disappointment with her. I recalled that before my past several years of adventures with alternative medicine and investigating its lessons of balance,
I would have just pushed myself through this tough period and not taken
time off. That symbolism was probably a reason why she was especially
irksome, reminding me of that part of my old self that had driven me into
the ground and now repelled me. I wrote: "No spiritual awareness. She
had no idea of experiences other than her own. She couldn't understand
why I need structure."

After I recovered from that rocky period and returned to my Chicago
apartment, I did take on my previous, more tolerant view of her exhausting behavior as quirks. My life was going much better career-wise and

with improved health management, and I was less defensive. Again, how I reacted to her, the very embodiment of success as a writer, often reflected more on what I was going through than on her life. For the next few years, I let her know about positive developments and she always sent me very supportive and positive notes of congratulations.

In an e-mail exchange we had in July of 2002, she was also thrilled to relate her own writing progress, being relieved that "Viking Penguin is ecstatic with the new version" of *The Chinese in America*, which would be published in early 2003. After some struggle with her editors there, she had met their tight deadline, after all. She was further celebrating that she and Brett had just moved from their Sunnyvale rental and bought a new house in San Jose, a few miles from his work. At the end, she said that she had more news to share with me later. "We should talk this summer—there's so much happening in my life right now, much more than I can summarize in an e-mail." I would later find out that the other news would be that she was expecting Christopher.

But even if I could have dismissed her quirks as quirks, I continued to look for clues about Iris' deteriorating state of mind during her last five years in California. I needed to know what those near to her observed, since I was no longer as close to her. This turned out to be a challenge because no one saw her as much after her child was born, as is often the case with busy new mothers.

In fact, Iris' closest friend, Barbara Masin (who declined to speak in detail about the mental illness), noticed that compared to the Nanking book, Iris was notably more relaxed with the subject matter of *The Chinese in America*, despite its common references to prejudice and desperate immigrants going insane and working themselves to death. "She considered that sort of her vacation after *The Rape of Nanking* thing," said Barbara. "*The Chinese in America* project was relatively benign. . . . It's not the same as disembowelment and murder of tens of thousands of people." But then she said that Iris returned to being disturbed by grisly stories in the last years of her life by researching her book on Bataan.

Yet, *The Chinese in America* was more stressful than the other books in one way, a tight deadline to write on a sprawling topic, and with very high financial stakes. Viking had signed up her book after a very heated auction, which had paid off big, she told me. I remembered Iris calling me in a total panic sometime in 2001 or 2002 that her editors at Viking had not liked her first version of the manuscript; it was, in their view, too unfocused. Making matters worse, they were insistent that she rewrite it in a very short amount of time, so that the book would be timed with a Bill Moyers' PBS special on the topic.

When I had seen her rambling first draft, earlier that year, which she had sent me to critique, I actually had felt a bit comforted. This was a natural part of the long process of producing books on very general topics. I wasn't the only one who didn't write perfectly in draft form.

Despite the hint of "other news," I was surprised months later to receive her 2002 Christmas card, and see what it contained. I opened it and pulled out several photos of her serenely cradling her newborn baby. I had not even known that she was pregnant. I chalked her previous odd silence about it up to possibly having previous disappointments getting pregnant, and not wanting to tell too many people about it. (I was also a bit surprised to learn in the card that her parents had moved a few houses away, to Iris and Brett's same San Jose subdivision. I knew they would help with child care, but also that Iris valued her independence.)

Others were just as surprised with her birth announcement. Iris told none of us that she was pregnant. Li Wen Huang said this was the case with her, even though the two had spoken often on the phone in depth about publishing matters during that period. She also was surprised because, like me, this had been a major earlier topic of conversation. Li Wen had stayed with Iris in about 1999, and remembered hearing then that Iris' effort to have a child "was a struggle, but I didn't know the details of the struggle. . . . The next time I really heard anything was suddenly it's like 'we have a baby!' . . . Suddenly there's this picture of Christopher, however many pounds and inches, and it was just kind of like 'Oh, I didn't even know you were pregnant.'" Soon after, Li Wen lost almost total contact with Iris, excusing that absence as a result of the time Iris had to spend with her child.

Barbara Masin said she thought Iris had taken too much on from that period starting in 1999, when Iris was trying to start a family and was also working on *The Chinese in America.* "She was trying to do so much. She didn't dial back on her career at all—her public speaking, her writing—she kept up all of that at the same pace as she had before. Then she had Christopher; that was an added responsibility. . . . You read about it in the *Wall Street Journal,* mothers that have full-time careers with children, don't sleep much, and I think that's what happened with Iris."

"She didn't recognize any limits, for better or for worse," I said.

"She was driven, and her goal was to meet her expectations of herself in every area."

"As a mother too?"

"Yes, that's right. She took it very, very seriously. She wanted to do right by Christopher, and she did a lot of reading and educating herself about child rearing in general. It wasn't just to make sure he doesn't fall down the stairs and get into trouble," she said, "but she wanted to do it right. She wanted to make sure he had the best start he possibly could have in life. To her that was a major issue."

But Iris was mostly secretive to friends about Christopher even *after* his birth. Her friend Iris Chang Herrera told me that none of her fellow activists in their Bay Area group even knew that she had a child, despite working closely together during that time. "She kept it secret from all of us. I mean none of us could even believe that this busy woman had time for a child. . . . When she passed away and we found out that she had a son, we were all in shock."

Others noticed her pattern of being particularly preoccupied after her son was born about threats against her from unnamed sources. Monica Eng remembered Iris telling her when she met her in the spring of 2003 not to mention her son in her upcoming *Tribune* article, since she didn't want to put him at risk.

Filmmaker Christine Choy recalled having almost that same conversation with Iris, about unnamed threats against her child. It was so extreme that she actually confronted Iris about it. That was when she visited Iris in July of 2003 in San Jose to interview her for a documentary on Tsien. After filming at Iris' nearby parents' house, where Iris had directed the crew in place of her apartment, they went to lunch. "I got in her car, I saw a baby seat and I said, 'Oh, you've got a kid,'" Christine recalled. "That's when she said, 'Shh, don't tell anybody.' I said, 'Why?' She said, 'Well, I'm really concerned about his safety.' Later on that day, Christine saw a similar pattern when she asked Iris about her husband. "I said, 'What does he do?' She said, 'You see that building it says "Cisco," that's where he works, but don't tell anybody.'

"I said, 'Iris what's wrong with you? Are you paranoid? What is wrong with you? . . . I've never met your husband. Are you okay?' 'Yes, I'm okay.' I said, 'You know, you've got threats or something like that? You are so concerned about your safety, do you think the Japanese are coming after you?' She didn't say exactly, but according to my recollection she said there are people harassing her in mail and by phone. . . . She said she didn't know. She wasn't quite sure who was after her."

Christine added that Iris seemed stranger than usual in subtle ways; she watched the front door during her on-camera interview, and wore a heavy long-sleeved dress, although the weather that day in San Jose was unbearably hot, likely over 100 degrees. But, Iris herself admitted on camera to Christine that she was always hard to figure out. After talking about being misunderstood by classmates in high school, Christine asked her, "What about now?"

Iris answered: "I think today there seems to have been a lot of respect for me, but also a sense that it's hard to get close to me."

I wondered about the observations of veterans whom she had interviewed for her book on the Bataan Death March in 2003. According to media interviews after her death, these veterans thought that she seemed sharp and professional. I observed this myself watching a video of a 2003 interview, and snippets from others that she had done at that time posted on a veterans' Web site. Here, her typically extreme focus was an asset to convey her seriousness to her subjects. At first, some were a bit wary of her motives, given that she was Asian—how they identified their previous captors. But, upon meeting her and hearing her slight Midwestern twang and how educated she was about their experiences, the men soon realized that they had more in common with Iris than not, with their shared Midwestern backgrounds.

Iris was profiling the men of a single unit, the 192nd (Provisional) Tank Battalion, one of two tank units captured by the Japanese in the Philippines, all of whom were from Illinois, Ohio, Kentucky, and Wisconsin. Iris was clearly emotionally involved and sensitive to their cause. That was the pattern I saw on the videotape of her, and the observations of one of her transcribers. She repeatedly exclaimed sympathy with what they had gone through and pledged to help them fight for justice, health care, and even reparations from the government. By some accounts, she did seem more serious than she had in past years; one historian who accompanied her to interviews told Monica Eng that in December 2003 she was "no longer the 'smiling Iris'" that he had known earlier. But, even when hearing the most grisly stories imaginable of torture and execution, she didn't seem, he said, disturbed or traumatized.

I heard similar observations of mutual bonding and trust with Iris from one of the more public former POWs, Ray "Hap" Halloran. I visited the eighty-three-year-old at his home in the hills of Menlo Park, near San Jose. Hap, who is a retired executive at a major freight company, coincidentally had just returned from visiting Iris' grave. "I haven't done that with anybody," he said, even members of his own family. "I guess I was saying [to Iris] 'you're not all alone.'"

Short for "Happy," he clearly got the nickname from his friendly attitude. But an undercurrent of something darker definitely flowed beneath his sunny countenance. After all, what he went through would traumatize anyone. Iris had interviewed him at his home for hours in October of

2003 about his experiences as a prisoner of war for seven months in Japan, after his plane was shot down over Tokyo in January of 1945. (This was before she narrowed the topic of her project from including all American POWs held by the Japanese to just those captured at Bataan.) As he recounts in the self-published book he coauthored, *Hap's War*, his imprisonment and torture included being held naked on public display in a lion cage while the allies fire-bombed Tokyo all around him. He is the last living soldier of his air crew of about a dozen men, five of whom survived their plane being shot down. He was slated for execution, but was saved at the last minute when his camp was liberated, the direct result of the bombings of Hiroshima and Nagasaki.

He says he can size up people he meets in about thirty seconds, and Iris had passed his test. "I wanted to help her, and part of that was because she qualified under my trust formula, and her dedication was obvious. And she looked you in the eyes." He remembered her intense interest and vocal reactions during the interview: "I did notice her leaning forward and saying, 'Do you mean that? Do you mean this? Do you mean that?' It was not only involvement, but it was almost a concern that she had about what she was hearing."

He also noticed a pronounced emotional reaction from her after they had a short argument. At one point, Hap, who is very staunch in his views, told Iris that her quest to get the Japanese government to officially apologize to China for the massacre at Nanking was futile. She became very upset. She retreated to the bathroom to collect herself, where she stayed for about twenty-five minutes.

Hap explained to me his view on this matter. Through the years, he has personally come to terms with the institutional denial of the top officials of the Japanese government, and instead had sought reconciliation with Japanese people. He has done this himself, by personal necessity, to heal his own emotional wounds. For decades, his recurrent nightmares about the experience of being beaten and starved were terrorizing him. His desperate screams for help during the night were loud enough to wake his children when they were young. In 1984, he finally found the only way to remedy them was to travel to the site of his imprisonment and befriend his former Japanese captors. Since then, Hap has traveled there many times and hosted numerous Japanese visitors in his home. This even included making friends, on a second visit in 1985, with the Japanese pilot thought to have shot down his plane. So far he has received personal apologies from about 200 Japanese citizens.

Iris and I had talked a bit about the veterans when I saw Iris for the last time, after her Harold Washington Library speech in Chicago in spring of 2003. Probably her only odd behavior then was that she didn't ask a single question of the friend I had brought along to dinner. I chalked up her lack of interest to being preoccupied with her book tour. We corresponded with short e-mails and updates for about the next year. In spring of 2004, she called at the last minute to say that she would be in Chicago that night and wanted very much to see me. I said I was sorry that I was on my way out of town (I was), but that I'd see her next time.

Over the summer, she called me a few times, including once on my cell phone as I was getting off a bus. I became anxious, afraid that she would keep me on the phone a long time and make me late to a movie, where I was meeting friends around the corner. She asked me a simple question, related to a routine question about locating a transcriber for her Bataan interviews. Then, to my surprise, she quickly let me go. That was that. I clicked the phone "off" and stared at it with some disbelief.

I became busier with my own deadlines and didn't even think of e-mailing her, until around the next time she called me and got me on the line: November 6, three days before her suicide, the first occasion when I had realized that something was seriously wrong.

How had Iris moved so seemingly quickly from reasonably sane—if quirky—to suicidally depressed? A few people who saw her during her final six months of life had mixed reports about her state of mind. Then-student

Jennifer Kong, who helped organize one of her last speeches, which happened at Stanford University in May of 2004, said she seemed "strong." "I must say I didn't recognize any irregularities," she wrote me in an e-mail. "I felt very inspired by her words, as did others." In fact, Jennifer went out with Iris and some other students afterward, where they had a long conversation about career choices.

Barbara Masin said it wasn't until the last few months of her life that she noticed signs of Iris' mental illness. She got a phone message from Iris from Louisville in August of 2004. "I forget the exact date, and she was very agitated and basically she said she had to talk to me immediately. And I didn't get the message until Monday because it was a weekend. And I don't know, I think I was gone or I wasn't checking the machine. Yes, so then I called Louisville and she wasn't in the hotel anymore."

Barbara then called Brett, who told her "there were health issues." So she had assumed the hospitalization was for physical reasons, such as maybe something on the order of dehydration. Two weeks later, she finally got a chance to talk to Iris and heard the true story: Iris had been institutionalized very much against her will.

Barbara visited Iris three times in 2004, in August, September, and then October. During those times, Iris seemed exhausted and her tone was "flat and detached. The fizz was out," she said. However, Barbara thought that the visits, involving hiking outdoors, "seemed to help her tremendously."

In fact, on the night of November 8, just hours before the suicide, Iris and Barbara talked on the phone to plan Iris' visit to Barbara in Santa Barbara for two weeks later. Barbara couldn't remember if she called Iris or if Iris called her, to spark that conversation. In any case, the phone call was uncharacteristically short. Iris was hesitant to make plans, and then Brett got on the phone urging her to go on the trip.

Before they hung up, Iris said, "I love you." The only other out-of-the-ordinary "good-bye"-like comment that Iris had made was several weeks before when she told Barbara, "You've been like a sister to me."

Despite knowing about the mental illness, as the only friend of Iris' who did, Barbara was still "shocked" by the death. "I think any time anyone takes their life it's a shock," she explained.

A few months after I met Dale, I called him for some follow-up questions. As usual, he was keeping unorthodox hours. As we had arranged over e-mail, his best time to talk that month, a short window when he wasn't working, happened to be the midnight before Christmas.

As we were wrapping up, he asked how the project was going.

I paused and answered, "It's not as depressing as I thought. I don't know why."

"That's because she has become a character to you. She is a subject now, something you're writing about."

I thought for a moment and realized he was right. For good and bad, Iris had become a character to me. She had turned into a piece of material, a thing. I was objectifying her. That detachment recently had even become true when I now read her letters and saw pictures of us together. I truly had become the amoral writer.

But I realized that I now was not all that surprised by this development, even if I hadn't seen it coming. I chalked up some of my ability to become dispassionate about my subject to a natural product of time passing. And maybe my growing professional detachment was even proving beneficial to me personally, as a survival skill. I realized that the last several months of research had *not* been terrible and traumatizing; plumbing the depths of Iris' despair had not plummeted me into my own insanity. Instead, this time had been quite stimulating. Iris was endlessly interesting to me in her contradictions and symbolism. As a character, but also as a friend.

But so far I had mainly looked at her life before fall of 2004, when her mental illness was publicly exposed by the suicide. I wondered if I'd be able to hold things together so well emotionally in delving more into the darkest parts of her life at the end.

I had learned so far about some of her earlier anxieties, but they did not reveal a sign of psychosis. They all were rooted in reality or shared by many others. As for her fears of Y2K, she was not alone. She was reflecting widespread fears already existing and being widely broadcast in the media. That was the same with her refusal to go into a whirlpool at a spa, which could make one sick. In retrospect, I wondered if she may have been pregnant and avoiding the whirlpool for additional risks of heat leading to a miscarriage. She had trouble having a child for years, so naturally she wasn't open about it. In not letting others, especially in the activist community, know that she had a child, she could have been taking wise precautions; her hate mail from Japanese right-wingers was real, and she had reported about assassinations of muckrakers like her. And, as I was finding out, the possibility of children getting autism through vaccines had been a heated mainstream topic of debate, regularly addressed in the major media and medical journals.

Most clearly, these fears revealed that she was losing more and more of her filters, a sign of mental illness, to reject *any* fears. To survive in modern society, one has to selectively pick and choose their fears; if not, absorbing everything that constantly floats around us—in print, broadcast, proffered casually in conversation—can be unbearable.

I was still on a quest to find out when Iris' bipolar illness came on, what her worst fears were before her death—and how much of them were truly based in reality. For that information, I would need to try again to contact the one person left who could possibly help me, her husband. This wasn't easy. Personally speaking, I wanted to leave him alone and not dredge up, yet again, his most painful experiences that he was working to put behind him. But as a writer, I knew I had to keep trying.

CHAPTER EIGHT

What Happened in California?

$\mathcal{F}$rom an October 22, 1991, letter:

Dear Li Wen,

> *There's something strange about California that I can't quite put my finger on. I don't know if it's the climate or the people. People here seemed detached from reality, drifting . . . drifting. . . .*
>
> *One man [who] told me "there's nothing I'd like more than to be a successful writer of fiction" confessed to me that he had not read a single novel—not even pulp novel—for months. ("I'm not interested in writing literature, just something that sells.") Almost everyone here aspires to write a screenplay or novel, but few take the time to actually read one carefully.*
>
> *People don't read out here as much as the on the East Coast. In Baltimore, I listened to a taxi driver quote Fitzgerald and Poe as he proudly wheeled the car around their old homes. I watched the librarians at Enoch Pratt crack open the crates of H.L. Mencken. I saw that the clerks at Printing Services studied at Hopkins at night and read Jane Austen at home, and even the soda jerk at the Tamber's fifties café tried to impress*

his customers by slinging around some Shakespeare. Baltimore
really IS the city that reads, more than any other city I have
lived in....

... I really miss Chicago—the bars and pizza joints along
Rush Street and the Tribune Tower on Michigan Avenue and
the long nights with my friends at Second City and the walks
with my friends along the glittering high rises of Lake Shore
Drive and the little cafés and boutiques in Lincoln Park.
... I even miss the 40-below-zero winters! Compared to
Chicago, Santa Barbara seems so bland, a never-ending en-
nui of sunny weather and highways and chain-store shopping
malls....

Love, Iris

When Brett first saw Iris, she was walking across the Quad in Urbana. It was then that he first saw "the intensity in her eyes." Three years later, when he first spoke to her in person at a party, he knew that he "wanted to spend the rest of my life with her," he had recalled at Iris' funeral.

And now, I had to ask him about the fur coat that he also described her wearing that day in the Quad, and how it conveyed her uniqueness (and lack of political correctness).

We were sitting in a sushi restaurant in San Jose in August of 2005, having the first of two interviews we'd arranged for that week. When I had arrived in the Bay Area, I had finally reached him over the phone, and he agreed to talk to me on two nights. We were starting our first interview with light—very light—questions, about how they met and their relationship before her mental illness. The next night, I'd have him fill in the gaps about what came after.

Brett explained that Iris' fur coat—along with other unusual pieces of her wardrobe—came from a friend of her family who shopped at Bloomingdale's. She liked to give Iris her castoffs because she enjoyed how elegant they looked on her.

It went at least down to her knees. Imagine walking through the Quad *in November, and you see all these students all dressed alike. And then you see this really tall beautiful thin Chinese girl wearing a fur coat. It's pretty hard to forget. . . .*

I don't know if you ever heard anybody talk about her "cold walk"? She was so thin, and she hated the cold, so she would literally walk with her whole upper body completely rigid, with a whole lot of leg motion, so it was also this very distinctive walk. People teased her about that when she was in Chicago [working for the Tribune*].*

Brett also had once noticed her coming and going to the offices of the graduate math department, where she had sought expert tutoring from a math professor she knew through her parents. Finally, they met for the first time right after homecoming in 1988, when Brett had seen Iris attract much male attention as she went by in the parade as a "princess." After a date, she appeared later at a party that weekend in his low-key engineering-focused fraternity, of which he had been president. That was actually one of many parties she had been invited to that night because of her courtly status.

"It was about twelve midnight, and I had a class the next day," he recalled. "And I was about ready to go upstairs because basically the party was starting to dwindle down, and there weren't that many people left. And then she walked in the door and I met her, and we spent about two hours talking."

Their first date soon followed. It was a night of seeing the movie *Jesus Christ Superstar*, having ice cream drinks, and then going back to Brett's room at the fraternity house. That was where the action soon took a nosedive.

"And this is where she just kept talking and talking and talking," he said. "And I was like rubbing her back and stuff, and she literally talked until she went to sleep. I mean she was talking, and then one minute later she went to sleep. So I woke her up and drove her home, and that was our first date."

On the second date, she continued to amuse and intrigue the usually introverted and subdued Brett. They went to a café where Iris introduced him to her typically elaborate—and original—ordering procedures. Even in a restaurant, she wanted to make her mark. Brett said:

> *Iris' family, when they go to a restaurant, ordering dinner at a Chinese restaurant is a long, long process. It takes about five minutes of discussion back and forth before they figure out exactly what they want to eat. I used to think it was a Chinese thing, but I think it's more of her family thing. Iris would take this to every aspect of eating, like when she would eat out she would take a long, long, long time to decide exactly what she wanted.*
>
> *So we went there [to the café], and they asked me what we wanted. And I ordered immediately. And then Iris started to quiz the guy about what he had. And they had Coke and 7-Up and Dr. Pepper, root beer, all this stuff. And then she said, "What can they put in it?" And they said they can put ice cream in the root beer, they can put ice cream in the Coke. They have chocolate sauce, strawberry sauce, you know. And so they went through all these things. And she went through all the permutations.*
>
> *And finally, after two or three minutes, she finally said, "I want you to have a cup of Coke, and I want you to take the fudge and I want you to just dump the fudge in the Coke." So that's what her drink was. She had Coke, and they dumped fudge in the Coke.*

As she told me through the years, Iris liked that Brett was a high achiever on his own—he was valedictorian of his high school class and a varsity athlete—and was not at all threatened by her extreme ambition. (That was a reason why I liked him also.) Soon, like with other couples from small towns experiencing their first serious relationship, he explained, they talked about marriage. But the level of intensity of the relationship did catch her by surprise. In November of 1988, she wrote to a friend:

> *Anyway, my life is pretty crazy at the moment. I met an electrical engineering graduate student two months ago, at a frat party, believe it or not! His name is Brett Douglas. The relationship is getting very serious, and we're already worrying about what to do when I graduate in May. I wasn't planning to fall in love; in fact, I wanted to cut loose all ties when I leave so I can start out fresh. But, it just happened. We see each other every day now.*

They married two years after graduation, in 1991, and Brett's support of her work didn't change though the years, even with all the attention she received. "You know actually Iris got so many more calls than I did that I just didn't answer the phone. She took all the answering machine calls. In general I always had people call me at my office." I asked if people called him "Mr. Chang." "Some people still call me, and they will go to Iris Chang's Web site, Irischang.net Web site, and then they'll get the phone number and they will call me and they'll refer to me as Mr. Chang. It doesn't matter."

"Why doesn't that bother you? Not that it should bother you, but the traditional . . ." I said.

"Well I always had enough success in my own career that I wasn't insecure about that."

"So you weren't measuring yourself against Iris; were you two competitive at all?"

"No, not really. We were different enough. She was a lot better writer than I was, and I was a lot better at technology and with numbers than she was. . . . I was always driven towards my career stuff, and her things were different enough that there wasn't competition. I helped her with her computer-related things and bookkeeping. And I helped her with contracts and things like that, so it was always sort of like 'Team Iris Chang,' and I was a player on that."

Brett recalled many instances of playfulness in their relationship from when they first were married and living in Santa Barbara. One involved a nude beach. Many of his humorous stories about her had that theme of what he called her "attention surplus disorder," such as her misadventure of almost getting trapped overnight in the National Archives.

> *Normally where we'd go for a walk was Hendry's Beach in Santa Barbara. Maybe about a mile and a half down the beach was a nude beach. And I think I just wanted to see how Iris would react because I didn't think she knew the nude beach was there. So we just started at Hendry's Beach and we walked down to the nude beach... There were maybe fifty to one hundred naked people on the beach. . . . It was maybe two hundred yards long and we walked all the way past it.*
>
> *At the time she was talking about doctors and insurance companies and how it's so complicated for the doctors to deal with the insurance companies that they are not focused on the patients or something like that, and she was completely focused on that. . . . We walked all the way past the nude beach, we turned around and we walked all the way past again and we got maybe fifty or one hundred yards past the nude beach and I said, "So what did you think about the nude beach?" She said, "What nude beach?"*

Iris' life in Santa Barbara and later in the Silicon Valley was not all work. She did listen to classical music and saw many movies. She and Brett would take walks every night before he went to sleep—and before she went to work in her office. Iris got into weightlifting and kickboxing, which did come in handy.

*We used to go for walks at about eleven o'clock at night. And
one time we were going for a walk and some stupid guy left his
gate open and this really big mean-looking black dog came
charging out at us. And Iris started doing her "Haa! Haa!"
kicking at the dog. And I heard this big dog running. I just
jumped back, and Iris charged out at it and she was kicking
at it, and the dog totally stopped. He didn't expect the small
human to be that aggressive, right, and so the dog was just
standing there sort of growling. And I yelled, "Can somebody
please get your dog?" And the owner came out and got his dog
and pulled it back. The next day at work I told all my coworkers what happened, and they were teasing me about hiding behind her skirt while she was protecting me from the dog.*

Iris' seeming fearlessness, of course, was not limited to dogs. In 1993,
during the second year of their marriage, she confronted some high military officials, face-to-face, in the People's Republic of China. "When she
was twenty-five years old, she went to China to research Tsien Hsue-shen,
the subject of her first book," Brett recalled.

*Tsien was a high government official in China, and there
were generals in the Chinese Army who reported to him. And
they decided that they were going to get her to write what they
wanted her to write in the book about Tsien. And they told her,
"Oh you don't need to do any research; we'll tell you what to
write."*

*So they got her into a room where there's this little twenty-
five-year-old woman from America, right, and they had a
couple of generals and colonels and majors behind them. And
so the generals are quizzing her saying, "Now what you're going to write about Dr. Tsien, he's going to be very happy about
this, isn't he?" And Iris says, "Well, I don't know, unless you
give me the opportunity to talk to Dr. Tsien," and they said,*

*"Well, there are certain things we wouldn't want you to write
about him." She would say, "Well, why don't you give me the
opportunity to talk to Dr. Tsien, and I can show him my material that I'm going to write, and I can get his feedback on
it."*

*So basically they were expecting to put pressure on her to get
her to say that she would write what they wanted her to write.
I mean that's kind of a cultural thing. And she did not give
one inch to them. And every single time she turned it around
and put pressure back on them. She said after a few minutes of
this that the general started to get more and more exasper-
ated, and their underlings behind them were laughing because they were having absolutely no success, and she did not
lose her cool at all. They were red in the face.*

Brett went on to describe the bigger hit she made at the Renaissance
weekends. In telling this story (about Renaissance weekends) and many
others, Brett used the word "beautiful" to describe her. But Iris herself
seemed oblivious to her beauty and its effect on men. When she worked
at the AP in Chicago after college, she took a commuter train to and from
the city from where she was staying in the suburbs. When Brett met her
afterward, she often commented about all the "nice businessmen on the
train" who gave her their business cards and showed him a pile of them.
Other times, she was continually surprised at more aggressive advances.
At her readings, she constantly had to fend off male admirers.

After my dinner with Brett that night, we went to pick up Christopher
at Iris' parents' house. I waited in the car as Brett retrieved Christopher
and buckled him into the car seat. I was suddenly choked up. That was
the first time I had ever seen him in person. He looked like the domi-
nantly featured parent, Iris, appearing to be fully Asian, with brown eyes
and black hair. He was also very tall, being able to pass for much older
than his three years. At that time, he also was showing signs of his
mother's intensity.

"He's really into numbers and letters," Brett had told me on the phone. There in the car, on the way to a playground romp, what had become their nightly ritual, I found out what he had meant. From his perch in the back seat, Christopher was looking far ahead of us and shouting out the contents of license plates that I could barely make out.

On the night of our second interview, Brett and I met for dinner at another Asian restaurant and sat outside at an umbrella table. It was in a brand-new shopping center, which looked like the rest of that area around Silicon Valley, with no history.

Then we got right down to business. From my interviews, I had suspected that the onset of her mental illness was about 1999, when Dale described her increasingly irrational fears. I also was curious about the effect of infertility treatments, which I surmised had started at about that time. But I still didn't know for sure when it started and which factors brought it on.

Brett made no hesitation in pinning down the exact date of the onset of Iris' mental illness—a much later one: May 1, 2004. That was when she came back from her grueling six-week book tour for the paperback version of *The Chinese in America,* which he mainly blamed for her breakdown. At that point she became obsessed with clearly irrational fears. "She was not the same person when she left in March and when she came back in May," he said.

Brett said that even Iris herself had been questioning how she would pull off the extensive tour, of more than twenty cities in thirty-one days, when in February she had seen the schedule in advance, although she had a similar tour a year earlier for the hardcover version. The dates were so tightly booked that Brett pointed out to her that it would be humanly impossible for her to get from one city to the next in time for the events. In response, the publisher shifted some dates around so she could make the flights.

One of the most tiring parts of the speaking engagements was what came after them; the organizers would ask her to go out and socialize. Iris always had trouble saying no to them. "I was talking to James Bradley about this—she would do all these events and then they would want to have her out for dinner and she would go out for dinner with them and stay out late at night and then come home to the hotel and call me at like one in the morning where she had been going since six a.m., you know. He said you have to just say, 'No, I have to go back and rest,' and she wouldn't do that."

A problem was that Iris had always gotten away with pushing herself in the past, so she didn't worry about later consequences. "When she was thirty and she did her *Rape of Nanking* book tour [in 1998], it was not quite as intense but it was much longer. She went to sixty-five cities promoting that book. And so I think that they thought she was just this machine who could just go nonstop forever. And I think when she was thirty-six, and she was probably tired from being a working mother when she started; it was just too much for her." He added that she "didn't have much more than average energy; she'd just push herself so hard" that it seemed like she had more.

We went on to talk about some of the demands of that third book, *The Chinese in America*, which involved high expectations to turn in a draft that was ready to be published. "I don't know that much about the industry," Brett said, "but the perception was that she got small advances for her first two books, so it was okay to turn in something that was so-so as long as she worked and improved it. . . . But she got a big advance for her third book, and so the perception was you have to turn in this masterpiece." Still, Brett was not condemning of her publisher, saying that much of the pressure Iris always put on herself was internal. He spoke about how her condition deteriorated in May, 2004:

> Basically the first thing I noticed was I could always go on a business trip and always have complete confidence that everything was going to go fine when I was gone. I was gone for a week in May, and I came back and she said "there were things wrong with Christopher, the nanny was not doing a good job." She needed to find a day-care center, and things sort of fell

apart. And just simple things, like she would get checks from a speech, and I would say, "Are you going to go deposit this in the checking account?" She would say, "Well, I want to start a business, and I can't really deposit the check until I have a fictitious business name set up and an account in that business name." I would say, "Just deposit the check; you can move the money later into the business account."

And then she started to lose her credit cards. She'd literally lose her credit card on a Monday, and we'd cancel the credit card, and we'd get a new credit card, and two weeks later she'd lose her credit card again. It was just subtle little things that just sort of gradually ramped up. . . . Another thing was her computer, she always thought her computer had a virus on it and it didn't have a virus. I'd run virus checks.

Through the summer, their full-time nanny, who came during the day, was able to keep order. But then Iris became "much, much worse" in August, before she left for a trip to Kentucky to interview Bataan veterans. (It was on that trip when she had a breakdown and was hospitalized.)

Gradually . . . [Iris] started to get on the nanny that the nanny was not feeding Christopher the right things, the nanny wasn't doing this right, the nanny wasn't doing that right. And eventually the nanny couldn't take it anymore, and she quit. That's when I had to come home all the time because Iris wasn't able to handle things. . . . There would just always be a crisis. When she was mentally ill, we'd start with a plan at the beginning of the day, a weekly plan, and by Monday at noon it would just be shot. Her mother would always call in a panic if something was going wrong.

At that point, they decided to send Christopher to live with Brett's parents in Illinois, to concentrate efforts on helping Iris. He realized he could not do both at the same time. "She was still mentally ill, but we led more or less a 'normal' life. I would go to work and then come home and check on her at lunch and come home as early as I could at night and make sure we did something together at night. So the last month we got to spend a lot of time together," he said, with some appreciation.

I asked about other exacerbating factors to wear her down, such as efforts to have a child, starting in 1999 and lasting until 2002, when her son was born. Although they did not realize it at the time, that period marked the official onset of her bipolar disorder, manifested by extreme mood swings and insomnia. (But he didn't consider her "mentally ill" until she was clearly out of touch with reality after her book tour in 2004.) Brett said that she would have problems getting pregnant and then miscarry repeatedly. That process, along with weeks of infertility-drug treatments, shifted her hormones wildly, which can have an impact on destabilizing brain chemistry. As I later learned, for someone with a genetic vulnerability to bipolar disorder, this can be profoundly disturbing on a mental level.

Certainly this was one of the greatest ironies of Iris' life. Her book proposal on the biological clock, which she was never able to sell despite her greatest effort, expressed tremendous optimism in scientific advancements to overcome women's most basic limits. But this process in real life, conducted without proper education and precautions, may have been a factor in her eventual unraveling.

I asked Brett if Iris had a genetic vulnerability to bipolar disorder, which is very likely to be inherited. It turns out she may have, from what Iris herself had speculated about one of her older relatives in her extended family. (But with that relative now deceased, and without her ever having had treatment or that official diagnosis, that is something I cannot confirm here.)

After May 1, 2004, some of Iris' earlier fears escalated and became obsessive. One of her most severe was that she had "given" Christopher autism, which she had told me in our last phone conversation. Now Brett told me how that fear started, years before.

I first saw this [article] that some people believed there was some link between vaccines and autism, and I forwarded this story on to her. . . . This was probably in 2003 when she read it. She gathered all the information, she said, "Okay, we'll find the vaccines that are really important to give him, and we're not going to give him any extra vaccines when he needs vaccines." And so all of that was fine, and she never worried about it. I mean we gave Christopher vaccines all the way through the end of 2003; she never worried about it at all. It was only when she came back from that book tour that she started worrying about it, and so then it just got worse and worse.

I asked about her friends' observation of Iris' fears growing more irrational in 1999, the year she started being rocked by hormone swings. As an example, I repeated Dale Maharidge's observation that Iris was terrified in the days leading up to the year 2000 that all her financial records would be wiped out by Y2K and she would end up broke. Brett downplayed their significance.

"Well, I think Iris was just excitable, right, and you could get her spun up on something, and so that was one example," he said. He gave another example of a worry of hers from 1999, also based on "scientific" articles, regarding the possible negative effects of power lines on her fertility.

"Well, some people believe it's bad for you—the radiation from the power lines, so she didn't like that. Actually, I don't know if you know this, but all the power lines in the whole United States are all in-phase kind of, and so if you're way, way, way, way out in space that's what you can detect. So you can be billions and billions and billions of miles away and you can detect the power lines in the United States."

Some of these fears about power lines were related to the struggle to have a child, which finally happened in 2002, when Christopher was born. Brett said Iris was successful only after she took matters into her own hand, ignored her doctors, and researched fertility herself. She discovered her problem—and corrected it. (He would not share with me any more detailed medical information at that time.) But this negative experience with what she considered inept doctors, and her "superior knowledge," had dire consequences in the last few months of her life.

Brett said: "She had the perspective that she was more capable than these doctors for understanding what was going wrong" when she became psychotic in the last months of her life. As a result, she did not trust psychiatrists and the drugs that they prescribed.

I was curious about how this trouble with having a child figured into the secrecy she had about her pregnancy. To explain that period of being withdrawn from friends, Brett said that she had been absorbed in the infertility research and finishing the first draft of her book. But he couldn't really explain why she never went out when she was pregnant and hid her child from everyone, including her fellow activists in the Japan war crimes reparations movement who worked with her regularly.

"I think she wanted to make sure that Christopher lived a normal life, and so she tried to keep him really sheltered as much as possible," he said.

"But even not going out when you're pregnant, was that all a part of it?"

"I don't know," he said.

Brett recalled the irrational fears intensifying in August of 2004, when he had still underestimated how deeply disturbed she was. On her research trip, she had a breakdown and was hospitalized by one of the elderly veterans she was interviewing.

So basically she went on this business trip on the twelfth of August to Louisville. I knew that week that she was staying up all night browsing around stuff on the Internet, but that wasn't unusual at all because she would often do that and then sleep all during the day. Then it turned out she wasn't sleeping during the day. She was up all night and all day for about four or five days straight. She started to get on to these things she was worried about that just didn't make any sense.

*I thought if she gets on this business trip, she'll be able to fo-
cus on her work and not worry about these things she was worrying about. It turns out she was too far gone for that. And
our nanny was the one who saw it more than anything. She
didn't speak English. And I didn't speak Chinese, so it's really
too bad.*

"The nanny was Chinese?"

"Yes. She told Iris's mother the day Iris left or something she didn't think Iris should have gone. . . . Iris effectively stayed up for four days straight. Then she went on this business trip, and she didn't eat and she didn't sleep another night. And that's when she had her breakdown."

"What was she up researching? What kind of fears? Like the government?"

"Yes, there were some fears about that," he answered.

"She had written [in her suicide note] that the government was trying to discredit her," I said.

He explained: "It was really bad, like a lot of things came together all at once. It was a political season, and there were government people contacting her, wanting her to give speeches for them. And then about five days before her breakdown we went to see *The Manchurian Candidate,* which is about the government messing around with peoples' minds."

Iris' specific fears of the U.S. government were also aggravated by her fellow activists in the movement to get reparations from Japan. They told her that they feared they were being monitored, so Iris assumed she was in the same boat. "They were saying things like, 'I think my phone is tapped.' I don't know if they were correct or not, but I had heard her say that she had heard that from them a lot."

I remembered journalist Helen Zia telling me about a creepy "spy sub-culture of ex-military and counter-intelligence types who are obsessed with Asian Americans," a group she had been exposed to while research-ing a book on Chinese-American scientist Wen Ho Lee, a true victim of U.S. government persecution. Real incidents like that had spawned much worry among many Asian Americans that they also were being monitored covertly. Iris herself had written about that past threat of FBI surveillance of Asian Americans for being threatening "foreigners" in *The Thread of the Silkworm* and *The Chinese in America.*

I asked Brett about that possible connection: "After she told me that about the government, I started to think, boy, the last book [about the Chinese in America] might have affected her more than *The Rape of Nanking.* It is all about the government screwing people."

"It was promoting the book that triggered her mental illness," he maintained.

"But do you think it could have been exacerbating—the material that the *Chinese in America* was about the Chinese being second-class citizens and the U.S. government?"

"No, because I think her philosophy was she'd never really experienced any discrimination in her whole life. . . . The first time she said anything about the government being out to get her was literally when she came out of the hospital."

Iris did blame the U.S. government itself for institutionalizing her in Louisville in August, as a part of its supposed vendetta against her. She had confused her Bataan interview subject, Colonel Kelly, with a government official trying to "recruit" her. Then the colonel and others involved with setting up the interviews—representing the U.S. government to her—forced her to check in to the mental hospital there. So, that was why she freaked out when he saw him, and wouldn't drink from a water bottle he offered her, I realized.

A series of events that built up that fall seemed to corroborate her theory that the government was going after her. Brett said:

> *She saw* The Manchurian Candidate, *and then they forcefully put her into the hospital, so that was frightening. And then her contact . . . Colonel Kelly who she met in Louisville . . . said something to her that "we want you to join our organization," and he said this to her right before she went into the hos-*

pital. But what he meant was their organization is people to try to tell the story of the Bataan Death March survivors. But Iris took this as all some big government conspiracy to discredit her and put her in the hospital. . . .

She kept telling me: "They recruited me and I turned them down, and now they're out to get me." I had asked her what's an example, and she would always come back to Colonel Kelly's statement: "I want you to join our organization." He told her that before they took her to the hospital. So she thought that there was some secret-sponsored organization to do something, and she didn't do the right thing.

"She didn't join Colonel Kelly, so they were going to go after her?"

Yes, and she didn't respond to all these politicians who wanted her to give speeches for them.

She wasn't making a whole lot of sense. But then once she got on that track, it's easy to find all kinds of information to support that hypothesis.

I don't know if you've heard of the Illuminati. She was worried about the Illuminati. . . . It's supposedly some secret organization. That fall they made a movie. . . . This is another bad thing. In October there was a Nicholas Cage movie that came out called National Treasure *about the Illuminati, and she was all worried about that.*

He also mentioned the election early that November as additionally depressing Iris. She had been involved in numerous legal efforts through the years for veterans to get reparation from the Japanese government, and the Bush administration had continually struck them down, one by one. "I think it was that the Bush Administration wanted Japan's support in the war on terror, so they didn't want to antagonize Japan. So maybe she perceived that as the Bush Administration was out to get her or something, I don't know. Basically she needed stronger medication to get rid of these worries; she couldn't get rid of them."

"Is there something that she found that she uncovered? She said she found things 'at high levels.'"

> *Once you get into that mindset that there are government conspiracies, you can find a huge amount of information to back up that theory. I mean there was stuff on the Illuminati, right, that there's a secret society of people that control things that go on in this country and other countries. I don't even know all the details about it. Then she got on this Web site of a watch list of all the people that the CIA was monitoring and she knew people on there.*

"She didn't discover any of this, this was stuff that was already out there. She didn't originate this stuff."

"Right, right. But I think in her mind it was all coming together. She was seeing all these different things."

He added that the vast amount of conspiracy information available on the Internet accelerated that process.

> *You saw* A Beautiful Mind, *didn't you? About how he believed he was seeing all these codes in magazines. It was certainly easy for her to find—I mean it would have been much harder if you were John Nash in the fifties and you believed there was a conspiracy. You couldn't just go on the Internet and find hundreds of conspiracies in one day. . . . In the magazine he saw random words, and he started to believe he saw codes in there. Well, imagine today if he started seeing things and he started doing searches on Google! I mean he'd find hundreds of things right away, and that's what she would do a lot. Basically I would catch her doing this, going through all this conspiracy stuff, so I'd try to get her off the computer.*

I asked if she had tried to take her life earlier, between her hospital release and her death. He replied that she did have a somewhat ambiguous suicide attempt in September 2004 when she checked into a hotel with sleeping pills and vodka. I asked him which hotel it was, and he pointed directly ahead to the towering Crowne Plaza in the distance.

"She checked in, and how did you find out about it?"

"I was on a business trip. My mother was there watching Christopher, and her parents were there helping to care for her. And they just called me in the evening and said what she did."

"How did they know?"

"Basically I think she told them she was going to be gone for a while, she'd be back at six. And so she checked into the hotel, and she went to sleep, and she woke up at eight. So her mother expected her to be back at six, and she called 911. [When Iris returned home after eight,] Iris said she thought she took sleeping pills, and they took her to the emergency room and she hadn't taken any sleeping pills."

However, even though he knew about the sleeping pills, Brett was skeptical that it had been a suicide attempt, considering her mother's tendency to worry. But then, a week before her death, he realized it was real when he found a receipt from her buying the suicide how-to book, *Final Exit*. He also found out from the receipts that she had brought a quart of vodka to the hotel room.

"That's when I immediately contacted the psychiatrist and said, 'Hey, this is not just Iris's mother just worried about Iris committing suicide. There's a good basis for this worry.'"

But work with the psychiatrist did not go well. "It was hard to find a psychiatrist who was specialized in her area. I don't know why. It seems like there is a huge demand and a very little supply for psychiatrists. We saw three different psychiatrists, and the third one seemed to be good. He would actually do a lot of psychotherapy with her, and he saw her three times a week. The other two—one guy just saw her once and was like, 'I'll be in Europe for a month; call me back in a month.'"

"You said her area, what area was that? Bipolar?"

"Bipolar, yes."

"And with medications then, I'm assuming that she started taking medication at that point."

"Yes."

"How did that go? I know from experience that taking a lot of drugs for pain it's a lot of trial and error."

"Yes. So from day one they gave her Risperdal. That's an antipsychotic. The problem was she wouldn't take very much of it. It made her kind of drowsy and she didn't want to be drugged up, so she would fight taking it. Then they tried some various antidepressants with her. So she was on two different antipsychotics, two different antidepressants, and one mood stabilizer within the course of three months."

"Did anything seem to help?"

"The Risperdal helped a lot. But she wouldn't take enough of it. She would fight taking it."

"Do you think it could have made her worse at all? Sometimes you can take the wrong stuff," I said.

"Well the dangerous stuff they say—I mean I'm certainly not a psychiatrist and don't claim to be—but it was going on and off the antidepressants is the really dangerous thing, they said."

"So when she died was she in a transition with drugs? Or what kind was she getting off?"

"I knew it was, antidepressants she was getting off, and they were getting ready to get her on another one."

"They took her off gradually, or did she just stop taking it?"

"They say Asians respond more to these medications, so she was always on relatively small dosages."

He added: "Iris was always able to 'keep control' of the situation."

"What do you mean?"

One of the psychiatrists suggested that we put her in the hospital, and she made it clear to us that she did not want to go back into a hospital because she was terrified the first time she went in one. And so neither her parents nor I would be the bad guy and say, "You have to go into the hospital."

She insisted on seeing the psychiatrist by herself, and she kept a lot of stuff away from the psychiatrist. She didn't even let the psychiatrist know what a lot of the issues were. I went in there once with her, and he would say, "You never brought this up; you never brought that up to me." She felt like she had to be in control. . . .

In general the last week of her life she was pretty good; she was pretty coherent. I mean you heard her [just before] the last night of her life. But the weekend before I thought she was actually getting better. I think she had decided she was going to kill herself, and she was kind of like enjoying the last few days of her life.

I thought how she had sounded truly awful when I spoke to her then, wondering if she put on a better act for Brett. "Do you know when she had decided? She called me the Saturday before. I mean it was before that she had decided."

"The first gun she bought was on the fourth of November."

"She called me on the sixth."

"I think she bought two guns on the fourth· and she bought one on the eighth.

"She bought a total of three guns?"

"Yes."

"Why three?"

"She bought bigger and bigger guns, and she used the big one."

"Why?"

"I think she didn't want to try and fail. After she killed herself I looked at *Final Exit,* and that's what they tell you, is that you need a big gun if you want to commit suicide. And so she bought a big gun."

"Did she get all three of them at the same place?"

"I don't think so. I think she bought them at different places."

He talked about how hopeless she was at the very end over her late-October diagnosis of bipolar disorder.

> *Her parents had taken her to a support group up at Stanford in early October of people who were suffering from bipolar disorder. And so the people in the support group were not people who had overcome bipolar disorder and were leading productive lives; they were people who were actually walking around like zombies. That was early October, and that really upset her and she said, "They are not going to put me on these drugs." We said, "Well, that's not what your problem is. You're not suffering from bipolar disorder."*
>
> *Then we finally found this psychiatrist who was good, and he diagnosed her with bipolar disorder. . . .*

"So it became an issue that bipolar means 'you become a zombie' [from drugs]?" I asked.

"Yeah, and I knew that's how she was perceiving it, so I asked the psychiatrist, please give me the names of people who you successfully treated and are leading productive lives. And he did, but she never would call and talk to them."

"Why wouldn't she contact them? She was so far gone?"

"Yes, I think when she was diagnosed with that, that's when she got the idea she was going to commit suicide."

"Why did that trigger it? She didn't want to live as a bipolar person or a zombie with medication?"

"Yeah."

"When did they tell her she was bipolar?"

"My guess would be October 28th. So they told her this, and she went to a gun shop and got this gun safety course [pamphlet]. Her mom found [it], and we told her, 'What are you doing? You don't need to buy guns,' and she said she was doing it to protect herself from the government. . . .

"And then a lot of things all lined up at the end of October. She was diagnosed with bipolar disorder, they changed her medication, George Bush was reelected, she thought the government was out to get her." I asked him to explain why the election would be that unhinging. "I mean the election was literally on the second and the results were announced on the third, so the same government that was out to get her was going to be back in power for four more years," he explained. "She bought her first gun on the fourth."

We were done eating, and a child crying at the next table was starting to interrupt our conversation. So we moved to Brett's house. On the way, in the car, with the tape recorder off, we talked about how Iris grew more suicidal as she felt less and less in control. In a perverse way, suicide is the ultimate act of control, I thought.

We pulled into the garage, which was filled with dozens more boxes of Iris' papers. Brett explained that many of those papers were about Bataan and were headed for the Hoover Archive at Stanford. The living room, where we then sat, was simply decorated, resembling something like a hotel room, on the order of a Hampton Inn, early 1990s. The walls were white and the only décor was a mirror, which he told me Iris had bought. The furniture was mainly a black futon couch and two black leather recliners. Brett said this was the most decorated any of their homes had been; they had just bought about everything there from the prior owner.

In the front entryway were the only overt signs of Iris herself, in the form of family pictures showcased on a table. One was Iris happily cradling Christopher. Others were of Iris and celebrities, including a well-known Asian-American astronaut.

Referring to the boxes containing the Bataan research, I asked Brett about the effect of that research on her mental health. Brett downplayed its depressing influence—and that of her other dark research topics—still insisting that the main stressor was her book tour. "She worked on that Bataan project for almost a year. I didn't see any change in her personality. And then that book tour, the difference from the beginning to the end was just very striking."

"What about *The Rape of Nanking*? Everybody assumes that that really depressed her. Was it hard for her to work on that? Her mother was quoted saying it 'made her sad.'" Iris had indeed told many reporters, and friends, about what a strain that experience had been on her, mentally and physically.

"To be honest, I do not remember that. I mean other people have said that. Supposedly she's told other people that. What I think is she knew this was an important subject to write. And from the time she started in '94 to the time when she did all the final paperwork in '97, she was just totally focused on getting that done. And I didn't really see any personality changes in her during that time at all."

"Did she tell you that it was affecting her or talk about it?"

"Never did."

"Did she have an outlet for talking about this stuff?"

"Sure. She would tell me if she wasn't feeling good. Definitely if she was feeling upset about something she would tell me. She never did really."

Brett also said that Iris talked with her interview transcriptionists and other friends about this dark material. He said that nothing was "real" to her until she processed it out loud.

Brett did concede that the Bataan book may have had an influence on depressing Iris because of how elderly and infirm her typical subjects were. She felt intense pressure to interview them as soon as possible, before they died; many whom she had befriended had passed away within weeks of her meeting them, which was tough on Iris.

At the end, no matter what the effect of the actual material on her, she was certainly feeling isolated with the Bataan project. I brought up how in an interview with Monica months earlier, Brett had stated to Iris that he didn't want to hear her recount stories about Bataan. He agreed that this is what he had told Iris.

She would interview those survivors, and just have one horrible story after another and just tell me. And I finally said, "Look, I don't want to hear it anymore. If you want to write

the book fine, but I don't want to hear the stories anymore."
That was probably sometime in 2003 when I told her that, be-
cause she was just gathering one after another. And normally
what she would do is she would read a book or do an interview
and then come back and tell me everything—and I didn't
want to hear them.

At about that point, I heard someone unlocking the front door. I got up, expecting Christopher's arrival from his grandparents' house. It was more or less the time that we had picked him up after our interview earlier that week.

In walked a petite Asian woman. Brett came to life and walked over to hug her.

"Paula, this is Iris," he said.

"Nice to meet you," she said, with a Chinese accent.

I collected myself and said, "Nice to meet you, too."

"Yes, she is thirty-six, and her name is Iris," Brett said, recognizing the irony.

The woman offered to go upstairs until we were done, which would be just a few minutes. He explained that he had met her via online dating several months earlier and thought she was playing a sick joke on him when she first told him that her name was Iris.

I took this in and asked myself: how many Irises were there? Just meeting Iris Chang Herrera had surprised me, and, to say the least, this was even more unexpected.

Now, I was now starting to lose my detached coolness, which I had consciously cultivated over the months. I didn't blame Brett; he had gone through hell for many months and had suffered enough. I knew that it is common for a widowed man with a child to start dating relatively quickly after the death of a spouse. But his moving on like this was an undeniable sign that she was gone and was never coming back. I felt myself start to feel more unsettled.

I looked over my last questions.

"Is there anything that you want to say about any misunderstandings about her or about bipolar illness and suicide, these issues and what you wish you would have known?" I asked.

"I guess the key thing is that it would have been better for us to let more people know, and get more help from more people."

"More openness?"

"Yes. We were in over our heads with the small group of people that knew about her problem. Especially if you have a family, and one of the spouses gets bipolar disorder. I mean normally you've got two people caring for X-number of children, and then when one of them gets mentally ill, now you've got one parent caring for a mentally ill adult, and all the children. So we definitely would have been better off enlisting help from more people."

"What kind of people?"

"More relatives. I mean she had a whole lot of relatives, and calling friends. We didn't come up with that idea of having her call friends until the last two or three weeks of her life."

I answered: "My first response afterward was I could have given her advice because I've gone through a lot of stuff, but the more I learn about what she went through, it's almost like the advanced stages of cancer or something. I really don't know if this could have been prevented."

"You can't second-guess yourself if your spouse has cancer," he agreed.

"Yes. Like 'I should have seen that coming,' and 'that was a sign,'" I said. Just as I was learning to not blame myself, I also knew I had to be understanding of Brett's own oversights.

I paused and said, "How are you doing these days?"

"I'm doing better, yes. It was really tough. I was basically living alone for two months, and then when Christopher came back I was a single parent with a demanding job and a two-year-old who had been spoiled rotten by his grandmother, so that was tough. I was able to get a handle on that by February or March, and then when I started dating Iris, that helped a lot too. Life is more normal."

"That's good. It still hasn't been that long, but you seem like you're as good as someone could be in this situation."

"Yes. Actually I just had a week where I went to a conference—the first business trip I've had since Iris got really mentally ill. It was good to get out of here and then come back. I'm in much better shape than I was even a month ago."

I hesitated and asked: "Is Iris a popular Chinese name, like Iris' Chinese name Shun-Ru is really 'Iris' or something?"

"Iris is an English name. We were talking about this."

"You translated it?"

"Iris Shui's Chinese name is Jiebing [phonetic] and Iris Chang's Chinese name was Shun-Ru. They are not related at all. They just choose an English name. So there are tons of Chinese women named Iris, Daisy, Lily, Rose. . . . "

"Oh, I never noticed that."

"It is very common."

"So, a lot of flowers."

"A lot of flowers, yes."

"It helps to explain it. Is Iris from China?"

"She is."

"Can I ask you what she does?"

"She's in marketing."

That was the end of that tape.

$\mathcal{N}$ow at the end of my Bay Area trip, I had time to visit a site that I dreaded but knew I had to visit.

I got out my map and looked for directions to get to Highway 17 in Los Gatos. I knew the exact spot I wanted to pull off to near Bear Creek Road; Monica Eng had e-mailed me the location the day before.

On the way, I saw a sign for the "Winchester Mystery House," open for tours, and thought of the consuming fears of another famous former San Jose resident, Mrs. Winchester. I had first learned about the notorious Winchester house the week before seeing a photo installation on it at the San Francisco Museum of Modern Art. Apparently, the house, with its 160 rooms, was now quite a tourist attraction in San Jose. The former owner of the house, the widow of the Winchester gun magnate, who had helped to capture the Wild West, was convinced that spirits were responsible for a series of tragedies in her life. A medium told this Mrs. Winchester that she could keep the demons at bay if she kept adding rooms to her house to confuse them. In 1884, she started around-the-clock construction of mazes of rooms and winding staircases, some which led up to nowhere, just to walls or open windows. The constant ruckus of construction didn't end until thirty-eight years later, just minutes after Mrs. Winchester's death.

To distract myself, I turned on the radio, and hoped it would suppress, rather than bring out, my own unresolved demons related to Iris. A week before, when I had arrived in the Bay Area, that move had backfired. I had turned on the radio, and thought I had heard Iris' voice filling the air. A few seconds later, I had realized it was a rebroadcast of a taped interview with her about *The Rape of Nanking* on National Public Radio. I also couldn't stop noticing that the announcer had some kind of affected accent, not British but something else, and kept calling her "Iris Chong." Later during that week, it seemed that every time I turned on KQED, they were rerunning the interview or doing a promo for the interview "with the late author Iris Chong who died last year of an illness." I knew it wasn't a haunting, but it felt like it, just the same. I was also feeling a chill from the cold-bloodedness of Iris' planning of her own death, which still wasn't quite believable.

Her voice on the radio had also been disturbing because at that time I was also being repeatedly haunted by Iris via another medium, my voice mail. At that point, I still was not able to bring myself to erase her last November 3, 2004, two-line message to me, about wanting to talk and catch up. Every two weeks, it would come on as I logged into voice mail. Then I would have the choice to press "9" to save it or "7" to delete. I always pressed "9." And yet I would still be startled fourteen days later to hear it again.

I concentrated more on the road, which started winding more sharply, and harrowingly, as the darkness of the night started to descend. I noticed many emergency call boxes dotting the road, just like the one by which Iris had parked her car in her final minutes.

I also remembered how Iris must have traveled this same road years before that, in 1999, on her way to visit me for a day in a rural part of the mountains of Santa Cruz. I had been staying with a friend there. When it had gotten dark, I had asked her to stay the night. I was worried about her trip home to San Jose back over these mountains, mainly because the roads leading out were not well lit. She insisted on going home anyway because of a FedEx package she was expecting the following day. You just couldn't argue with her.

I wondered what she had been hiding during that visit, when she had seemed relatively normal but likely had just experienced at least one disappointing miscarriage. Again I found myself wondering if I ever really knew her? Do you really ever know anyone?

I was getting very nervous with the relatively high speed of the traffic combined with the increasingly winding narrow roads. I realized it was too dark now for me to even determine the exact spot where she had stopped that morning, ten months earlier, to begin that three-minute ritual of loading and firing the gun. Had I passed it already? And, now feeling flooded by emotions from the interview with Brett, from meeting his new Iris, and from the week in the Bay Area, I didn't want to find it anymore, anyway. I was getting very tired.

In any case, I very likely had passed the exit at this point. I was climbing higher and higher over the mountain, beyond where she would have gone. And the many cars speeding close behind me were making me even more nervous, especially at every sharp turn.

As I turned off on the next exit, I remembered Iris' quote from 1998 in the *Champaign News-Gazette* about the madness of her experience in the public eye with *The Rape of Nanking*. She had compared it to "being strapped to a roller coaster and not being able to get off." Later, with the burden of mental illness, that ride became even more accelerated, unpre-dictable, and terrifying. No longer bearable.

I was relieved, myself, to now be off that road. Those closely trailing cars were no longer behind me, and I was able to collect myself. Very slowly and deliberately, against the flow of traffic, I caught my breath and turned the car around.

CHAPTER NINE

What Were Her Demons?

*F*rom *The Rape of Nanking:*

> *There are several important lessons to be learned from Nanking, and one is that civilization itself is tissue-thin. (220)*

Now, I thought, since more than a year has passed since her death, I will finally be able to handle it. In early 2006, I sent a check for $18.05 to the coroner of the County of Santa Clara. Soon after, I received a manila envelope with a sixteen-page packet.

With a conscious effort of emotional detachment, I opened it and saw that on the cover sheet listing the basic information about the case were some blacked-out lines, just like the FBI files that Iris had found for Tsien. Inked out was a box describing her medical history, along with her home contact information.

Still legible were detailed descriptions of the body: how it was found on the scene, and studies from the later autopsy. Page after page followed detailing the grisly nature of the injuries: "Decedent's teeth appear broken and there is blood exuding from the mouth." Apparently, she had put the gun in her mouth and fired upward. One section listed an inventory of her clothing, most of which was "blood-stained."

Yes, the coroner's report concluded, it was a suicide. They had found traces of gunshot residue on her hands (revealing that she was the one who fired the gun), and in the front seat was a box full of gun accessories, "such as black powder, lubricant, patches, tools, and lead ball ammunition."

Also convincing was the psychological autopsy, characteristic of such suicide reports, looking at evidence of intent. The investigator had gathered testimony from the gun shop salesman about the purchase, and from the family about her history of such planning. In a heading, "EVENTS SURROUNDING DEATH," the investigator said: "Decedent was known to be suicidal and apparently decedent's mother had been cautioned the day before not to let decedent out of her sight. . . . A note of suicidal ideation was found on the home computer."

In his final summary, the medical examiner, whose marks concluded the report, agreed:

OPINION: Based on the medical investigator's report and the autopsy findings, Iris Chang, a 36-year-old Asian female died from a self-inflicted gunshot wound.

CAUSE OF DEATH: Intraoral gunshot wound.

MANNER OF DEATH: Suicide.

Signed 12/23/04

At about that time, the mail carrier delivered me another document, a book, which also starkly elucidated some of Iris' elaborate planning in her final days. I had ordered this copy of Derek Humphry's *Final Exit: The Practicalities of Self-Deliverance and Assisted Suicide for the Dying*, which Brett had mentioned to me.

Some of my greatest surprise with this book was not its cold-blooded contents, but how easy it was to get. I had been a bit afraid that, upon receiving my order, Amazon.com would report me and then a helicopter-propelled SWAT team would descend upon my apartment building roof, and then take me away.

But, as I saw on the book's Web page, I was far from alone in my order. It turned out the book had become a "#1 *New York Times* bestseller," was published by a division of the mainstream Random House (after Humphry's incredibly successful jump start in self publishing), and has been translated into eleven languages. This was just a regular business transaction; not only did Amazon.com *not* report me, they asked me if I wanted it gift wrapped before I completed my order.

The author's suicide "do" method of choice: sedation with large amounts of lethal drugs, while suffocating with an ample plastic "turkey bag" fastened over one's head. That bag "can be found in the 'Foils and Wraps' aisle of a supermarket," he advises. (125) Later I read in Dr. Kay Redfield Jamison's illuminating book on suicide, *Night Falls Fast*, that *Final Exit* has been so popular that it made asphyxiation deaths via plastic bags go up 31 percent.

The book is actually a typical example of a larger body of readily available literature, much of it online, which gives such calculated directions. These days, according to textbooks on suicide, a standard part of the post-suicide period for loved ones is often finding this book or the URLs of such Web sites. (Humphry even advises the reader to leave a copy of his book near their body, so family will know this was a conscious, rational, and active decision.)

Humphry explains that his goal is to help people pull off "a good death," defined as easy and painless and quick as possible. While therapists often refer to suicide as "hurting yourself," his aim is not to actually hurt the person, but to help them die as painlessly as possible, to take control of what they *can* control. He does warn that his directions are meant only for the terminally ill, those suffering from a physical ailment— not "the deeply depressed and mentally ill," whom he recognized as having abused the book. (xv)

He also qualifies that his book does not discuss the *ethics* of "self-deliverance," referring the reader to other sources to answer that question.

Assuming the reader is already at peace with this decision, he goes on to deliver a remarkably methodical and dry "how-to." A sort of death DIY. In fact, he recommends that one should read the book twice because "a good death requires courage, support, and strict attention to details." For example, if you do insist on going against his recommendation of the turkey-bag method, and instead take cyanide in a glass with water, make sure to get up to rinse it out at the sink before dropping dead. That way, no one else in your family will drink from it by mistake. If you choose death by drugs, "be careful about the contents of your stomach. Tea or coffee, toast or a bun, are acceptable. Nothing heavy or difficult to digest." (144)

Skimming through the book, I immediately noticed how Iris, ever the researcher, paid attention to Humphry's minutest details. While he discourages death by gunshot because of its messiness and relatively high failure rate, he does grudgingly give advice. That includes directions on how to position the gun in the mouth and to buy as big a gun as possible. "The bigger the gun, the more likely it is to be effective," he advises. (45) Ironically, as his example of someone who made a failed attempt with too small a gun, Humphry gives General Tojo, whom Iris described as one of a handful of executed Japanese war criminals in *The Rape of Nanking*. At the end of World War II, as Allied troops advanced to Tokyo to arrest him, Tojo aimed at an "X" he had his doctor mark over his chest in chalk on his clothes. He shot the gun and missed, only wounding himself.

Another of Humphry's recommendations that Iris took was to do the deed away from home, where your family will not be traumatized by finding your body. One option was to go to a hotel—which Iris did for her first muddled attempt. (I don't know if she took Humphry's suggestion to leave "a generous tip for the motel staff to compensate them for the disturbance caused.") (94) Iris ended up following his advice to do it in one's car, in order to be eventually found by a professional first-responder, such as a police officer, who is trained for such circumstances.

Another tip that Iris heeded: "Tell those around you the complimentary things that might have been left unsaid due to the strain of illness. A simple 'I'm grateful for all you've done for me' or similar remark goes a long way to comfort those you will leave behind."

Yes, Iris had said good-bye to me personally, and now, after meeting with Brett, I had most of my most mysterious questions answered about her greatest fears of her last weeks. But I was still not comforted. I was still confused, basically more disturbed about the facts of her death than ever.

Although—as I now knew—Iris' illness was likely genetic in origin, and aggravated by hormone upsets and stress, I found myself having flashes of irrational thoughts of her being possessed. Her last actions were so extreme, violent, and seemingly sudden that it was as if she were brainwashed. It was like someone or something just took over her mind, maybe using *Final Exit* as a tool for murder.

Obviously, despite some basic knowledge on mental illness, I was still lacking specific information—about the long-evolving biological and cultural aspects of Iris' mental illness, and how severe hormone swings from pregnancies and infertility drugs fit into that picture. And the best way I had found through my life to vanquish irrational fears was by addressing them directly, head on, and seeking the facts. It was time to hunker down and learn more facts about bipolar disorder, and how it develops over time.

After all, the issue of imbalanced brain chemistry was the foundation of what happened to Iris. That was the one limit in life she was not able to overcome, even with the most iron of iron wills, a healthy bank balance, good looks, fame, a loving family, and the most lofty ideals to "have it all."

The bottom line was that no amount of retracing her last steps or analyzing her life stressors would tell me more about her motivations for suicide. These bizarre final acts and fears didn't give a picture of her true self, but only of the bigger failure of her brain to be rational.

It was now clear to me that earlier I had been following a natural coping pattern of friends of suicide victims, to investigate recent external circumstances as being at the root of such a death, while overlooking the most basic factor of biology. In her book *Night Falls Fast: Understanding Suicide*, psychologist and noted expert on bipolar disorder Kay Redfield Jamison points out: "Most people know little about suicide or the psychiatric illnesses most closely associated with it and therefore flail about, trying to make sense of an often senseless act. They inevitably focus on the events of life—broken or difficult relationships, financial concerns, job-related stress—as the reasons for suicide." (299)

After all, as she writes, *everyone* faces hardships in life, but suicide is mainly a response of the mentally ill.

> *Everyone has good cause for suicide, or at least it seems that way to those who search for it. And most will have yet better grounds to stay alive, thus complicating everything.* . . . *(74)* *It is clear that these or similar setbacks hit everyone at some point in their lives. Unless someone lives an unthinkably boring life, has no hopes that can be shattered, no love that can be lost, or transits from birth to death in a bubble above the frays of earth, he or she experiences the same griefs or strains that, for a few become the "cause" of death. (199)*

Personally, I knew about the dominating powers of unbalanced neurotransmitters, also at the root of many kinds of chronic pain. I was only able to learn to manage my own chronic head and neck pain, still with some ongoing struggle, when I understood it as "a genetic disorder with external triggers"—and realized that external stress was not the root cause. While reducing stress is certainly helpful in reducing pain (and every other physical and mental illness) the root cause for me has been overly reactive brain chemistry. As with bipolar disorder, for someone with chronic pain, even minor changes in routine—such as in hormones and sleep patterns—can exacerbate or trigger the underlying genetic problem. And in the case of those with these predisposed vulnerabilities, more extreme stressors, such as an extended nonstop book tour to dozens of cities in a short time, perhaps, could do much greater long-term damage than with others.

Ironically, I learned that chronic head pain and bipolar disorder are often related, on a chemical level. People with chronic daily headache and bipolar disorder, as well as those with epilepsy, typically take the same drugs to calm down an overactive brain, including Depakote, an anticonvulsant medication, which Iris had taken at the end of her life (and which I had also been on at one point, along with many other drugs of that type). In fact, someone with any one of these problems is more likely than others in the population to have multiple ones, because of similar underlying brain chemistry imbalances.

Like with my own chronic pain, bipolar disorder is laden with cultural myths. In general, "invisible" illnesses—that is to say those that do not immediately "prove" themselves as "real" with an overt sign of injury, such as a cast or cane or results on a CT scan—carry a strong double standard. This is the case no matter what your culture. This attitude of denying biological realities when they are invisible goes way back. In ancient times, common knowledge was that demons, literally demons, caused what we now see as mental illness. Another entrenched belief is that the souls of suicide victims are more restless than others, and more prone to nightly perambulations.

In our age, we often are not that much more enlightened, although our language sounds more scientific. For the past century, a common "modern" catchall framework for explaining all ills has been psychoanalytic theory, which posits mental illness as the victim's "subconscious" world expressing itself. While such introspection can be helpful for a patient, a common result is denying real medical treatment. The patient is blamed for maladjustment and for not dealing adequately with stress, leaving him or her more shamed and isolated than ever. An example is how postpartum depression was treated for more than sixty years after Freud: as the woman's subconscious rebellion against being a mother, instead of as a brain chemistry imbalance due to the biological effects of pregnancy. While psychological factors, such as any ambivalence and stress about motherhood, are useful to address, it's been damaging to focus on those exclusively—and not offer these women proper medical care (drugs).

The more I studied about bipolar disorder, the possible effects of infertility treatments, and the possible role of Iris' culture to mask the problem—the more I understood what Iris experienced. It gave insight into her final months, when she became psychotic, as well as earlier in her life, as the problem evolved. This suicide was more deep rooted, and less impulsive and sudden, than I had imagined. In fact, while I'm still not sure if her death could have been prevented, I started to realize that Iris had fit the profile for someone at great risk for suicide, not only in her last weeks, but for years before.

The label "bipolar disorder"—and the more old-fashioned term for it, "manic depression"—are a bit misleading. They do convey the reality of a disorder of the moods, that the patient suffers from extremes on both poles, both up and down. But, as many people don't realize, bipolar disorder is much more than that. One of the most dangerous aspects of bipolar disorder is that it often does involve *psychosis*, or losing touch with reality, during either end of the mood spectrum. That can include visual or auditory hallucinations, or delusions of grandeur or persecution (paranoia). This state of psychosis is one of the most torturous parts of the illness, creating the feeling of being perpetually hounded by such fears. Indeed, not only the content of these fears, but also their sheer exhausting presence can drive someone to end it all. In her suicide note, Iris had described her utter exhaustion in having to face one fear after another, of feeling like she "was drowning in an open sea."

Those with psychosis are at especially high risk for suicide and are more likely to use violent and bizarre methods. For this reason, and as a result of the dangers of both the depressed and manic states, bipolar disorder is a very dangerous illness, killing about 10 percent of its victims through suicide. About half of those with bipolar disorder attempt suicide, as compared to about 20 percent with depression.

Besides the psychosis, characteristics of both depression and mania can lead to suicide. In the state of depression, the brain loses its capacity to cope with the negatives of life. The depressed person is more likely than others to interpret their past experiences as failures, focus on them, and lose hope for the future. In other words, they can't just "go with the flow." "Much as a compromised immune system is vulnerable to opportunistic infection, so too a diseased brain is made assailable by the eventualities of life," writes Dr. Jamison in *Night Falls Fast*. (93)

Iris no doubt was depressed in this way; her intense self-blame for "giving" her son autism is a good example. On one hand, she was reacting to widespread and mainstream media and medical discussion at the time speculating that vaccines can cause autism. That argument was in the air. And, it turns out that she did certainly witness early signs of such a problem in her son at that time. (After our interview, Brett did let me know that Christopher since had been diagnosed with Asperger's Disorder, a milder variant of autism.) But her coping skills were off; she wrongly condemned herself as the cause of such a problem. At the time she told me about these fears, in November of 2004, she couldn't begin to understand a life—for her son and also for herself, having been recently diagnosed with bipolar disorder—that did not resemble the "normal" one that she had planned.

But suicide attempts themselves usually happen while the bipolar patient is in a manic state—or in an even more dangerous and agitated mixed state (one with both depression and mania). In any state tinged with mania, the patient has the energy and drive to commit the act, which he or she may be missing while depressed. Sleeplessness, which Iris long suffered from, is one of the strongest elements to trigger manic states. In *Night Falls Fast*, Dr. Jamison describes its typical characteristics: "With mania, there is a vast, restless energy and little need for sleep. Behavior is erratic, impetuous, and frequently violent; drinking, sex, and the spending of money are excessive." (107)

However, this is just a general guideline. Mania isn't always easy to detect because it takes many extremes and many forms. As I only recently realized, Iris' behavior, even at the end of her life when her condition was most extreme, did not neatly fit the standard profile of mania. While I sensed some manic leanings with Iris through her adulthood, such as in the fatiguing marathon-length phone calls, I was thrown off because she did not appear to manifest some of the most typical and well-known behaviors of mania: sex and shopping. I had thought that if she wasn't sleeping around wildly or racking up the bills on her Visa, she couldn't be bipolar.

This is where an understanding of one's culture comes into the picture, to understand what mania can look like. As Dr. Jamison herself explains, the way someone exhibits the typical recklessness of mania depends on one's culture and gender. A manic man may get caught up in violence, such as in causing a car wreck, while a woman shoplifts or gambles to an extreme. As an example of culturally defined mania, she describes an Amish man using a public telephone. For him, that's reckless behavior.

It turns out that I, along with many others were using a very "Eurocentric" model in overlooking Iris' mania. That was the observation of Dr. Aruna Jha, a scholar and activist on the issue of Asian suicide based in Chicago. She explained to me that Asians' typical range of accepted behavior is much *narrower* than that of Caucasians. For a greater number of them, such "reckless" behaviors of promiscuity or shoplifting would be unthinkable, even in the most unhinged states. "People raised in Asian cultures are expected to adhere so closely to a very narrow range of behavior that's considered appropriate," she said.

As a result, white people, like Iris' husband, might have overlooked some of Iris' "excitable" behavior which would have seemed in the range of "normal" for a white person, but could signal spiraling mania for a typically less expressive Asian. "It would take another Asian or a very sensitive person to realize that she [Iris] had gone past all the limits of what Asian human beings tolerate at this point," Dr. Jha said. And even when white people do recognize extreme behaviors in Asian friends or coworkers, such as nonstop work for days, they may accept that as a normal characteristic of the Asian super achiever or "model minority." She added that compounding inaccuracy of diagnosis, even for trained professionals, is an extreme lack of clinical research into nonwhite subjects and how they experience mental illness.

But Iris did follow some standard profiles that cut across ethnic background. As I read Dr. Jamison's book on suicide, I was repeatedly jarred to see how she fit classic clinical characteristics of extreme risk in the last months of her life. An attempted suicide, which Iris had apparently experienced in September of 2004, is the single biggest predictor of an eventual suicide. People with mood disorders (depression or bipolar disorder) are more likely to kill themselves early in the course of their illness, when they have fewer coping skills and more fear for the future. That often happens after their first attack of severe depression or release from a mental hospital, which happened to Iris in August of 2004. As with Iris, and her *Rape of Nanking* heroine, Minnie Vautrin, the suicide often comes at a time when the patient has been described as "improving," perhaps when they have more energy to commit the act.

The risk for suicide is even greater in cases of superachievers who have a relatively late onset of psychosis. Jamison points out how these types are less able to accept the illness, while fearing they have more to lose with a recurrence. She writes: "Patients who do well socially and academically when young and who then are hit by devastating illnesses such as schizophrenia or manic-depression seem particularly vulnerable to the specter of their own mental disintegration and terror of becoming a chronic patient. For them and many others there is a terrible loss of dreams and inescapable damage to friends, family and self." (84)

One of the most seemingly unusual parts of Iris' suicide, the use of a gun, I found, was actually more common than one would think. While women are less likely to use violent means than men, that is changing. A growing number of women are using guns, which account for about 60 percent of all completed suicides.

A major red flag from the start of Iris' life may have been simple genetics, the most powerful indicator of bipolar disorder. Brett had speculated that a relative of Iris' may have shown such signs.

Iris also fit a profile as being at higher risk for a mood disorder as a creative type. It turns out that some of the stereotypes of the writer as depressed are based in reality. And that pattern in artists of all kinds can be difficult to detect because it can be easily confused with the extremes of the creative process. In both mania and creative thinking, the individual makes leaps in thinking and connects new dots to make original discoveries. This process can be instructive, or destructive, depending on the person's state of mind. Dr. Jamison explains how "extremes in emotions and thinking, when tightly yoked with a disciplined mind and high imagination, certainly can advance the arts, sciences and commerce." (180) In contrast, in a state of psychosis, they are likely to connect dots, such as with wild conspiracy theories, that should not indeed be connected. As examples of populations prone to mania in her book, Dr. Jamison continually cites artists and scientists—the professions that define Iris' family. Dr. Jamison herself, who is bipolar, is the daughter of a scientist who also suffered from the illness.

Dr. Jamison writes: "At least twenty studies have found that highly creative individuals are much more likely than the general population to suffer from depression and manic-depressive illness. Clearly, mood disorders are not required for great accomplishment, and most people who suffer from mood disorders are not particularly accomplished. But the evidence is compelling that the creative are *disproportionately* affected by these conditions." In short, insane people aren't particularly creative, but creative people are particularly insane.

That confusion can certainly be true in interpreting the behavior of ambitious and in-demand authors, even after the writing is done. Their typically nonstop promotional efforts of being "on" for days in a row and hardly sleeping can be indistinguishable from mania. "I will say that I never had an inkling of Iris having a bipolar disorder," said novelist Amy Tan, a friend of Iris' whom she had interviewed for her book, *The Chinese in America*. After the interview, they stayed on the phone for a few hours, when Iris asked her advice about coping with the demands of being a popular author.

> *I remember one of the first things she [Iris] talked about was how tired she had been from doing a book tour, and she had been up for several nights without any sleep, and that she had to do an interview somewhere. I don't remember if it was television or radio or in front of a group of people, but suddenly her brain just stopped functioning and she was caught there without being able to say anything. I think she was mortified. And I said, "You know that has happened to me so many times." You're exhausted and you don't even hear the question, and suddenly there you are on live radio you don't say anything or just say, "I'm sorry; I haven't had any sleep in forty-eight hours and I have no idea what you just asked me."*

She stopped and chuckled a bit. "It never occurred to me she was not sleeping because of any other problems that she had with her health. You just naturally assume that you don't sleep when you're on book tours." Tan added that not only could the demands of a book tour resemble mania, but they can also feed into that cycle.

As I've written earlier, Iris' fame, along with her good looks, also shielded her from the scrutiny of outsiders. In a typical pattern of such patients, she also likely was *actively* hiding her depression and smaller-scale manic periods for years, even purposefully projecting an image of absolute perfection. Her veneer of perfection was so extreme to her friends that it couldn't have just metamorphosized on its own. For years, she may have also chosen to surround herself by people, like her low-key husband, who gave her plenty of space to hide it. Furthermore, as I was realizing, her "demons" were not new, unique to her last months; after all, her lifelong fears all had the same "paranoid flavor," as my therapist terms them, dealing with safety issues. She had a long-established pattern of such fears, not just in her last months. Even one of Iris' stated motivations for joining a sorority—to be "safer" living in its fortified house, instead of an apartment—could have been part of this pattern.

The easiest stage of bipolar disorder to hide, which she likely suffered for years, is depression, when the person is naturally keeping a lower profile and is less flamboyant. Thus, a person is more likely to only be hospitalized and diagnosed while in the manic—and more obviously mentally ill—phase, as is what happened with Iris. But, even in her last days, she was still certainly very actively covering it up. This is a common pattern. About one third of previously hospitalized patients who commit suicide look completely "normal" to their friends, doctors, and family in the minutes or hours before it, as Jamison describes in *Night Falls Fast*. This calm can be explained by the person feeling relief about the decision to kill oneself, or may be just plain deception to throw others off the path.

The fact that mania comes in different extremes also diverts others from the trail. Bipolar disorder itself, along with mania, happens in a spectrum and is widely variable. In recent years, clinicians have expanded definitions of bipolar disorder greatly to refer to those beyond the severely bipolar, diagnosed as bipolar I, which represents 0.5 to 1.5 percent of the population. Among other milder classifications, they have (with some controversy) defined bipolar II, including up to 5 percent of the population, which is typified by mild manic episodes followed by depressive ones. These types of mild manic episodes are called "hypomania." Far from troubling, this is a form of mania not prone to psychosis, which could even be quite productive and desirable. The symptoms may also include decreased need for sleep, obsessiveness, flights of ideas or racing thoughts, and distractibility, among others. Indeed, it is quite normal for someone with bipolar disorder not to want to miss these periods of creativity and exuberance by medicating them—when they can do difficult things quickly, like conducting major scientific research or writing an entire novel—all carried off with very little sleep.

While medication is not always necessary for those with bipolar leanings, recognition of such tendencies is useful because the status may worsen over time. A person can go from being charmingly exuberant (bipolar II) to dangerously manic (bipolar I) in a short time, especially when left totally unmedicated and if the stressors are extreme. A major factor in diagnosis, explained Dr. Jeanne Watson Driscoll, the coauthor of *Women's Moods* and *Postpartum Mood and Anxiety Disorders*, is "frequency, duration, and intensity." These are the criteria for diagnosing other mental health problems, from paranoia to depression, which everyone suffers from once in a while, but may be more serious in others.

Looking at common patterns in women, I agree with Dr. Driscoll's observation to me that Iris' state likely evolved from the more low-key bipolar II to the more flagrantly serious bipolar I. Clinicians understand the development of the more severe bipolar I as "additive," meaning that it can build with the introduction of more and more upsets in someone's life. Those stressors can actually change the brain chemistry over time, acting like fault lines before an earthquake, which is a metaphor Dr. Driscoll uses in her book. When the fault lines become more numerous, then the earthquake, or the mental health breakdown, happens. While it likely had been building for years, this disruption may seem sudden, triggered by only one fault line, say a stressful and busy book tour.

As with Iris, for many women a major fault line on the road to bipolar I is the onset of dramatic hormonal shifts. According to Brett, Iris went through six weeks of taking infertility drugs, and two years of multiple failed pregnancies—all of which can have a profound effect on worsening bipolar disorder. At our interview, Brett would not go into specifics with me about which infertility drugs Iris took, but the most typical ones go right to the limbic brain, the mood center, and strongly affect all neurotransmitters, such as serotonin, at every stage. Standard infertility drugs, like Clomid and Pergonal, greatly elevate hormones to stimulate the ovaries to make many eggs. "When on these drugs, women have estrogen levels ten times higher than during natural menstrual cycles. This is what increases the probability of mood shifts," write the authors of *Women's Moods*. (65) Also typically influencing all the mood pathways in the brain is progesterone, a common treatment given to women to help establish a pregnancy after the egg has been fertilized.

In fact, one of the most startling facts I learned while researching this book was just how extraordinarily sensitive those prone to bipolar disorder are to *all* major hormonal shifts. Immediately after Iris' death, I had only considered the possibility of her vulnerability to depression in the postpartum period, which has gotten more press as a threat, and not during the complete range of "hormonal events," such as the unsuccessful pregnancies and infertility drugs. Besides right after childbirth, vulnerable times include onset of menstruation, the days preceding menstruation (when "PMS" hits), the duration of pregnancy, menopause, and any time high doses of artificial hormones are prescribed: such as in the form of certain birth control pills or infertility drugs. In addition, anxiety disorders also tend to emerge for the first time during these hormonal events. All these episodes can serve as a useful predictor of future problems with postpartum depression or psychosis; if someone experiences dramatic emotional upset with infertility treatments, for example, she will likely be more vulnerable to problems later after giving birth.

This onset of bipolar disorder can happen at a much later age than I had thought. Women's peak periods of bipolar disorder are from the ages of twenty-five to forty-four, which coincides with their childbearing efforts these days. Such an onset can even happen as late as menopause, especially after decades of accruing stressful events and hormonal changes.

Women with bipolar disorder can be so sensitive to hormonal change that an estimated 70 percent of them get clinically defined postpartum depression (when not medicated), compared to only 10–15 percent of the general population. And about 10–20 percent of women with bipolar disorder become *psychotic* in the postpartum period; this contrasts to only 0.1–0.2 percent in the general population. This close correlation of bipolar disorder to hormonal upset is why researchers are beginning to define postpartum psychosis basically as a mood disorder, not typically experienced out of the blue by women without this predisposition.

Probably the most overlooked patient who's at risk during these hormonal events is the one with bipolar II, whose disorder may be too mild to notice. They do not suffer from psychosis, which is the first point of the illness' progression that many family members (like Iris' husband and many of her friends) may define as "mental illness." But, again, this condition of agitation and mood swings can evolve into something worse on the bipolar spectrum, and the differences between bipolar I and bipolar II are not often black and white.

"When it comes to bipolar II disorder, it is easy to be confused," write the authors of *Women's Moods*.

> *This is the most unrecognized and under-treated mood problem we encounter in our practice. . . . We are always on the lookout for it, since misdiagnosis can lead to worsening of the condition. The brain pathways in a woman with bipolar II disorder are exquisitely sensitive to the fluctuations of hormones. . . . Unless this disorder is diagnosed, women who suffer from it have a difficult time with their moods throughout their childbearing years. (69)*

Dr. Driscoll pointed out the difficulty that these women even have getting properly diagnosed, and hence treated. In her dissertation, she followed eleven such women, who took an average of seven to eight years to be diagnosed. "Once they were on the right medication, their life totally changed," she said.

I also didn't realize that the effects of hormonal events can be cumulative. This means that not just recent events in a person's life, but also past events, can have an influence in the present. Just because infertility treatments had taken place years before Iris' death doesn't mean that they didn't affect her later on. In that vein, I had misunderstood postpartum depression, which I thought she also likely suffered, as limited to affecting a woman temporarily, for only the months after pregnancy.

In her critiques of the infertility industry, Dr. Driscoll continually emphasizes the importance of these clinics doing in-depth investigations of a patient's past: of family history, stressful life events, and negative reactions to prior hormonal events. "You can't just assume that seeing them at this moment is what it has been like for the past two weeks. The words we use all the time are, 'How did your brain get in this room? What happened to your biochemistry through your life—that we are not seeing—to present these symptoms?'"

Unfortunately, such in-depth and sensitive communication is rare, with women often going completely unaware of the hormonal risks to their mood disorders. "Consideration is rarely given to women who enter programs with a mood disorder and find themselves worsening during [infertility] treatment," write Driscoll and her coauthor, Dr. Deborah Sichel, in *Women's Moods*. "In fact, it is rarely mentioned that most of the medications used to augment hormone levels or to stimulate egg production generate mood swings and depressive symptoms." (165)

At best, typical infertility doctors may broach the topic by asking a woman during intake if she "has a psychiatric history." However, a patient is unlikely to identify this status, especially if she has never had therapy or taken medication. Of course, she may not be aware of the existence of such a thing as "bipolar II," and the reality that milder symptoms of mood disorders could evolve into something worse. Dr. Driscoll also explained that a woman like Iris with hypomania may actually benefit from that energetic state and not want to "treat" it. "We love it because it's highly productive, and they [hypomanic patients] are successful," she said. "But we *don't* love it when they become psychotic, and then we get terrified of them."

Another typical conflict with infertility drugs is that the entire focus may be on the goal of getting a baby, period. As a result, the woman's particular mental health risks can be a secondary concern to the mother or the doctor, or both. As long as a baby gets born, that's all that matters.

"I think what needs to be said strongly is that every woman is unique, and we can't assume that all the biological things we're doing to help people get pregnant do not have a cost. And I'm not talking financially, which is already quite high, but emotionally," Dr. Driscoll said. Summing up this dilemma is a noted quote from the 1930s infertility treatment pioneer, physician Sophia Josephine Kleegman, who said, "In no field of therapy has the human body been so frequently assaulted as that of the barren woman."

More improvements in education also need to take place beyond the clinic. The major researchers on this topic point out the lack of data on the effects of infertility treatments on mood disorders. This is true across the board regarding research about women and all kinds of hormonal events, even pregnancy. "Despite the undoubtedly great clinical importance of the female reproductive life cycle (the menstrual cycle, pregnancy, postpartum, breast-feeding and menopause), remarkably little is known about its impact on the course and treatment of BD (bipolar disorder]," write contributors to the 2005 psychiatry review, *Mood and Anxiety Disorders During Pregnancy and Postpartum.* (53)

One explanation for this gap is that doctors in the past followed the longtime myth that a woman's hormones were designed to "protect" her from emotional upheaval during a pregnancy. Also as a result of Freudian psychoanalytic theory, they have tended to see such mood swings as purely "in the mind," as the result of ambivalence toward motherhood and not brain chemistry. Another major problem is that researchers through the years have resisted using women as test subjects for medications, especially women who are undergoing hormonal events; instead, men have been the standard, for their lack of "complications" in research. Also, companies that make the drugs have failed to research their long-term effect on patients with mood disorders; after a drug has been approved by the FDA, they have little incentive to rock the boat and conduct negative research on their products' adverse effects on a subset of bipolar patients. Certainly, the fact that mental illness has been so stigmatized—especially among new mothers—has also been a factor in these patients themselves not speaking up more to complain about the effects of hormonal treatments.

Also missing for doctors and patients is research specifically on how individual cultures shape the presentation—and the denial—of mood disorders. As I found out looking at a new breed of activism in the Asian American community, this work is just beginning. After all, it's no small feat. While every society has stigma about mental illness, that stigma is extreme, by all accounts, in this one.

At a park district field house in Chicago, in May of 2005, a leader of a discussion group of mostly Asian-American social workers is listing "the four S's" on a chalkboard:

- STIGMA
- SHAME
- SILENCE
- SECRECY

She is referring to her community's longtime reaction to mental illness—and meanwhile is challenging that pattern. "We have to be loud in saying suicide is a mental *illness*," she said. "There is no shame in asking for help."

This action reflected the wider purpose of the afternoon's groundbreaking gathering, "Seeking Light in the Darkness." The event, addressing both healthcare providers and family members who have survived a suicide, was the first known public rally—in Chicago and beyond—to raise awareness about the issue of suicide among Asian Americans. It was also the inaugural public meeting of the newly formed Asian American Suicide Prevention Initiative, which had started the year before in reaction to a spate of suicides—six in a very short time—in the local community.

At the opening remarks of the event, Dr. Jha, a cofounder of the group, tried to put those assembled there—social workers, patients, and

families—at ease, discussing her longtime and most fundamental approach of compassion to this very sensitive topic.

> *I want to welcome you to this circle, where you may find a*
> *space to grieve, to search, to listen and to reach out. Each one*
> *of us brings here a story, the story of our brokenness and our*
> *sorrow, but also the story of our survival and the need to get*
> *more out of life. In coming here today, each and every one us*
> *has demonstrated tremendous courage, the courage to face our*
> *innermost fears and our pain. . . . We need to break the barri-*
> *ers that surround us as a community. We don't have to close*
> *ourselves off. We can talk about our pain and grief. . . . Our*
> *intent is not to cause more pain, but to allow the wounds to*
> *breathe. . . . Asian Americans find it difficult to express feel-*
> *ings, and some of this may feel contrived. But we are compe-*
> *tent in dealing with this situation and so will carefully walk*
> *you through the afternoon.*

Following her were speeches by family members who had lost loved
ones to suicide, and then smaller discussion groups of survivors and clinicians. This event, and then a higher profile meeting on that topic at the
New York University School of Medicine that fall, were hopeful signs of a
very new movement to reach out to the Asian community about the issue
of suicide.

Clearly, the next generation of Asian Americans, assimilated into
American culture and publicly recognizing an epidemic of suicides, is expressing less tolerance for such secrecy. As well as building awareness on a
community level, they are also working to better train the next generation
of clinicians to be aware of cultural taboos and pressures.

"Research has shown that Asian Americans end up seeking mental illness services only when the disease has become completely unmanage-
able," Dr. Jha later told me. "The individual will try to tolerate it and
compensate for it, and the family has a very high level of tolerance for it."

Indeed, if Asian Americans ever do get therapy, it's only in the eleventh hour of an extreme crisis—as Iris had done. The only time that Iris had ever seen a therapist in her life for mental illness or gone on medication was in the few months before her death.

This quest also taught me about Iris' further enormous post-death symbolism to Asian Americans, which went beyond being a historian of World War II atrocities, to casting much-needed light on the issue of depression. She became a lightning rod in the Asian community to reveal the cultural tendency to keep mental illness—and other negative realities—a secret. I was continually startled at the deep entrenchment and power of this secrecy; one Asian person after another whom I interviewed for this book admitted to me long-hidden depression in their families.

This ethic of "saving face" in public, long advanced in Asian culture as an honorable trait to uphold, was even reflected in the most basic literature I was reading; Maxine Hong Kingston's classic literary memoir, *Woman Warrior*, starts with the story of her family's decades-long cover-up of her aunt's suicide in China. The first words of the book are a quote from Kingston's mother, about to recount a family story to her daughter: "You must not tell anyone." Later, Kingston's mother laments over the younger generation of Asian Americans being too brazen in revealing such secrets: "The emigrants confused the gods by diverting their curses, misleading them with crooked streets and false names. They must try to confuse their offspring as well, who, I suppose, threaten them in similar ways—always trying to get things straight, always trying to name the unspeakable." (5) She also says, "The work of preservation demands that the feelings playing about in one's guts not be turned into action. Just watch their passing, like cherry blossoms." (8)

Unfortunately, suicide is indeed rampant in the Asian community. American college students of Asian descent are twice as likely to seriously consider suicide as their white peers. Furthermore, Asian-American women between fifteen and thirty-four are twice as likely to actually commit suicide as their white counterparts. China alone accounts for a staggering 40 percent of the world's suicide deaths and more than half the world's female suicides.

Dr. Jha explained to me that suicide itself is culturally more accepted in Asia as "an option to resort to in a personal conflict." It's not as heavily linked as it is in North America to mental illness, which is at the root of the vast majority of our suicides. While mental illness is highly stigmatized in Asia, suicide itself is not, relatively speaking. She said, "And that is why there is the high tolerance, because it's rationalized as a logical response to certain situations." For example, a Chinese woman might be more likely to perceive suicide as a way to preserve her family's honor if she has shamed them, or even as a retaliatory gesture against someone in a quarrel.

Dr. Jha, fifty, a soft-spoken yet assertive woman with a lilting South Asian (Indian) accent, has felt that stigma personally in trying to raise awareness of the problem in the Asian community. When she started out in the field in the early 1990s, no one had studied the problem or organized against it. In fact, when her mentor suggested that she fill that gap with her studies, Dr. Jha was taken aback. "My mentor was a psychiatric nurse, and she literally had to very, very lovingly keep nudging me. It was like, 'Aruna you've got to do it, you've got to do it,' and my thing was no—I don't want to. . . . I remember saying to her, 'I don't want to touch it with a nine-foot pole.'"

She feared a backlash against her—which is exactly what happened. Soon others were "spreading rumors about my motives," she said. "Most often it came out as 'she has an ulterior agenda, you know.' 'She's in it for the money.' 'Yeah, but she's not really compassionate.' 'She's pointing fingers.' And 'it's intrusive and painful for families if she addresses the issue'—'that it is best to let sleeping dogs lie.' 'This is a family shame, and it cannot be supportive to the family if you talk about it.' 'Let it just be.'" She also faced the widespread fear that focusing on the suicide would detract all attention from the person's life, and end up defining who that person was.

Many whom I interviewed explained the high Asian suicide rates in North America partly by the pressure people feel to live up to the "model minority" expectation. That view of Asians as naturally successful may also discourage others from reaching out and treating them, said journalist Helen Zia, author of the history *Asian American Dreams*. For example, in universities, a mental health professional might not target groups of Asian students who get all A's.

Zia explained to me that adding to the high expectations and pressure is that a disproportionate number of Asian-American families have a history of prominent careers in the sciences. That is because of immigration policies that have favored these skills. This sets the bar high for their children. Iris' parents themselves came to the United States in the 1960s as a part of such Chinese immigration waves regarding the sciences. In addition, Asian-American women are well known to feel additional pressures to be "superwomen," to excel both in a family life with children, and having a high-powered career in the professions, such as becoming a doctor or a scientist.

Some of the pressures are common to immigrants in general. Zia commented that Asian Americans are disproportionately immigrant populations—and *every* new generation of Americans, no matter what their race, has a greater achievement ethic than those who have been here longer. In addition, Dr. Jha said, any "pioneer" faces specific pressures of being in-between worlds, of feeling at home neither in their immigrant communities nor in their new American ones. Further, minorities in general are less likely to seek mental health care and admit weakness, perhaps being more insecure about their status as Americans or too preoccupied with work.

Immigrants in general also have relatively high rates of bipolar disorder. In her book *Exuberance*, Kay Redfield Jamison explains that the characteristic high energy of these individuals, which often makes them more successful, could be a factor in their decision to emigrate in the first place: "Individuals who sought the new, who took risks that others would not, or who rebelled against repressive social systems may have been more likely to immigrate to America and, once there, to succeed." (297)

Iris' friend Iris Chang Herrera agreed about the stigma of Asian immigrants getting help for depression, especially considering the relative ease of life in the United States.

> *It's taboo. With my parents, too. When I was growing up, if I*
> *was "depressed" or not having a good day or whatever my*

mom said, "Get your act together, suck it up. You have noth-
ing to be depressed about."... They had it so hard, and now I
have it easy—and we do as Americans. You have to really
think about how fortunate we are. I've got a roof over my
head; I've got food to eat. I might not be the richest person, but
I've got all the basic necessities, and there are a lot of people in
this world that are not as fortunate. But I am very fortunate.

I talked about this more with Li Wen Huang, Iris' friend who had come to the United States from China at the age of three. I asked her about the general Chinese opinion toward mental illness, and very bluntly, she stated, "We like to hide our crazies."

She explained: "I'm thirty-six years old. I didn't find out until last year that there's a history of mental illness in my family, so it's definitely something that isn't talked about." She explained part of the family motivation in not wanting to "burden" others about negative things. In a close family, one's burden, once disclosed, becomes that of the others. "When my grandmother died, I didn't know about it for like three months afterwards because both my brother and I were in college. And they didn't want to tell us the news because they were afraid it was going to affect our school."

Because of its symbolism, Iris' death proved to be a tremendous force in the Asian community in raising such dialogue and questioning these stigmas. Although few specifics about her case have been known, she still has been a major public figure discussed in educational sessions. After her death, the country's largest provider of mental health services for Asians, Asian Community Mental Health Services in Oakland, California, reported a doubling of the numbers of Asian women seeking help for depression.

Now, by studying some of the emerging research on all these topics related to mental health, I myself was finally connecting the dots about Iris. While I couldn't ever really fully understand what happened to Iris, I was as close as possible. This biological and cultural information seemed key. I had found out how Iris' mental illness fit the profile of an evolving bipolar disorder, especially considering her gender and ethnicity. While her culture was not all-defining, it very likely had a role in how she reacted to her mental illness, in denying and hiding it.

That seemed to be what I needed to finally end the investigation. But still, despite my apparent conclusion that her demons were all "internal," a few nagging questions—or perhaps irrational fears—of mine about her last months remained. In her world of high-stakes publishing and constant challenging of people in high places, figuring out which threats to her were indeed "external" would become my necessary challenge.

CHAPTER TEN

Just Because You're Paranoid, Does That Mean They Still Aren't Out to Get You?

From early childhood "Secret Spys [sic] Iris's Notebook,"

Rule sheet (typed out):
1. *No criticizing.*
2. *No talking or laughing while spying.*
3. *When taking notes, write in code form.*
4. *If caught spying, don't panic. Just run silently away.*
5. *Be serious and don't laugh during club hours.*
6. *Don't run away while spying. Only run when caught.*
7. *Only eat at snack-time.*
8. *Be quiet while spying.*
9. *If someone starts to laugh, stare at him.*
10. *Always follow the rules from above.*

Excerpt from Iris' "My Pledge to America" submission to Illinois Veterans of Foreign Wars (VFW) essay contest, May 1985, age seventeen:

Liberty and individual human rights were not always attainable in the past history of the country and this world. They were priviledges [sic] that the founders of this nation had to fight for and even die for so that we may enjoy them today. . . . As I appreciate our special freedom, I am also determined to do all that I can to insure that we keep it forever. . . . Lastly, I pledge to preserve opportunity in America. The US is a land of opportunity because our society is based on a meritocracy and capitalism. Any person can be successful as long as he is determined to work hard. All that counts is the amount of effort, time and energy a person is willing to spend on his work. . . . As ex-president Nixon once said, "Hard work is what made America great."

In Iris' note cards for preparing autobiographical speech, 1998:

Dilemma of being writer:
Try to remain sensitive and tough.

Iris quoted in June 2003 interview in the Web magazine *Identity Theory*:

It's important for me to write about issues that have universal significance. One of them that has resonated with me all my life has been the theme of injustice. Some people as they write, they might dwell on love, other people on money or the acquisition of great riches, but for some reason I seem to be bothered whenever I see acts of injustice and assaults on people's civil liberties.

"Are you taking your meds?"

That is the question that a panel of government officials starkly poses to an agitated Ben Marco, played by Denzel Washington, in the 2004 remake of *The Manchurian Candidate*. At that point, Ben, a Gulf War veteran who has rightly suspected that he was being monitored by the government, heroically rebels.

He states: "I have had over a dozen years of experts telling me that I have post-traumatic stress disorder, that I have Gulf War Syndrome, and every mood disorder that you can name. In those twelve years, I've been a good soldier, and I've denied what every nerve ending in my body has been telling me is more real than not."

Through the rest of the movie, as he becomes increasingly disheveled and wild-eyed, he races against time to expose a real secret plot of the government to brainwash him and recruit him as an assassin.

Throughout his perilous mission, even his best friends advise him of his folly, blaming his actual perceptiveness on mental illness. They chide that he is "delusional," has "full-blown schizophrenia," and refer to his "slim hold on sanity" and "bipolar war." They dismiss his online conspiracy sources, saying "the Internet is the sacred sanctuary of idiots and nutters."

At the end, we clearly see that he is, indeed, the sanest one in the film, a real truth teller, trusting what he calls "the truth deep inside us."

The so-called "crazy" person as brave crusader is also the theme of *National Treasure*, starring Nicholas Cage as the misunderstood hero/challenger of the U.S. government. This film came out weeks after *The Manchurian Candidate*. According to Brett, both fed into Iris' fears.

Here, Cage's character breaks into Iris' beloved National Archives in Washington, D.C., to brazenly steal the ultimate primary source of our country, the Declaration of Independence, for a treasure map it allegedly contains. Despite a constant barrage of dismissive accusations from others that he is mentally ill, Cage does not waver: "If there is something wrong, those with the ability to take action have the responsibility to take action," he states. In contrast to the doomed Ben Marco, his ending is glorious; the last shot is of him walking away with his new wife, a beautiful National Archives administrator, to their mansion built on his cut of the recovered loot.

For both heroes, the sources of their problems were external, and not internal, indeed. But in real life, such distinctions aren't always as easy to make.

While at the Hoover Archives at Stanford University in February of 2006, I didn't expect to make any major discoveries about Iris' inner world; her family had sealed off her personal writings contained there from the last years of her life, along with her Bataan research; those boxes wouldn't be available to the public (me) until 2015. I also knew that none of the 261 open boxes contained any of the journals that Iris likely had kept through her life.

Still, I was also overwhelmed at the sheer volume of the collection. Even in death, Iris was still testing my stamina. Apparently, she did not feel that the undocumented life was worth living.

But, from my first moments there, I saw that the visit would be useful to help me confirm my own observations so far—into how deep-rooted her fears were, and how intense her later work-related pressures became. I even got a glimpse into her thinking in her last week. Upon arrival, I asked the archivist in charge of her papers if Iris had contacted him soon before her death, as in the case of the University of Illinois archives, and as I had just learned a few months earlier, her second collection at UC Santa Barbara. Indeed, she had called archivists in both of these places in the weeks before her death. She was alerting them that she was about to FedEx them CDs containing hundreds of personal photos from her life to include in her collections. This was yet another indication of how premeditated her death was.

It turned out that Iris hadn't sent him photos. But, yes, she had left an urgent voice-mail message for the archivist the week before her suicide. He had managed to reach her that Friday, November 5. At that point, "she couldn't get off the phone fast enough," he told me. Iris sounded severely depressed and uncharacteristically abrupt, just holding on long enough to ask him which Bataan interviews of hers he already had, and which he still needed to complete the collection. She had explained that she was in the process of organizing them. That was the last he would ever hear from her.

But, as I soon discovered, her personal observations and thoughts weren't limited to her sealed-off papers, or the journals still in her family's possession. Reflecting the fact that her personal life and her work were inseparable, she had often jotted down personal recollections in notebooks and on note cards used for her research, which became ad hoc journals. I deciphered what I could of that scrawled writing on often undated materials. This was one of many signs that these papers at Stanford were different, less clearly "edited" and processed by her than the other two collections. In contrast, her smaller collections of papers at Illinois and UC Santa Barbara were strictly limited to her professional life, not her personal one. The most "polished" collection was the UC Santa Barbara one of about seventy boxes, in which she had perfectly stacked and aligned documents, without so much as an ink or coffee stain—with completely legible handwriting throughout, no repeated pages, and files all scrupulously dated and numbered.

This more sprawling collection at Stanford was more "flawed," and, well, human. She had only personally vetted about thirty of the boxes, those regarding research for *The Chinese in America*, which she had personally transferred herself in the summer of 2004. Brett had shipped the rest sometime after her death, apparently straight from their San Jose garage. After my first request of ten boxes arrived on a cart, I opened one box, reached in, and extracted, with some guilt for my continuing personal intrusion, a long black hair. It was Iris'.

I also found a large box of note cards she had used to construct her proposal on the biological clock, many of which seemed like diary entries of hers. On some cards, she recorded her early sense of anxiety about such biological limits, such as in high school feeling "intensely jealous of two men who have prof. degrees and family" who had no such "slim window" on what they could professionally achieve. ". . . I had only 8 years to prove myself [before giving birth]," she wrote.

In one section of cards in another box on the topic of feminism, I saw several with my own name on them. She had taken notes on my suggestions for books to read regarding feminist thinkers' mixed views of reproductive engineering. Over and over again that week, I saw such references to myself in her notes, such as the many reminders to herself she had jotted down in the margins of pages of reporter's notebooks to call me about specific publishing questions she knew I had considered. "Call Paula re: adaptation of book," was one. In a box of hundreds of business cards she had collected from people in film and the media, I came across mine, with my current home address at the time. This experience seemed surreal, of traveling across the country to a distant university archive, where I found traces of my own life.

This collection of her papers at Stanford also stood out from the other two in revealing her earliest creative life. Here I found some of her childhood fiction stories and art projects, including a spy manual she had made out of construction paper. Attached to it with a string was a tiny booklet written in a secret code, composed of symbols like spirals, swan necks and asterisks. Nearby were reams of correspondence with friends from high school and college, including one pile from a Chinese-American boy she had met through Mensa as a teen. He started off writing on letterhead from his prep school and then continued the following year's letters on letterhead from Harvard. They talked about the unromantic topics of SAT scores and PASCAL and BASIC computer programming languages. Later, the tone got more personal, with him asking her "how long she had been an atheist" and tentatively signing his letters with the word "love." (He commented after that in parenthesis that he was taking a chance in doing so.) Indicating her early ambition was a long and meticulously detailed list from high school of "things to do this summer," which included studying karate, computers, Chinese, calculus, and math "every day," and writing poetry.

I turned to folders from college, including an upbeat sorority memento book with a kitten on the cover, which she labeled in cursive as "Precious Moments Last Forever." Also included were things more somber in tone, specifically stories and poems of hers from the college literary magazine she founded and edited, "Open Wide." One of the two published issues included the poem "End of the Mirror Tunnel," about the two selves that she sees in the mirror. One viewed endless possibilities and another, who got the last stanza of the poem, was destructive: She was "waiting for me/ and smiled/ Light was glinting off/ Her long, sharp/ Knife."

In a large box of note cards marked "personal thoughts," probably from about 1997, she included cards with personal strategies for her own success. The boxes included pages of observations from many popular self-help books, such as Harriet Rubin's 1997 *Machiavelli for Women*, "a book that celebrates a woman's unique gifts: passion and intuition, sensitivity and cunning." One line of her notes that she circled: "Think big." Iris also had taken detailed notes from the works of the famed Chinese early-twentieth-century-revolutionary/philosopher Sun Yat-sen, who talked about "speed as a strategy," she noted. I thought back to the quickness of her suicide, which did indeed serve to foil attempts against it. Another box was filled just with audio tapes and notes from "Educational and Motivational Courses," public speaking primers among them.

Indeed, she *was* strategic; that step-by-step planning was not something I had just imagined she was doing. While some of these self-help books and courses seemed embarrassingly simplistic to me (despite my own use of embarrassingly simplistic alternative medicine books to get by), she was able to extract apparently useful tactics from them.

Iris also recorded many personal reflections among note cards she had used to plan a speech about her life that she gave at her high school in June of 1998. She was there to collect a major award and to give career advice to the students. As I read through the cards, I found them to be more and more intimate about her personal state, revealing patterns in thinking that would become more extreme in her later years. (I assumed that most of them never made it into her speech; newspaper stories about it talked about only her career advice, nothing so personal.) She talked about being "a loner at heart": "It is far more terrifying for me to be stuck in an office, working with the same group of people than speaking in front of hundreds of people in a lecture." She also wrote: "Not a day goes by that I don't dream of being more rich and more famous." One detailed the ways she had "changed as the years went by," including being "less likely to divulge personal problems to friends." Again, I had not imagined that.

Revealing another obsession, the subject of Hollywood—and the possible film adaptation of her Nanking book—was everywhere. She included course notes from screenwriting classes. Many notebooks detailed her meetings with top stars and executives from 2000. Some observations: "It's way too shallow (kissing-kissing, false friendly)."

Indeed, these personal papers also revealed a fact of life for the writer, even for the most ultimately successful: rejection. Included in her papers from college were piles of rejection letters for internships, such as from the *Chicago Tribune* for the summer of 1988, a year before she ended up working there. Files with her later freelance work contained some rejected articles.

And then, in box 265, there it was. I found the file, which I had only guessed had existed. It was simply labeled "Excerpt published in *Newsweek*, 1997 December 1."

I skimmed through the dozens of pages, and as I had hoped, this folder was the best documentation I could ever expect to find of "the *Newsweek* incident." This is how she referred to what she felt was an attempted quash by Japanese advertisers of a much heralded excerpt of *The Rape of Nanking* in *Newsweek* in November of 1997, just as the book was being released. Now I had the tools to finally figure out, after about a decade of speculation and rumor, what had really happened here. This was a part of a bigger ongoing quest to figure out which of her fears were imagined, and which were based in reality. Just because she was paranoid later in life, that didn't necessarily mean that some people in high places weren't out to get her.

The *Newsweek* incident was a defining and extremely upsetting episode in Iris' career. For years, she had talked about it to me and most of her friends as symbolic in her life. She had never exposed it in the wider press, as she had seriously considered doing. Whether it was true or not, it could have been an explosive story, especially in the Chinese-American community, which might have rallied against *Newsweek* at that time. She said the Chinese reaction would have been tantamount to a Jewish reaction to a long-overdue exposé on the Holocaust being stopped because of protests from Mercedes-Benz. When Monica Eng was working on her February 2005 story on Iris for the *Chicago Tribune Magazine*, we regularly talked about this incident's significance in Iris' life—as reflecting Iris' fears about Japanese influence against her. It had spooked Iris so much that she was even still talking about it as late as spring 2003, when she first met Monica. But, in the end, Monica was never able to find the specific and sufficient documentation that her editor required for her to write about it. Finally, she had to cut out a long section on this conflict from her piece. But, as she observed, and as this file confirmed, many of Iris' fears of Japanese influence at *Newsweek* were based on compelling circumstances that would have raised an eyebrow with any writer addressing such a controversial topic and challenging powerful corporate interests.

To others who heard about this incident later, after Iris' death, it was also symbolic: of Iris' paranoia. Monica's editor at the *Chicago Tribune* had stipulated that she could only talk about the incident if she framed it as evidence of Iris' losing touch with reality. After all, Monica's knowledge of the incident was vague, and a *Newsweek* spokesperson denied it ever happened. When *Newsweek* was originally presented with Iris' allegations that the excerpt was delayed because of Japanese ad issues, *Newsweek*'s then-communications director Ken Weine asked for time to respond and after a few days came back with a "No Comment." When I called a *Newsweek* editor named in the file myself, he advised me at the end of the interview: "I do think that you can't underplay the mental illness part of it. Because that's key to explain it all, too."

This file did help me to understand this incident better, seeing Iris' fears as based in reality: of the Japanese not wanting to advertise in the same issue as her excerpt. By all appearances, there is a chance that *Newsweek* did intentionally postpone her excerpt, so as not to lose a dozen profitable Japanese corporate ads in that issue.

But Iris likely overstated the Japanese corporations' impact on and malevolence toward her personally. I interviewed two *Newsweek* editors involved with the controversy, who pointed out that *Newsweek's* timely printing of the article, two weeks after its initial last-minute delay, was an ultimately positive sign. They said that showed the Japanese advertisers had not censored the story, even if they had, in the worst case scenario, attempted it. And, with many facts still unclear, I do not have solid proof of such an effort, or that *Newsweek* management had decided to delay her article so as not to jeopardize that original issue's large number of profitable Japanese ads. It is most likely that the Japanese advertisers exercised their right to not appear in the same issue as the excerpt, but that doesn't mean that they were responsible for any manipulation of editorial content.

But according to what Iris wrote in the folder detailing the incident, she seemed to have a reason, at least at first, to get so upset. On the surface, it had seemed like an open and shut case, as a clear case of wrongdoing, which had become "hot" enough to gain the attention of the highest levels of both *Newsweek* and Iris' publisher Basic Books.

At the urging of her editor and new agent, Susan Rabiner, Iris had kept a log of what happened and named everyone she spoke with at the time. She also kept copies of all e-mails exchanged on the matter. One of her logs states how it started: "Message from Tom Maslin [*sic*] on voice mail, November 7, 7:29 p.m.—'Iris, it's Tom Maslin at *Newsweek*. I'm sorry to tell you that we've had to hold the excerpt because the magazine has (he pauses for a long time) shrunk by four pages, which is what we had for it.'" She adds: "Tom's voice seems strained and uncomfortable. Brett and I agree that it doesn't make sense. Why would four missing pages make a difference? How would it throw off the layout? Brett said the Japanese are probably behind it because Maslin's message sounds like a flimsy excuse."

The next day, three other editors told her that about four ads had been pulled the night her story was put on hold. Then she called an old friend there, then-"Periscope" section senior editor George Hackett, who was not involved with the story, "and asked him why my story was held. He said he wasn't at *Newsweek* last night but heard that *Newsweek* had lost four to five ads last night. Inadvertently told me that Toyota pulled their ads. Promised to make some phone calls to find out details." But then he called Iris back right away and said "not to worry, that the advertisements had nothing to do with the excerpt. Wouldn't tell me who the advertisers were when I asked him."

On November 11, as Iris noted, *Newsweek* seemed to change its story, saying officially that "the Seymour Hersh book on JFK is what bumped everything back," referring to an excerpt of another book, *The Dark Side of Camelot,* which did run on November 17. In an e-mail to Susan that day, Iris asked her to ask *Newsweek* why "she was told by FOUR different *Newsweek* staffers over the weekend that four to five major ads were jerked out of the magazine late Friday night and THAT was the reason for holding the excerpt? And why did one *Newsweek* staffer tell Iris that he heard that Toyota pulled their ads? And why did Tom Maslin inform Iris late Friday night by voice mail that the magazine SHRUNK, not EXPANDED, in size?"

The situation heated up fast. On November 12, Susan Rabiner e-mailed Iris that Jack McKeown, then the CEO of Iris' publisher, called Maynard Parker, "the highest person at *Newsweek.*" Rabiner e-mailed Iris that *Newsweek* and her publisher "are now terrified that you will say anything public about *Newsweek* suggesting that they caved into pressure. The results would be disastrous for all [of them]."

Susan ended the e-mail asking Iris to remain silent and expect the excerpt to work out. According to what Parker had promised, the excerpt would run soon. But Iris concluded that this meeting between Parker and McKeown was an incriminating "showdown," as she had told her friends. In an e-mail back to Susan, Iris agreed to remain silent, expecting things to work out, but added that she didn't understand why *Newsweek* and her publisher:

are terrified about the possibility that I may go public with the story. If there wasn't any truth at all behind it, then what would there be to fear? If the pulled ads weren't Japanese, Newsweek *could have easily told us which corporations DID pull the ads and nipped the matter right in the bud. They would have told us—let that crackpot Iris Chang make the accusation, we have PROOF that it was Chrysler or Ford (or whoever) who pulled the ads and what's more, we can get spokesmen from Chrysler or Ford on the phone with the press to back us. Believe me, this matter would NOT have gone to Jack McKeown and Maynard Parker.*

Then, *Newsweek* did run the excerpt, in an unusually low-key way, as she noted to her friends, without a reference to it on its cover, in its December 1, 1997, issue.

An easily traceable paper trail—of advertising placements that Iris pointed out—does suggest that Iris' book was a factor to Japanese advertisers, something for them to avoid. Iris' expose on the Rape of Nanking was definitely delayed by two weeks, to an issue on December 1, 1997, virtually without Japanese ads (just one from an American-managed Japanese copier company, Ricoh USA). It had been originally slated to run in the November 17, 1997, issue of *Newsweek*, right at the book's time of official release. (Both a printed announcement in the *New York Times* for a companion *Newsweek* radio show on the topic and an article on the book in the November 1997 Johns Hopkins alumni magazine had announced that as the original excerpt date.)

When that November 17 issue ran, without Iris' article, it had eleven ads from Japanese companies—about twice as many as usual. (The surrounding issues contain a more even number: with seven in the November 24 issue, four in the December 8 issue, and eight in the December 15 issue.) This high number suggests that it was an unusually profitable issue for *Newsweek* regarding these advertisers—providing incentive for a delay of Iris' article.

Iris' folder on the *Newsweek* incident also revealed at least the appearance to Iris of other possible Japanese-influenced censorship of the story. It included Iris' records of some last-minute editing of the story. Her *Newsweek* editor had tried to take out some sentences on the bloodiest acts of the massacres, such as "hanging people by their tongues." Iris described the surprised reaction of the editorial assistant, Jennifer. "Jennifer baffled by that—thought it was important but her boss, some woman editor, thought it was too much." That was the night that Iris got the call from Tom Masland that her excerpt was being cut from the issue.

These files also underscore some of the larger frightening forces, likely backlash from the right-wing Japanese, fanning the flames of Iris' fears at that time. In one of her first entries in her log, Iris writes on November 9 that she received "an obscene phone call last night. 2 am they asked for Shau jin [*sic*], said it was from Brett, and it was all nonsense on the phone." This was an intimidating phone call from someone who clearly knew these personal details, of her father's name and husband's name.

Adding to Iris' anxiety were concerns from others. In her first log of *Newsweek*'s delay of her article on November 8, she wrote about Susan Rabiner's response: "Now you know how the real world works, she said. She's seen books cancelled because they threatened important interests." In that entry, Iris continued that "Mom wondered if I should keep my mouth shut, not afraid of sabotaging my career with *Newsweek* but afraid that 'an evil force' (Japanese) will hurt me if I tell the world about the *Newsweek* situation, but Dad and I insisted that silence is not going to protect me—I'll be safer if I tell others. Mom said it is a good thing my book is out—afraid that Japanese would buy HC [HarperCollins] and cancel it." In this first, most emotional log entry, she also writes that [her parents] speculate that "our phones are being bugged."

To explore these points, and separate fact from speculation in this case once and for all, I needed to get the side of the story of the numerous *Newsweek* people whom Iris named in her folder as being involved.

Unfortunately, the then–senior writer Tom Masland (whom Iris calls "Maslin"), who had told Iris about the delay with a tone of discomfort, had since been tragically killed in a traffic accident in October of 2005, five months before I found this folder. I wasn't able to talk with the editorial assistant Jennifer, no longer at *Newsweek*, who did not return my e-mails.

But, I did reach Senior Editor George Hackett, the editor friend whom Iris reported as first telling her that Toyota had pulled out of her issue. It turns out that he was a longtime friend of Iris', dating back from the time of her college internship there in 1988. He basically told me what he had told Iris in his follow-up call to her from November 8, 1997, as she records, that the ads were not a factor in delaying her excerpt. "Articles in *Newsweek* might influence advertisers, but it's not the other way around. And I think that's what happened in this case."

Hackett pointed out that the only possibility of advertising shifts related to her article would have been if Japanese advertisers had wanted to avoid placement in the specific issue of her excerpt. But that would not have influenced editorial content, only advertising content. And this is all a matter of policy. He said that the magazine might inform advertisers in advance of editorial content that might be noncomplementary to their ads. He gave as an example their coverage of a plane crash, "and we have an airline ad in the magazine that week. We'll inform the airline that we're doing an article on this plane crash, and they would prefer not to have their 'come fly with us ad' near the article."

I asked him about the specific comment he had allegedly first made to Iris about Toyota pulling out, which got her thinking along the lines of a conspiracy. "I think it would be unusual for me to know that Toyota had pulled an ad. I don't think I would have had that knowledge," he said. He explained that he could have offhandedly repeated to Iris "hallway gossip" about that advertiser, a "rumor that I felt that could have lessened the blow" personally to Iris of her article being cut, that it wasn't the fault of the article itself.

He said: "There certainly was corridor talk. Let me put it this way, everyone knew that this was a controversial book that was unpopular among the Japanese, right? And that was mentioned in every review about it and even some news stories. . . . I think that was reasonable that was something somebody might have heard or might have supposed." He added that the Hersh excerpt on JFK could have been a factor, that they would NOT have run two book excerpts in one issue. (The Hersh "excerpt" was actually a long article about the book; it did, as I found, have a tie-in to a television event that month.)

As far as last-minute cutting choices, Hackett said that book excerpts are often a logical move because they are not as timely as other content, such as breaking national news. In cases when they lose space, "they're not going to take out the first four pages of the national affairs section," he said. The book excerpts also do represent a specific block of copy that is easier to cut than other articles. He added that even "in the worst case scenario," if Japanese advertisers had dropped out of the issue of Iris' excerpt, *Newsweek*'s response would have been to run the article then. With the advertisers already gone, *Newsweek* wouldn't have had any reason to hold the story. He said he also would not have told Iris about the identity of any advertisers who might have pulled out because of magazine "policy," not due to a cover-up to protect them. In going over the ads myself, I found that Toyota was an advertiser in the November 17 issue, not having pulled out, after all.

I also talked to Iris' actual editor for that excerpt, Deidre Depke, who also denied that the Japanese advertisers were an influence in the delay— or in her editing suggestions. "I don't remember what the specifics of that issue were, but we did run the excerpt. So I think that negates the argument. If we had really been worried about what Toyota and other Japanese advertisers were, their feelings were, we just never would have run it. We didn't have to run it. I don't know—that seems a little conspiracy minded."

Depke also said that delays of book excerpts are common, even at the very last minute. "The reason why some things get delayed is basically because we're putting together a weekly magazine, and things happen, and news pushes out things that are more set features. In fact, when we take an excerpt, we generally excerpt it for a period of time. In other words, we usually give ourselves something like six weeks so that we can kind of do it whenever the time is, you know, when it works out, basically when we have the space."

She agreed that she may have suggested cutting out some of the goriest parts of the article, as Iris' copy of her editing shows, but ultimately let most of them run. "It was probably a combination of sensitivity about the reader, because we are fairly mainstream and have to be sensitive about what you're putting out there. But I'm glad to hear that I kept it [the most gory parts] in. I listened to her argument and considered it, which is what you hope to be as an editor."

While she denied wrongdoing, Depke agreed that "it's possible that they [Japanese advertisers] did not want to run [in the same issue] with the excerpt. I guess that's a possibility. A lot of times advertisers, they have certain provisions in their agreements with us, so that airlines get pulled out of issues where we're talking about crashes and that kind of thing. And I think that Japanese advertisers are not anxious to be in WWII-related content, no matter what you're writing about. Even if you're writing about Germany, they are not interested."

What about Tom Masland sounding "uncomfortable and strained" while informing Iris of the delay, as Iris had written? Hackett said, "He was a very nice guy, and no one likes to call somebody that this exciting thing, your book was just about to be [run], and is no longer. It's not a call you like making." Depke added: "I think it is important to remember the context of that time period, too. That was pre-9/11. I was foreign editor then for a few years, and it was an extremely frustrating period to be covering foreign news in the American media. There just wasn't any interest in it. And Tom's frustration was that they had rolled up our section yet again, for probably the fifteenth week in a row, and I think we both at that point were extremely frustrated by that. And the news climate since then, of course, has changed dramatically, and that's no longer the case. The foreign editor here has tons of space in the magazine.

"But I do remember the excerpt very well, and I remember being proud of it and proud that *Newsweek* had run it. "

Once again, I had entered Iris' inner world and felt some of her same fears. Once again, in the end, I had wondered if I was getting paranoid myself in even asking such questions.

But the fact checking in the *Newsweek* case had helped me, in the end, to emerge with greater clarity about what had happened. I knew I had to do the same thing in examining Iris' greatest fears at the end of her life, which were still the topic of widespread online rumors. At some points of my research, after learning just how actively involved she had been in the controversial POW reparations issue, I wondered if she had more in common with *The Manchurian Candidate*'s Ben Marco than I had assumed.

After all, as the current headlines told me on a daily basis, these were strange times. As she had expressed over and over again in her book tour for her third book, Iris had been deeply concerned about an erosion of civil liberties post-9/11. And she had a point. She was not the only cultural critic to compare what was happening now to other periods of crisis and paranoia, mainly the McCarthy years of Communist witch hunts in the 1950s.

The similarities between then and now seemed especially striking to me during the week I spent in early December 2005 at the California Ethnic and Multicultural Archives at the Davidson Library of UC Santa Barbara. I was there to see Iris' papers, related to research on her first book, which thoroughly investigated the effect of the Cold War of the 1950s on stifling scientists. This especially applied to foreigners like her subject, Dr. Tsien Hsue-Shen.

The scary tenor of those times came alive to me as I looked over some of the hundreds of copies of FBI documents, in the form of letters and reports, which Iris had uncovered from the time. They looked like stereotypical fifties FBI documents, with the words "SECRET" and "CONFIDENTIAL" stamped repeatedly all over their margins and many typewritten lines blocked out in black ink. Most of these documents had been declassified in the 1980s, but some pages were still missing, indicated by page-long "access restricted" forms. These documents went to the highest levels of FBI command, with most addressed to its notorious director of the time, J. Edgar Hoover.

A typically creepy file from that time was one on ongoing covert microphone surveillance of Frank Friedman Oppenheimer, who was in that same suspected "communist cell" of scientists as Tsien. With his famous brother J. Robert as director, both Oppenheimer brothers had worked on the Manhattan Project during World War II to develop the first atomic bomb. Much of Frank's file is blacked out, including entire pages at a time. The file reveals that not much solid proof was needed in being suspected as a Communist; just idle hearsay of being a liberal was enough. One page describes testimony from another scientist, interviewed in 1943, who stated that he didn't think Frank Oppenheimer was a Communist, but that "the subject [Oppenheimer] was highly in favor of extreme liberal activities of the New Deal, interested in social reforms, and always took a favorable stand on racial minorities. The subject's wife was a liberal in her opinions as was the subject." These investigations took a toll on the career of Frank Oppenheimer, as well as many other scientists Iris profiles in *Thread of the Silkworm*.

After a week spent going through these dozens of boxes in Santa Barbara, I needed a rest, but my efforts to do so all backfired. One night, I sat down at a café with a newspaper and was alerted by that day's front-page story: "Patriot Act Deal Reached in Congress." That night I saw the movie *Good Night, and Good Luck*, about the persecution of heroic newsman Edward R. Murrow by the opportunistic and ruthless Senator Joseph McCarthy. The film was in stark black and white, just like all those FBI documents which I had reviewed that week. Needless to say, that film, in no subtle way, also made the connection between those particular times and ours.

After that trip, I was again reminded in my daily life about the intensity of past U.S. government irrational spying behavior. I couldn't even watch

TV without such a history lesson. A special on cable and another on PBS reported how the FBI had tried to discredit such important figures as Martin Luther King Jr. and John Lennon. One of the FBI's biggest files ever, totaling three thousand pages, was on liberal Eleanor Roosevelt.

Also highlighting questions about Iris and the U.S. government, I was finally getting around to looking at the transcripts of Monica's interviews for her *Chicago Tribune* profile of Iris that she had given me to use as background information for this book. She had intensely focused on Iris' work on behalf of American POWs in Japan and interviewed many activists involved in that movement. Some activists expressed some seemingly reasonable fears about Iris' death that seemed worth further checking out. That had to do with Iris' long-term involvement in championing the rights of former Bataan POWs to sue for compensation from Japanese corporations that had enslaved them during the war. In the two years before her death, the National Archives was reported to have finally declassified some supposedly sensational U.S. government documents from that period, which Iris had allegedly seen. One activist veteran that Monica interviewed speculated to Monica that Iris had found a "smoking gun" there of the Allied negotiator John Foster Dulles "selling out" the veterans to placate Japan, a needed ally in the Cold War. Another activist pointed out that she and Iris had e-mailed a lot about these apparently suppressed documents and that Iris was "angry" about some that seemed to be present one day in the National Archives for researchers, but then "missing" the next.

This issue of the enslaved GIs in Japan had long been controversial, with strong passions flaring on both sides. The veterans felt betrayed by their government, and the State Department feared endangering relations with its ally Japan. Not to mention, people in the State Department resented being cast in the role as "bad guys" fighting in court against our greatest national heroes.

And, apparently, Iris had thrust herself right at the center of that battle. In 2001 and 2002, the issue came to a head as the Bataan POWs took the State Department to court for the right to sue Japanese corporations, and lost. At the same time, a bill in Congress enabling them to privately sue Japanese corporations lost steam. With the support of the Bush Administration, the State Department had successfully argued that the U.S. was obligated to instead honor the 1951 peace treaty with Japan, which had, on its face, prohibited such actions from private citizens against Japanese companies. In turn, the activists were still arguing that the treaty had a major loophole, in Article 26, which seemed to allow such suits. In the meantime, in related news, other authors—such as Sheldon H. Harris in *Factories of Death*—had been waging startling allegations against the U.S. government regarding biological warfare experiments. They wrote that the U.S. government had helped to cover up Japanese chemical experiments in World War II, some allegedly targeted to American POWs. Further inflaming Iris, such books commonly pointed out preferential U.S. government treatment for formerly enslaved American POWs of German corporations, who seemed to have been much more significantly compensated with a highly publicized recent collective settlement of five billion dollars.

I called Iris' activist friend Linda Goetz Holmes, the author of *Unjust Enrichment*, another book critical of the U.S. government for letting the Japanese off the hook, based on documents from that time that she had unearthed in the National Archives. Holmes described Iris' attention in her final years as shifting from anger toward the Japanese government to that for the U.S. "As time went on with the POW issue . . . Iris became more and more outraged." Holmes described Iris as "passionate and so involved with what happened to other people. . . . She became angry and frustrated at how our government treated these men." Holmes recalled Iris being "furious" at the attitude of the U.S. government at a major conference in San Francisco in 2001 celebrating the fiftieth anniversary of the treaty with Japan, and the continued alliance between our two countries. In fact, she and Holmes had participated actively in a controversial counter-conference there.

Reflecting her intense and high-profile focus on Bataan vets, Iris published an op-ed piece on December 24, 2001, in the *New York Times*, headlined "Betrayed by the White House," that harshly criticized the Bush Administration's efforts to block the lawsuits. It concluded: "Our leaders must not be permitted to sell out the men who gave so much for our freedom. . . . If we are to have another 'greatest generation' we must duly honor the rights of the first one." And of course, later on, Iris was planning a high-profile book on the Bataan veterans that likely would have greatly challenged the government's refusal to allow American POW lawsuits against Japanese companies.

Now, I realized just how openly critical Iris already had been of the U.S. government in all three of her books, which all concluded on that note. Most notably, *The Rape of Nanking* ends with Iris' criticism of the U.S. government for, in contrast to their treatment of the Germans, letting the Japanese escape justice with their 1951 treaty, and allegedly returning records of Japanese atrocities to the Japanese without copying them first. Also compared to the Germans, she writes "the Japanese have paid next to nothing for their war crimes." (222)

Iris ends *The Chinese in America* with a chapter, "An Uncertain Future," pointing to U.S. fear of China's military might. That was alarming to her because past discrimination against Chinese Americans has always coincided with the U.S. government's fear of China itself, such as with the notorious Chinese Exclusion Act of 1882. In her tours for that book in 2003 and 2004, a common theme she discussed were eroding civil liberties—and parallels between current unfair persecution of Muslim Americans, and that of Asian Americans in the past. She also mentioned the cases of exonerated Taiwanese Los Alamos scientist Wen Ho Lee and of the recent accusation of espionage against Captain James Yee, an Asian-American Muslim and former chaplain for at the Guantanamo Bay federal detention camp.

Iris repeatedly pointed out how the government did not have to be rational in order to justify such witch hunts. Referring to the apparent railroading of Tsien in *Thread of the Silkworm*, Iris told documentary maker Christine Choy in 2003: "It tells you what happens when you get caught up in the government machinery; it doesn't have to make sense. In fact, you can get chewed up in this arbitrary reflex of power.

"What was also terribly ironic about the whole thing was that the original reason why the government had put him under house arrest was to protect national security. But in the end the decision to deport Tsien caused the U.S. to lose one of the most brilliant missile scientists in this country, and it also caused the PRC to gain one."

It was clear that Iris had been publicly outspoken and heavily involved with the Bataan POW activists, who were more organized, controversial and impassioned than I had ever imagined. Now that bizarre e-mail from the State Department lawyer from December of 2004 about that topic finally made sense. She had been defensive about Iris' (and my) apparent glorification of their cause, and wanted to make sure I had considered the other, less sensational side.

My remaining question was whether Iris indeed reasonably had anything to fear from the government for these specific agitations. Had she, as she had told me on the phone during our last conversation, uncovered anything special in her research that "people in high places" wouldn't like?

Of course, I knew that Iris' career-long modus operandi was researching in archives, particularly at the National Archives (officially the National Archives and Records Administration, NARA) based in D.C., one of her favorite places in the world to spend time. And I had heard in researching the POW issue that the NARA in the past several years had agreed to open up long-classified documents regarding Japanese war crimes. I wondered if Iris, at the forefront of that search, had indeed found any "smoking gun" there. Like the complicated accusations against *Newsweek*, the alleged conspiracy regarding the U.S. stifling the records of the POWs had weighed on my mind for months. And I knew I had to take direct steps to examine it, to clear up any remaining doubts. I planned a stop at the National Archives during my already-scheduled personal trip to the D.C. area in the coming weeks.

Specifically, I hoped to visit Iris' old friend there, the legendary intelligence archivist John Taylor, who had guided most of her research efforts in the past on the U.S. government. If anyone would have known what she was researching, he would. He had advised her on all three of her books, including helping her track down John Rabe's diary in Germany and finding Japanese war crimes trial testimony. In a profile of Taylor in the *Baltimore Sun* on October 19, 2003, Iris voiced her appreciation of him: "Every time I went back to the archives to see him, I felt I was visiting a mentor. He was so learned. He'd go out of his way to suggest books to read and papers to look at." In fact, he was renowned for guiding countless authors through the years, including many of those represented in the hundreds of books of the "John E. Taylor Collection on espionage and intelligence" at the National Archives.

But a question remained if Taylor, who had started work at the archives way back in 1945, was still there—and if he was still alive. A Google search revealed a recent Congressional tribute to him with wishes that he have "an enjoyable and fulfilling retirement." There was no e-mail address for him anywhere. But after I left a phone message with another archivist, I got a call—with a very old Southern-accented voice on the other end. It was Mr. Taylor. He told me he had been shocked to hear about Iris' death, and that he did have some interesting observations about her last months that he'd tell me during my visit the following week.

The meeting that followed with the tweed-jacketed Taylor was far from cloak and dagger. I went to the front desk of the massive glass-covered NARA building in College Park, Maryland, where most of the archives' eight billion pages of documents are stored. (The more famous building is the original one in D.C., the one that Nicholas Cage broke into in *National Treasure*.) The guard called Taylor and reported that he was on his way down from the second floor. I waited. I waited for a long time.

After about twenty minutes, I thought of calling upstairs again to make sure there hadn't been a mistake. Then, across the lobby, I saw a hunched and jowled man, in seeming slow motion, get off an elevator and begin to inch his way to me, step by step. I went to meet him and saw he looked much older than his eighty-four years. He was further hobbled by a broken pinky finger that resulted in his entire left hand being disabled in a cast.

Since it was lunchtime and he had already made the trek downstairs, Taylor and I agreed to have lunch in the cafeteria. Many there seemed to know him, even the cashier who reached down to unscrew the lid of his juice bottle on his tray after checking him out. He told me a bit about his storied sixty-year career at the archives. During World War II, he had been rejected by the army after he had told them he was blind in one eye. When he applied for a job with the federal government, he did not make that mistake of full disclosure again. Soon after, he was hired in the archives. After all, he had always gotten along despite a long record of poor health; on his father's small plantation in Arkansas, he had kept the whole family up at night with his wheezing from asthma.

Later he led me, very slowly, up to his office. I noted that he opened door-locking mechanisms with the light-sensitive badge around his neck, and not his finger prints, as I had just seen was the case for the National Archive officials portrayed in *National Treasure*. He also clearly did not resemble the main archivist of that movie, a foxy blonde PhD, who had joined hero Nicholas Cage on his subversive treasure-hunting quest. Again, needless to say, that movie was at great odds with what I was finding in reality.

Our interview that followed, while interesting in its details about their long friendship, did not produce any revelations about her research on the U.S. government. He told me that when he met Iris in 1991, when she was seeking material on Tsien, they clicked right away. I asked him why that was. "She was very attractive," he said.

In fact, as with many other authors (even the unattractive ones), he had given Iris his home number, and she had often called him there on nights and weekends. I asked Taylor if this was common practice of his. "Sure. This job I like; it is a wonderful job. I don't mind. I get a lot of calls at home." On the phone, she often asked him about his health and if there were any new files there he thought she'd be interested in.

Apparently, as Taylor recalled, Iris hadn't been at the National Archives to look at documents in years, not since her research in about 2000 for *The Chinese in America*. But I was still curious about the reportedly newly declassified and long-censored documents about Japanese war crimes, if she had any special access to them through other channels. Taylor introduced me to the main expert in charge of this collection, Dr. Gregory Bradsher, who also had communicated regularly with Iris. He would know.

Compared to Taylor, Dr. Bradsher, wearing torn canvas sneakers, looked like a college student; after all, he had only been working at NARA since 1977, for about thirty years. His office walls, desk and floor were overflowing with stacks of folders and videotapes and books, including documents he had famously helped locate in the 1990s on stolen Nazi gold. During that effort, he had collapsed twice in the stacks due to exhaustion and had to be taken to the hospital. At my feet, one of the few places where I could see the carpet, were piles of prisoner records from the Dachau concentration camp.

He first explained his role with the Japanese documents. He was in charge of initially implementing the Nazi War Crimes and Japanese Imperial Government Records Interagency Working Group (IWG). The group had been formed by order of President Clinton in 1999 to find, release, and declassify all federal documents of Nazi war crimes; the U.S. had recently requested that other countries, such as Switzerland, take this step, and now it was our turn to do the same. In 2000, partly under pressure from POW activist groups, Congress officially ordered the IWG to take the same action with documents regarding Japan.

As an expert on all aspects of archiving papers, Dr. Bradsher then gave me a good lesson about how conspiracy theories, like this case regarding the government allegedly hiding Japanese documents, can get started. He also expressed how difficult it is to debunk conspiracy theories when documents are involved because of the sheer amount of hands-on research and effort often required. In the end, I saw how unlikely it was that Iris had found a "smoking gun" on how the U.S. government had sold out the vets, or that such a document would even have been actively hidden by the government.

His first, most basic point was that the great majority of NARA's documents on Japanese war crimes have, in fact, already been available for decades to the public—not actively suppressed. To follow its government directive, his IWG group actually had only to declassify a tiny minority of total Japanese war crime documents, about one hundred thousand. Its main announcement was that the millions of pages of records on the subject already had been declassified and available there since at least the 1970s—with only a small portion of them ever utilized by researchers. "The records are here; they've been here for thirty, forty, fifty years. They don't need to be declassified because they already are," he told me. In fact, NARA has as many documents on Japanese war crimes as it does on the more combed-through German ones. But a difference over the decades has been much more interest by researchers and the U.S. government in the European theater over the Pacific one. And all these documents are widely scattered among the files of many different government agencies.

As an example of a "lost" Japanese document that probably no researcher had yet seen, he showed me a book of Japanese war reports describing internal operations in the Philippines on thin yellowed onionskin-like crinkly paper. The United States had declassified it way back in 1958. "The thing is that somebody might come in here and see this and say, 'I've never seen this in the book before,' and say, 'newly declassified,' to make it look like the government has been sitting on it. And it happens every week."

The sheer volume of these documents, numbering in the millions, along with their lack of indexing by subject and thus scattered whereabouts, can also make searching time-consuming and difficult. "Every week I get a call from Sotheby's, Christie's, the Metropolitan Museum, some art place saying 'we have a painting and we think it might have been stolen.' And I say, "Well, as you know, there's probably about nine or ten different places you'll have to look here." And most people go, 'Aaahhh!' So it's just overwhelming. If you go into a library or a bookstore and you say 'where are all the books on cooking?' And you just point over at the shelf. Well, archives are arranged by the government agency that created or received them." He gave an example of how he'd help a researcher in a quest for material on the Rape of Nanking: "Well, you start thinking, OK, the American embassies and consulates in China collected information. The State Department would have stuff because they got involved. Then we have military and naval attachés in China in the 1930s; they would have created records. You start walking through it after the war, the general investigator for war crimes, then there's the National Tribunals. You start going and pretty soon you're up to ten or twelve places where stuff related to the Rape of Nanking is."

In other words, looking for documents on a given topic, such as "Bataan POWs," is rarely as simple and instantaneous as something like a Google search. As a result, many documents get overlooked at first and then are found later and mistaken as previously "hidden." The finding aids, or indexes, develop over time according to demand on a topic and the cumulative, often decades-long work of archivists. Following demand in the wake of the publication of Iris' *Rape of Nanking*, Dr. Bradsher has put together such a finding aid for the Rape of Nanking. Before Iris' book on the topic, it was the target of many fewer requests; it happened before the U.S. had even entered World War II.

In fact, in response to the recent outcry by advocates of the American POWs in Japan, Dr. Bradsher was at the time of my visit putting together such an index on Japanese war crimes documents. A year later, in January 2007, his 1,700-page finding guide was made available, as a CD-ROM, on the NARA Web site, along with essays giving direction and historical perspective to researchers. At that time, NARA also made an announcement that it would soon make available online a database of 1,400 of these documents.

Dr. Bradsher discussed other factors regarding archive operations that have added to the confusion of POW-conspiracy theorists. Often a document is declassified by one department, and not by another. So a researcher can find a document marked "declassified" that actually had been available through other channels. Dr. Bradsher said that whatever documents have remained intentionally classified usually are for good reason, not because of "embarrassment" of the government, but because of a possible challenge to current security, such as including the name of an operative in Afghanistan tracking al Qaeda, or the recipe for a new grade of anthrax. The misfiling of documents or confusion over their rightful place also commonly leads to such allegations. I brought up Iris' anger over her friend telling her that she saw records in a folder there one day, and not the next. "The records didn't disappear; she just didn't find them. They were here," said Dr. Bradsher of that particular case. "We told her it was in box 27 and she asked for box 28."

"That researcher e-mailed Iris about it, and Iris got all upset that the government was hiding stuff," I explained.

"'The government' is like John and I. We don't hide the stuff," he said, with some irony. "We're too lazy to go out in the stacks and hide stuff." As an example of such a possible misunderstanding, he gave a recent request by a *Time* magazine reporter for a specific war-crimes document it wanted to run on its cover. It set him into a panic. "Well, I went out there and I couldn't find it. I was going crazy. . . . *Time* magazine is going to run this and I can't find it. What are they going to say—'a government cover-up'? And I started going through the box and I found out Miriam [the other archivist] had put it in the wrong folder in the same box."

Some of Dr. Bradsher's final contact with Iris was e-mailing her in 2003 an early draft of the finding guide to Japanese war crime documents. She had been one of the few researchers to see it in its early form. I asked if that guide, along with any of the newly indexed documents of the 2000s, contained any shocking revelations about the POWs. He said that they found less than expected. Not located was any suspected letter from Secretary of State John Foster Dulles selling out the veterans. They also did not find evidence of biological warfare conducted directly on the U.S. POWs with U.S. government permission, as also had been anticipated by veteran groups.

I asked him if anything found by the IWG was a "smoking gun," and he said the documents mostly confirmed past views on Japan. But a highlight was (already declassified but previously overlooked) U.S. government documents about the notorious Japanese Unit 731, which conducted biological warfare, and the release of its director, the notorious General Ishii (the Japanese counterpart to Dr. Josef Mengele). Ishii was also symbolic as one of the many the Japanese war criminals who *did* escape prosecution with the help of the U.S government. In his case, the U.S. spared him in exchange for information on the results of his gruesome human experiments. In addition, the finding guide now allows the possibility for researchers to find much more information on the topic, and possibly challenge current theories of that history.

Whatever happens in the future, researchers will always discover that there is no one formula for finding records, with the finding guides and collections constantly changing. "Every situation is a little different. There's not . . . a recipe. You have to make a subjective decision and weigh different factors. And people bent on conspiracies don't know in most cases what all the facets of making records available are, why something is missing. The entire government keeps only one percent of everything it creates. . . . We make a subjective decision of what the future should know about the past. And I've made mistakes when I have recommended that things be destroyed, one mistake at least," he said chuckling. "Conversely, we keep things that fifty years later somebody says, 'Why the hell did we keep this? Who cares about this?'

"And so people who are caught up in all these conspiracies, caught up in issues, faced with large records, faced with missing records, faced with records that are declassified—each of those has an explanation if you dig hard enough to find it."

I asked: "Did the State Department ever try to influence any of the releasing of documents from the IWG or sort of interfering in their work?

"No," he said.

In fact, Dr. Bradsher said he was disappointed that Iris never had a chance to see more of these newly indexed documents herself, many of which related to her past work on the Nanking book. "I think she could have even had a more devastating well-documented story than she did—but that could be true of a lot of peoples' books," he said. He turned to her book and pointed out a conspiracy-tinged paragraph that especially had irked him, which he had wanted to discuss with her personally. On page 177, she wrote how the U.S. government "inexplicably and irresponsibly" returned incriminating war documents to Japan in the 1950s. For these reasons, she wrote, we are missing crucial information about Japanese war crimes today. (She was making that conclusion from her own interviews—with a Georgetown professor who had access to the microfilm in the 1950s and a former worker at the Library of Congress who had both heard rumors about the case—as well as by repeating what even prominent authors had written through the years.)

But Dr. Bradsher said that NARA does have copies of significant numbers of these documents, which the government microfilmed after their capture in 1945. He added that the U.S. government had "fully exploited" them in war trials. "In fact during the war we had thousands of people translating these documents. And in this building today, even though the originals have gone back to Japan, thousands and thousands and thousands of boxes contain this stuff, which has also been available." Also, it's standard policy to return original captured records back to their country of origin; this was not a special case of being favorable to the Japanese.

"This is not to say that these people [American POWs in Japan] did not suffer unbelievably. I mean there's no question about that. Maybe Congress should pass a special law saying that these American POWs should get additional compensation, but that's something Congress would have to do. But to believe that somehow the U.S. Government took the evidence and snuck it back . . ." he said as he shook his head.

We also talked about widespread conspiracy theories that formerly enslaved U.S. POWs of Japan were "sold out" compared to those held in Germany, who (with their lawyers) had recently won massive settlements. But he said that, unlike in the case of Germany, the U.S. government had set up a special fund for the POWs of Japan to be compensated right after the war. That was taken from billions of dollars of Japanese property that the Allies had confiscated. As many vets had forgotten over the decades, and which the government can document, they did receive a settlement after the war equivalent to twenty-three thousand in today's dollars.

While not a lot, especially considering the sheer hell they endured as slaves for years, that is even more than was recently obtained for those POWs enslaved by the Nazis, who were due to receive from two thousand to seven thousand dollars each, according to the State Department.

Looking over State Department documents regarding the Bataan POW trials of 2001, I also saw that the federal government had other good points. The State Department had argued that disregarding the 1951 treaty and allowing such private lawsuits could open the door to countless other litigation by people in Allied countries against the Japanese, as well as Japanese citizen claims against the U.S. concerning its use of atomic bombs. It argued: "There is a serious danger that, if the U.S. were to engage in a revisionist, post hoc reinterpretation of the Treaty out of a well-intentioned desire to obtain additional pecuniary compensation for the Bataan POWs and other former POWs of Japan, the GOJ [Government of Japan] would then feel free also to reconsider its Treaty undertakings, with a consequent potentially adverse impact on important U.S. interests regarding regional security issues and on bilateral relations." Another document stated: "Moreover, this is the way that war claims have been dealt with since our nation's founding—by treaty and Act of Congress." It also denied widespread conspiracy claims that the U.S. government had forced returning vets to sign forms binding them not to speak publicly about Japanese atrocities.

What's clear to me in all this is that basic facts can be forgotten over time, especially with such a massive volume of documents involved and with a topic so emotional. And this is especially true in a case like this, where real injustice has been committed by the government with the release of Japanese war criminals. Many veterans reasonably still feel cheated by their government, unable to forget the promised provisions that never arrived and led to their disastrous surrender at Bataan.

Of course, while illuminating, I knew that the interview with Dr. Bradsher at NARA was not the final word to deny the possibility of an organized government campaign against Iris. In the remaining research time I had for this book, I did what I could. I followed up with her husband and again asked him if Iris could have found a "smoking gun" among these documents. He assured me over e-mail that "Iris never had any classified documents in her possession. . . . Iris had no information that was not readily available to anyone else. . . . Iris was in very bad shape at that time, and every time she visited a 'Conspiracy Theory' Web site, she would believe whatever she read."

And then, to really cover my bases, I decided to file a final Freedom of Information Act request, this time to the State Department. As the most recent months of my research had clearly revealed, if any department of the U.S. government had an axe to grind with her, it would have been that one. The State Department was in charge of maintaining that crucial 1951 treaty with Japan, a valued ally on the War on Terrorism, and was vociferously against these incendiary Bataan POW lawsuits.

In January of 2006, I sent in my request for any files on "Iris Chang" to the State Department FOIA office, expecting to receive a one-page letter of denial of any records soon after. This had been the case with my earlier request the year before to the FBI—and later on with the National Security Agency (NSA) and CIA.

The weeks passed. A month later, I got an e-mail from the State Department assigning me a case number.

Then, in late October, I received a bulky five-pound package on my doorstep. It was from the U.S. Department of State.

Inside the package were twenty-six multipage documents, dating from May 1998 to December 2005, all of which contained references to Iris Chang. Almost all were from the U.S. embassy in Tokyo. A third were cables (internal memos, at a level higher and more official than an e-mail), and the others were press summaries from the conservative Japanese media. Most were marked "immediate" and "sensitive." A few had been classified at one time. They had all been sent to multiple high-ranking officials in the U.S. government, including the White House, various defense and intelligence agencies, and many U.S. embassies through Asia.

What they did show: Clearly, Iris was a true thorn in the side of the State Department. This was the most direct link I had found between Iris' Nanking work and its threat to greater U.S. relations with Japan. These dispatches were all reporting about Iris' activism—and trying to manage its impact on the sensitive Japanese government. They made a direct link from her Nanking book to the growth of the troubling movement of Bataan veterans. Her work with the POWs, and the effects of their potential lawsuits on relations with Japan, was of the most concern.

But: The documents reveal no misdeeds—or even any sinister behavior—by the U.S. government. At least according to the materials they had disclosed to me, the State Department was not tracking Iris personally, as she had feared, from a white van or by opening her mail or tapping her phone. These papers did not talk about any classified documents or any specific "smoking gun" that Iris had uncovered at the end of her life.

The first documents, apparent excerpts from the right-wing Japanese media from April and May of 1998, set the tone. They are marked as very high priority and "immediate," and report on the "female Chinese-American journalist Iris Chang . . . who appears unable to constrain her own negative reaction to Japan and the Japanese." One article cited points to fears that Chinese politicians would use the book's popularity in the West to exact an apology from Japan during an upcoming visit of its president to Japan. In another, a conservative pundit sums up Iris' threat, with a bit of grudging praise, while condemning her book: "She is clever as a writer on the point that she took up the Nanjing Massacre, which is widely known in Japan but hardly known in the U.S., and depicted the incident vividly. She has proved herself to be eloquent also in her speech. But most of the descriptions shown as facts in the book are unreliable and uncertain."

The U.S. ambassador in Tokyo, in charge of such dispatches, also felt that Iris' work was important enough to mention in at least four personal cables that year addressed to the U.S. Secretary of State and other high-ranking officials. They were mostly marked "immediate," and the first two had been classified until 2003. All basically warned about the sensitivity of her book, for them to keep in mind during state visits with Japan.

In a typical move of caution, the first reported a Japanese diplomat's recent "noting [of] the popularity of Iris Chang's book, 'The Rape of Nanking,'" and his hopes that "historical issues would not cloud" the upcoming visit to the U.S. by the Japanese prime minister.

Following that, through 2001, were mainly media summaries from Japanese right-wing newspapers specifically decrying Iris' activism on behalf of former POWs of Japan. Typed in all caps, they escalate in alarm, reporting on growing numbers of veteran lawsuits, which had yet to be struck down. Like others, this media excerpt from September 6, 2001, directly makes the connection between Iris' book and this issue:

WHAT PROMPTED THE CAMPAIGN IN THE UNITED STATES TO MAKE JAPAN PAY POST-WAR REPARATIONS WAS THE BOOK, THE RAPE OF NANKING, BY CHINESE-AMERICAN AUTHOR IRIS CHANG AND PUBLISHED IN 1997 IN THE US. DEMANDING COMPENSATION FROM JAPANESE FIRMS FOR FORCED LABOR DURING WORLD WAR II. FORMER U.S. SERVICEMEN HELD AS PRISONERS OF WAR (POWS) BY THE JAPANESE, AS WELL AS OTHER WARTIME VICTIMS, HAVE SINCE TAKEN LEGAL ACTIONS IN SUCCESSION.

The same report quoted Iris' speech at the 2001 San Francisco anti-treaty counter-conference:

"IF JAPAN WANTS ITSELF TO BE TREATED AS AN HONORARY CIVILIZED NATION, IT SHOULD CHANGE ITS PATTERN OF ACTION. IT SHOULD FIRST OFFER A FORMAL APOLOGY TO THE WAR-VICTIMS. NEXT, IT SHOULD PAY COMPENSATION TO THEM AND THEN SHOULD CLARIFY THE WAR CRIMES IT COMMITTED DURING THE WAR."

THE ABOVE REMARK WAS MADE BY IRIS
CHANG, THE AUTHOR OF THE RAPE OF NAKING,
A BOOK THAT DENOUNCES JAPAN'S PAST AC-
TIONS, IN A SPEECH ON THE 7TH. SHE RECEIVED
A LENGTHY STANDING OVATION FROM THE AU-
DIENCE.

The press reports are very similar in condemning Iris' book as giving an unfair and "masochistic" view of their history, all calculated to help other countries pry yet more money out of Japan and further China's political ends as its heroic adversary. Besides, they write, China is hypocritical in such demands for apology, considering that it slaughtered millions of its own citizens under Mao's regime. They deny her death toll reports for Nanking—and especially recoil at her book's comparisons of Japanese to the Nazis.

But, despite trying to be sensitive to the Japanese, the U.S. officials are far from hysterical. In a formerly classified February 1999 cable marked "sensitive," U.S. Ambassador to Tokyo Thomas S. Foley does opine that her book ultimately is not a threat to U.S/Japanese relations. Instead, he says it is ultimately significant in how it reflects remaining "ambivalence in Japan over its wartime role":

IF THE BOOK IS EVENTUALLY RELEASED IN JAPA-
NESE, IT IS UNLIKELY TO ATTRACT THE READER-
SHIP OR MAINSTREAM MEDIA INTEREST IT
ENJOYED IN THE U.S. AND CHINA. THE THUS
FAR SUCCESSFUL EFFORTS TO SUPRESS EVEN ITS
PUBLICATION ILLUSTRATE THAT WORLD WAR II
REVISIONISM IS ALIVE AND WELL IN JAPAN.

There are no documents on Iris from 2002, and then media reports from 2003, which praise the Bush Administration for helping to strike down the POW lawsuits against Japan, mention Iris in passing. They note

Iris' Nanking book as background for getting the whole controversy started in the first place.

The final two documents included in this package, cables from 2005 from U.S. embassies in China, reveal that Iris' symbolism as a controversial agitator remained prominent after her death. One, marked "confidential," from an official in the U.S. embassy in Shanghai (with the name blacked out for reasons of privacy), discusses the massive protests going on at that time in China over Japanese revisionist textbooks: "Japanese claims that their approval of the texts is a free speech issue are undercut by their previous banning of Iris Chang's The Rape of Nanking." The last cable, from Beijing, reported mixed public reaction to a pro-U.S. book on fighter pilots. One angry reader had written on a much-trafficked Web site on the topic that the author "must be killed by a bullet just like Iris Chang."

These documents ultimately reveal the extent of Iris' symbolism, at very high levels. She was symbolic to the Japanese government—and conservative press—as inflaming the West against it. She was symbolic to the U.S. government as a nuisance in relations with Japan. And, finally, she was symbolic to the Chinese as an ally against the Japanese.

They also show how successful Iris ultimately was in her goals to raise public awareness of Japanese misdeeds in World War II. Despite her paranoia at the end of her life, she did still raise some very legitimate questions about Japanese war crimes with her book and activism, which have resulted in dramatically enhanced public access to records on the topic.

Indeed, the National Archives thought her questions were sound and relevant enough to spur their release in 2000 and beyond. In fact, the introduction to the 2007 online NARA publication, "Researching Japanese War Crime Records: Introductory Essays," begins with describing the influence of Iris' work in these efforts, including the passing of the 2000 Japanese Imperial Government Disclosure Act by Congress.

The author of the book's introduction, historian Edward Drea, credits Iris' book on Nanking as "markedly" changing attitudes regarding and spurring activism about Japanese war crimes—in the U.S. and around the world:

> *The best-selling book spurred a tremendous amount of re-*
> *newed interest in Japanese wartime conduct in China, Ko-*
> *rea, the Philippines, Southeast Asia and the Pacific. The Rape*
> *of Nanking raised many issues that demanded further expla-*
> *nation. Why were the Japanese not punished as severely as the*
> *Nazis for their crimes? Did the United States suppress evi-*
> *dence of the criminal responsibility of the activity by the em-*
> *peror to ensure a smoothly running occupation of Japan? Did*
> *the U.S. government protect Japanese medical officers in ex-*
> *change for data on human experimentation? (3)*

Drea goes on to talk about the further U.S. government need to respond to numerous conspiracy theories regarding the documents, including Iris' charges in her book of the U.S. "'inexplicably and irresponsibly' returning confiscated wartime records to Japan before microfilming them, making it impossible to determine the extent of Japan's guilt."

Clearly, Iris ultimately raised questions of great interest and relevance to the U.S. government. As a result of these efforts, future scholars on World War II will be able to find more answers and discern truths, helping us to learn valuable lessons from, and even shift our views about, some of the most violent chapters in recent history.

In investigating her influence, I've also become more aware of the significance of historical documents in general to transcend speculation and rumor—and shed light on even the most convoluted and misunderstood events of the past. They can help reveal the true magnitude of past events, as with the priceless Rabe diaries that Iris found in documenting atrocities in Nanking. Conversely, they can also help to trace the origins of—and ultimately quell concerns about—conspiracy, such as with her files on *Newsweek,* and my FOIA request of the State Department. Iris' case also shows that effectively using documents from the past is not always simple. It usually requires patience and time, collaboration with others, and savvy about understanding and navigating great systems of bureaucracy. During most of her career, as a researcher Iris embodied those traits, and now has emboldened other scholars to do the same.

Who Were the Villains?

*I*ris describing anti-Chinese California senator John F. Miller's argument in 1881 in *The Chinese in America*:

> *Comparing the Chinese immigrants to "inhabitants of another planet," Miller argued that they were "machine-like . . . of obtuse nerve, but little affected by heat or cold, wiry, sinewy, with muscles of iron; they are automatic engines of flesh and blood; they are patient, stolid, unemotional." (130)*

They say that before you die, your whole life rushes before your eyes.

For Iris, I know that was true in the weeks before her death. No doubt, hundreds, more like thousands, of images flashed before her then.

This is not a guess. She did burn exactly thirty-one CDs of her life's photos, of which she sent copies to two archives weeks before her death.

After getting official permission from her husband, I finally got a chance to review them, during my final archive trip to the University of Illinois Library in spring of 2006.

In turn, her life flashed before my eyes, as well:

There was her class photo at Yankee Ridge School from 1976, then some other ones from grade school, all with a contemplative smile. Family vacations from all around the country, one to Stanford with her standing before the Hoover Archive. High school friends with eighties big hair clowning around. Her desk from the sorority house basement, with her published newspaper stories posted on the bulletin board above. At sorority parties, her dressed as a hula girl, then an Indian girl. In a convertible in the homecoming parade, with the brightest smile of all. Dad wearing "Illini Dad" sweatshirt in photo with her. Sitting on the grass in Central Park with the other magazine interns in New York City on Earth Day. Brett and her at a dance, her holding a rose. College graduation, us smiling in our robes, with her towering above me. A very proud Professor Reid. She and Brett, beaming at their wedding.

As an archivist walked by, I muttered to myself, "Her life looks so normal."

"Yes, more normal than normal," he agreed.

Then more: Iris standing in front of the Tribune building, on the campus of Johns Hopkins, at the Library of Congress. A university in Nanjing. Speaking at a podium before hundreds. With Barb Masin and then Dale Maharidge in Santa Barbara. Parties with celebrities: Is that Martha Stewart? News guy Peter Arnett? Hillary Clinton?

Even after all I had found out about her struggles in the past two years, it still did look like the perfect life. And in all these ways pictured here before me, it truly was. Her life did contain all these wonderful moments, and she did touch all those people pictured.

Thinking of where the pictures left off, I looked back at the time that had passed since her death. I regretted that she wasn't there to reap the many still-ongoing rewards of her labors. A documentary film, *Nanking*, about the Western heroes of the massacre that she had profiled in her book, was just shown at the Sundance Film Festival in Park City, Utah, in January of 2007. The documentary, produced by AOL mogul Ted Leonsis, who had been moved by Iris, featured the voice of Mariel Hemingway as Minnie. Iris also would have been thrilled to see the 2006 release of her friend Barbara Masin's book, *Gauntlet: Five Friends, 20,000 Enemy Troops, and the Secret That Could Have Changed the Course of the Cold War*—which she helped to inspire. Of course, she would have been ecstatic that another author friend, James Bradley, now had two blockbuster movies out, made from his best-selling books, *Flyboys* and *The Flags of Our Fathers*.

Most strikingly, she was missing her son grow up. He was now being cared for by his father, paternal grandmother, and his stepmother, Brett's second wife, Iris Shui, whom he married in early 2006. Christopher now also had a little brother. They moved back to central Illinois in May 2007.

At that time, as this book was nearly complete and he was giving me those last-minute updates, Brett filled in some other gaps regarding on-going questions about Iris' last years, specifically about some hidden "weaknesses." One, which I had long wondered about, was that her son really has autism (a less severe form on the spectrum, Asperger's Disorder). Once again, an "irrational" fear of hers (that she personally was to blame for "giving him autism" with vaccines) was based in reality: real autistic behavior that she was observing in him as a toddler just before her death. This was also a major source of self-blame and inner torment.

I had not even suspected the next disclosure.

We were reviewing Iris' seemingly odd behavior of hardly leaving her house and seeing people she knew while pregnant. Brett then stated that was because *Iris was never pregnant with Christopher.*

"Christopher had a surrogate mother," Brett explained. "That is why nobody saw Iris pregnant."

Christopher is Iris' and Brett's biological child, but he was born to an-other woman, who had carried him to term. Needless to say, this means that Iris was not suffering from postpartum depression, as many, such as myself, had thought.

It turned out that Iris realized that a pregnancy was too risky with her physical health problems of thrombophilia (blood clotting), hyperthy-roidism, and other conditions. She had also suffered miscarriages for a few years, which a doctor finally diagnosed in 2000 as being caused by "incom-patible DQ-Alpha numbers"—basically meaning that the mother's immune system attacks the fetus because of a clash in the parents' combined genes.

She didn't want to take immune-system suppressants to treat the problem, which could worsen her other ailments.

It turns out that Iris did *succeed,* with real bravery, in using the latest child-birth technologies, which she had heralded earlier in her life. But, she may have paid a price. Iris did take infertility drugs for six weeks in the end of 2001 while following the process of in-vitro fertilization (IVF)—extracting her own egg to be implanted with the father's sperm in the uterus of the surrogate. That involved the standard types of hormone-rocking and egg-stimulating drugs, such as Clomid and Pergonal, commonly used to make women more fertile, regardless of their use of IVF. However, her hormones were mainly on a roller-coaster from her constantly being pregnant and miscarrying from 1999 to 2000, before the incompatible DQ-Alpha numbers problem was diagnosed.

The added influence of stress, from her years of grueling book tours and grisly subject matter, was certainly at work, contributing to the onset of the bipolar disorder. The combined influence of these factors—genetics, hormones, and stress—can compound the effects of an imbalance of brain chemicals and gradually result in a breakdown. The mere weight of keeping secrets was a stressor in itself.

Above all, Iris' very intentional "cover up" of her use of a surrogate reveals the intense pressure that she felt to appear perfect. Again, it wasn't just coincidence that all of her friends had this impression of her. She was *actively working* to produce this image. We didn't just come up with it on our own.

Indeed, she took extreme measures to hide this "flaw" of not being able to carry a child to term, something that clearly shaped her definition of a woman. She never directly lied about it—she never told anyone outright that she was pregnant—but she allowed everyone to assume that she was. According to Brett, she hid the fact of the surrogate from almost everyone, even keeping it a secret from some close family members until the final weeks before Christopher's birth. These new details from Brett—Christopher's autism and the surrogate—reinforced just how much remains unknown to me about Iris, that there are things I never will know. But, compared with two years earlier, I am much more aware of the long history, intensity, and depth of her inner torment.

Besides a renewed sense of regret for all she had suffered, I now also felt a new sense of closeness to Iris. I realized I had lacked that during her life, when I saw her on a pedestal, as more of a superhuman, a breed apart from the rest of us. Now that I knew more about the full textured picture of her life, beyond the idealized images and sterling résumés, she was now a more authentic person to me. Instead of diminishing from her achievements, her flawed human qualities made them all the more meaningful and poignant.

Of course, as she expressed to me in our final conversation, her enemies may well use this, the fact of her mental illness, against her. Indeed, she was in a particularly sensitive situation in trying to maintain her credibility in the wake of exposing "controversial" facts about the Rape of Nanking. But no matter what her fears—she always ultimately had managed to produce solid and influential work—she asked some very good questions that have stood up to the test of scholars and critics over time.

In truth, we all have weaknesses that others can use against us. Like almost every other major writer or leader, she fought private battles that do not ultimately deny the validity of her public ones. This point was hammered home to me recently when I bumped into a fellow author, who had graduated college several years before Iris and me. When he asked me the secret she was hiding, I reported that Iris had bipolar disorder, as if this were a major revelation. He shrugged, totally unfazed, saying, "*Of course*, she was bipolar. We all have something. I'd be surprised if she didn't."

Now she was more of a real person to me, less of a machine, like the "Iron Chink" she had described in her last book and recalled in speeches. She wrote that a century ago—and clearly long before such a term would have been acknowledged as politically incorrect and insulting—its manufacturers had named a newly efficient fish-butchering machine the Iron

Chink "in a twisted acknowledgement of the enormous work capacity of these immigrants," whom the machine had supplanted. (74)

Indeed, during her life, like many people, I had seen her as melting in with the super-industrious robot-like immigrants she had profiled throughout *The Chinese in America*, the ones who intensely toiled on the railroads and worked assembly lines and, for that matter, got all A's at MIT—only stopping at the point when they dropped over from sheer exhaustion. I had too quickly associated her with the breed she had described working in the Chinese laundry for twenty-hour shifts, including those who reportedly hung a piece of bread from a string above them so they didn't have to take a break to eat. In the meantime, these immigrants with their "slavish work ethic" (169) attracted the scorn, confusion, and envy of the "real Americans" who couldn't quite explain the greater success of the immigrants and their children.

Iris' life showed how being a symbol, even a much-admired and apparently superhuman one, can be a very tough road. Others overlook the natural human parts of yourself, and over time, you do, too. As the mystique builds, your weaknesses only become more difficult for you and others to face. Others come to value you mainly according to what you do, how you're a verb, how you inspire them—not who you really are. They overidentify with you, overlooking aspects of yourself that are different from them. Then they're unprepared, to the point of being shocked, if you handle a situation differently than they would. The symbol just can't get a break.

Not that her life as a symbol—being a crusader for justice—wasn't important. She always emphasized the power of self-transformation and of the individual to make change, and her life was a testament to those possibilities. Her tremendous impact in exposing Japanese war crimes—and getting millions of documents on them officially released by the U.S. government—shows that the difficult and time-consuming work of digging beyond the surface matters, and that investigating dark topics can be very valuable. Another of Iris' most inspiring aspects was seeing past regular human limits. Leading by example, she taught other writers and activists to dream bigger. One of her greatest—and most unrealized—hopes was to further test womankind's limits, for smart and ambitious women to be able to fully realize their potential outside the family. What does it take for them to have "stellar careers," she asked. That's another important question to keep addressing.

But the challenge, of course, in thinking big is knowing when to stop, when to accept limits and get treatment. This is not easy. Accepting something very difficult like mental illness can be a long and difficult process. It means mourning the loss of your past self. It means recognizing weakness in yourself. It means no less than a total change in philosophy, of taking on the greater world view that not everything is in your control, a matter of sheer force of will. It means realizing that accepting an illness isn't necessarily giving up, a surrender, but an act of strength to address it, and then move on, as well as possible. It means searching for your own often scarce role models in this process. It means sometimes having a *"can't*-do attitude," and saying no to people and letting them down. It means asking for help.

I still don't know if Iris' death was preventable. As I told Brett at the end of our interview in San Jose, her bipolar disorder became so extreme in the end that it was comparable to an advanced cancer, a far-gone tumor. Because mental illness is invisible, and something like cancer isn't, there is a double standard in treating it, which dictates that controlling it is always within our powers. With all kinds of illness, there is a pernicious trend in our culture to blame the victim, not recognizing the frailty of the human body as a fact of life. All too prevalent, for example, is the myth of the "cancer personality" that blames the person for repressing anger, the cause of their problem. Even more extreme may be blaming the person with bipolar disorder for not knowing when to stop, for their overly ambitious attitudes. All this societal baggage makes illness a moral failing, and not a matter of physiology.

It was this real illness that was probably the main villain behind Iris' death. Not, as I've heard others speculate: her family, her doctors, her publishers, her editor, her agent, her grisly subject matter, her fellow activists,

Big Pharma, her desire to "have it all" as a working mother, right-wing Japanese opposition, the government of the United States, nor the government of China using her work for political gain. And making it even more lethal was its shadowy accomplice, the deep-rooted social stigma, dating back countless generations. It's the extraordinary shame about mental illness that prevents it from being recognized and treated sooner, not just at the eleventh hour.

Iris was hit with a double whammy of shame—a mood disorder combined with infertility problems. They each challenge the most traditional and idealized role of a woman as the protective mother; experiencing the two together can be particularly isolating. Not only did she have trouble carrying a baby to term, but she also had mental illness. Her secrecy surrounding both issues also denied her valuable education into her risks with these treatments, making her enter a very dangerous situation. I'm not even sure if Iris herself knew whether she was genetically prone to bipolar disorder, and if that was something that her family would have even shared with her.

Needless to say, in challenge to this barrier of shame, more public education on the long-term effects of hormonal treatments is critical, on many levels. Of course, it can aid in a basic way to guide individual treatment. A woman with a mood disorder who is properly medicated has a much better chance of going through fertility treatments, and even childbirth, without harm. In such cases, a very thorough screening, including asking about family history and past mood swings, can be vital. More research is also needed into the long-term effects of infertility treatments and other hormonal events on mood disorders, in the first place.

Also desperately lacking is research and public awareness about how gender and ethnicity can shape mood disorders. For example, women often experience mania differently; they "cycle" faster, or make rapid transitions in and out of the manic and depressive phases, even over the same day. Asians may react differently to drugs, such as being more sensitive to dose quantity. The Asian community itself, led by a new and more open generation, is just starting such work of addressing the issues of mental illness and suicide—and not just "watch their passing, like cherry blossoms." A major goal is raising awareness among therapists who treat those of Asian backgrounds, as well as among the greater community that contributes to and reinforces the overall shame.

As part of a more complete and holistic approach, Dr. Jeanne Watson Driscoll also emphasized to me the importance of the health-care provider, when possible, forming an ongoing long-term relationship with the patient, offering therapy, and not just acting as "someone who is writing out pill prescriptions. And that to me is a very important piece of women with postpartum or any kind of mood disorder need; they need the meds as well as the therapy, somebody with whom they can build a relationship with of trust that they don't feel like they are going to judge them and devalue them."

This relationship can work on a fundamental level to encourage patients with bipolar disorder to take their medications. These patients, like Iris, have a very poor record of compliance because of unpleasant side effects. Mind-calming drugs, like Depakote and Risperdal, can make a person tired and foggy. Often these side effects are not avoidable, particularly for large doses. But a good clinician can help to work closely with the patient over a long period of time to find the best combination of drugs and doses. This is typically an extended period of trial and error, which demands support and patience. It also requires the commitment of the patient, which I'm not sure Iris had.

Iris' tragic experiences also teach valuable lessons to all friends and relatives of those at risk for suicide. Mainly, don't be afraid to make a fuss. Family members shouldn't hesitate to take away credit cards, car keys, and checkbooks. Be the bad guy, and, if possible, have the person committed to a hospital if she or he is in serious danger. Then give the patient ample time for recovery before assuming all is well, knowing that suicide attempts are very likely in the weeks after a hospitalization.

Her death is also a wake-up call for self-care to many journalists and others who regularly deal with issues of trauma and violence. While Iris' mental illness was at the root of her problem, the abject lack of precautions she took in confronting such material certainly took its toll. I wonder how she could have benefited from at least regular therapy, or having a trauma specialist on site for the interviews, which is basic protocol for those in the human-rights field who interview torture victims. The challenge is to also follow the examples of first-responder professionals, such as firefighters, police officers, and psychologists, who get this information on trauma in their basic training.

Too long the ethic in journalism has been the short-sighted macho one of swallowing feelings, maybe compartmentalizing them, and facing trauma all alone, perhaps by medicating sorrows in drinks after work. Or reporters just leave themselves to feel the impact years later with a worsening of health. Journalism schools lack a basic curriculum to teach about trauma, along with a vocabulary for expressing it, the impact on victims, and its possible fallout to those who report about it. This is especially negligent considering that so much that journalists do involve trauma, from day one; typical first-year beat reporters pay their dues, as I did, covering crime and major accidents.

This blindness is deeply rooted in journalism. "The eternal culture of news organizations does not tolerate expressions of weakness," observed longtime newspaper reporter Roger Simpson. He is also the founding director of the groundbreaking Dart Center for Journalism and Trauma at the University of Washington in Seattle. He did give me some hope, saying that the ethic in journalism recently has started to slowly change. The Dart Center, founded in 2000 in the Department of Communication at the university, helps to educate journalism professors and organizations internationally about the process of trauma and its possible impact on journalists. Some of this corporate investment is out of common sense to keep reporters going over the long term, and some is out of fear of a major lawsuit for a news organization in the future. He described the center as following a greater national movement of trauma awareness, spurred by the past three decades of work by the women's movement in exposing such issues as sexual assault, and by psychological research on post-traumatic stress disorder.

Simpson's recently reissued coauthored book, *Covering Violence: A Guide to Ethical Reporting about Victims & Trauma*, points to the need for education of journalists on many specific dynamics of different traumas, including sexual abuse and domestic violence, terrorist attacks, war, and genocide. As he told me, a special challenge of tackling the topic of genocide is the typical denial involved, such as of the Armenian genocide in Turkey from 1915, still a hot-button topic there. Talking to veterans should also involve familiarity with post-traumatic stress disorder and managing it in the interview.

Iris' life also points to a need for education and in-depth treatment of journalists on the specific role of mental illness in suicide. Media treatment often is limited to early news reports of the suicide, concluding with the quickly-made judgment that "there were no previous signs." That coverage alone gives the misleading and lasting impression that it just happened out of the blue and for no reason, and that suicide is never preventable. This limited coverage follows Simpson's call in his book for more in-depth reporting on all types of trauma. He and coauthor William Coté point out the need for more of what they call Act III stories, which analyze greater social and economic issues around the story. This is in addition to the more standard Act I and Act II reports of trauma, which may be more superficial and sensational and happen in the first weeks after an incident.

Act III coverage with suicide means investigating the role of mental illness and describing its earliest signs and typical patterns of evolution. Progress has been made over the past few decades in reporting in particular about depression, but still lacking is analysis of the even more stigmatized issues of bipolar disorder and psychosis. As Dr. Kay Redfield Jamison observes in *Night Falls Fast: Understanding Suicide*:

> *Suicide is never the result of a single factor or event, but rather results from a complex interaction of many factors and usually involves a history of psychosocial problems. Public officials and the media should carefully explain that the final*

precipitating event was not the only cause of a given suicide. Most persons who have committed suicide have had a history of problems that may not have been acknowledged during the acute aftermath of the suicide. Cataloguing the problems that could have played a causative role in a suicide is not necessary, but acknowledgement of these problems is recommended.

Two years after Iris' death, I'm still haunted by this tremendous loss and tragedy, but am certainly less scared and dumbfounded. I finally was able to erase Iris' last voice-mail message to me, with no regrets. My education about all these issues surrounding her death—from mental illness to "secondary trauma" to the facts behind her conspiracy theories—was key in addressing my own demons. In addition, because of the education that I got, the whole process was not as traumatic for me as I had anticipated. While it was certainly tough and painful, I actually had a more balanced life than ever while working on this book. I was aided by regularly discussing it all with a therapist, and at points when it got to me and I wasn't able to distance myself from her as my "subject," I took some time off.

Instead of isolating me, driving me crazy, and making me obsessed with morbid thoughts, researching this book has actually made me feel stronger and more secure. I now know more about noticing signs of bipolar disorder in others. I know to pay attention to warning signs in myself, of escalating anxiety, which tell me that I'm taking too much on. I know more about the potential harmful effects of intense hormonal events, especially on those predisposed to mood disorders. I know that myself and my other journalist friends are unlikely to just go crazy and kill ourselves overnight without any prior warning. I know that "secondary trauma" from reporting about dark subjects can be monitored, and even avoided. I know that crusading for justice doesn't necessarily mean a total sacrifice of one's personal life and one's health. True, such research on trauma, especially involving any aspect of war, is inherently intense. And we cannot control a lot of how we react, especially when biologically rooted serious illness is involved. But it's good to get more of a realistic handle on what we can prevent and manage.

Some of my hope for the future, and for the power of education, is probably most clearly personified in one person I met along the way, Iris' protégée, Iris Chang Herrera. I met her in person where she was interning the summer of 2005, at the domed California State Capitol in Sacramento. After I went through the metal detectors, passed Arnold's governor's office, and took the elevator up to her office, she greeted me with a hug. The resplendently beautiful daughter of a China-born mother and Latino father, she looked like the true daughter of California she is.

She couldn't wait to show me a small sheet of official newsprint-like paper she was holding, a copy of a Senate bill she was working on. She was excited that it had just been passed through the Assembly Education Committee and was about to go before the Assembly floor. It provided encouragement to high school history classes to teach about the Asian experience in World War II, in China, Korea, and the Philippines. That part of world history is often sorely lacking in the state, as it is through the country.

"I know I definitely would not be going in this direction now if it weren't for Iris, working with policy, trying to make laws, change laws," she said.

She also said that she learned from Iris to "think big" and hopes to get involved to help implement similar policy across the country.

As she learned about her power as an activist from Iris, she also found out about the importance of self care to be able to go on for the long term. Of course, that awareness of balance does not ensure against trouble—Iris herself knew about it and often warned me in her letters to take time off—but it's a good start. It's a basic step to monitor for trouble and get treatment, if needed.

Iris Chang Herrera recalled her former view of Iris as a symbol, which was shared by her fellow Bay Area activists in the movement to recognize Japanese war crimes: "People knew that she needed to take a break. But at the same time we didn't really question it as much as we should because we just thought, 'Oh, she's a superwoman. She just keeps on going, doesn't stop.'"

Some of her wisdom of "knowing my limits" is, in fact, quite old. "My mom's family had this saying to not get too far into the cow's horn. The cow's horn goes from big to small, right? So the farther you go into the cow's horn, the harder it is to turn around. Iris Chang got too far in that. She couldn't turn around, and she ended her life that way.

"So you have to be careful, especially working with these issues that are depressing. They are negative. I mean these aren't the peachiest subjects," she said with a bit of a laugh. "You need to take breaks. You need to spend time with your family. You need to be with your loved ones. You need to go on vacation.

"You can't be so consumed in it that it takes over you. And that's what I think happened, in part, with Iris Chang.

"And it was really sad. She just kept pushing herself more and more and more. We all admired her for it, but I don't think that we recognized how painful it was for her."

ACKNOWLEDGMENTS

Special thanks for the generosity and insights of everyone interviewed, especially Brett Douglas. I also appreciate his permission for use of letters, poems, and archival materials.

Thanks for invaluable editorial consultation to: Monica Eng, Tamara Dean, and Kyra Auslander.

Thanks for making the book possible to: David Talbot at Salon.com; agent Daniel Greenberg; and editor Marnie Cochran and publicist Lissa Warren at Da Capo.

Thanks to "expert" reviewers of the manuscript: Dr. Aruna Jha, Natalie Greben DuBois, Dr. Jeanne Watson Driscoll, and Helen Zia.

Thanks for transcription to Sidney Schifferli of Transcription Professionals. And for other valued research and travel assistance to: Wendy Holt and Lindsay Lochner at Da Capo, Bridget Brown, Mike Ramsey, Ron Packowitz, Beth Schuman, Heather Barrow, Steve Rhodes, Barbara Seaman, Anna Minkov, Dr. Suzanne Parisian, Carolyn Shapiro, Rivka Solomon, Hilary Glazer, Carol Leschen, Rochelle Kopp, Christine Choy, Sasha Rubel and Dick Detzner, Stephany Creamer, Bob Simpson and Estelle Carol, Norman Solomon, Binnie Choslovsky, Matt and Huey Friedman, John Taylor, Marilyn Reid, Dean Ron Yates, Daniel Barenblatt, Cindy Vautrin, Emma Lyon, Shailey Merchant, Jennifer Sharkey, Marilyn Abildskov, Andrew Leonard at Salon.com, and Don Besom of the State

Department. Thanks also to Laura Haber and Howie Schein at Allen Hall in Urbana.

And thanks to the dedicated librarians and archivists at: the Woodford County (IL) Historical Society; University High School, Urbana; Yale Divinity School; The Hoover Institution on War, Revolution and Peace at Stanford University; The California Ethnic and Multicultural Archives (CEMA) of the Special Collections Department of the University Libraries at the University of California, Santa Barbara; and the University of Illinois at Urbana-Champaign Library Archives Research Center, especially William Maher.

On a personal note, thanks to my family—and to Dave Beazley for his support.

Contributions in honor of Iris Chang, and to continue her work, are being taken by:

The Iris Chang Memorial Fund,
an organization for public education,
a project of the Global Alliance for Preserving the
History of World War II in Asia.
www.irischangmemorialfund.org

The Iris Chang Journalism Award Fund,
a scholarship at the University of Illinois at
Urbana-Champaign. More information
is available at (217) 333-0810.
www.uif.uillinois.edu